W9-BGA-596

RELIGION

in the Modern American West

The Modern American West

Gerald D. Nash and Richard W. Etulain

EDITORS

Carl Abbott

The Metropolitan Frontier: Cities in the Modern

American West

Richard W. Etulain

Re-imagining the Modern American West:

A Century of Fiction, History, and Art

Gerald D. Nash

The Federal Landscape: An Economic History of

the Twentieth-Century West

Ferenc Morton Szasz

Religion in the Modern American West

Oscar J. Martínez

Mexican-Origin People in the United States:

A Topical History

RELIGION

in the

Modern American West

Ferenc Morton Szasz

The University of Arizona Press

Tucson

The University of Arizona Press
© 2000 The Arizona Board of Regents
All rights reserved
♾ This book is printed on acid-free, archival-quality paper.
Manufactured in the United States of America
05   04   03   02   6   5   4   3   2

Library of Congress Cataloging-in-Publication Data
Szasz, Ferenc Morton, 1940–
Religion in the modern American West / Ferenc Morton Szasz.
p. cm. — (The modern American West)
Includes bibliographical references and index.
ISBN 0-8165-1476-3 (cloth: alk. paper)
ISBN 0-8165-2245-6 (pbk: alk. paper)
1. West (U.S.)—Religion—20th century.   I. Title.   II. Series.
BL2527.W47 S83   2000
200´.978´0904—dc21
99-050963

British Library Cataloguing-in-Publication Data
A catalogue record for this book is available from the British Library.

Publication of this book is made possible in part by the proceeds of a
permanent endowment created with the assistance of a Challenge Grant
from the National Endowment for the Humanities, a federal agency.

Dedicated to
Mary I. Szasz and the memory of
Ferenc P. Szasz, and to
Margaret
Maria
Eric
Chris
Scott
Tyler
Sean
Matthew

Contents

Illustrations

Preface

For the past three decades I have taught American intellectual history at the University of New Mexico in Albuquerque. During this time I have been struck by the prominence of three overarching themes in American culture: (1) the role of literature and the visual media, (2) the impact of science and technology, and (3) religion. Although historians have devoted a good deal of ink to the first two, they have generally given the third a wide berth. This has been especially true for historians of the modern American West.

During the last twenty-five years of the twentieth century, many scholars reinvigorated our understanding of western history with approaches that ranged from the traditional narrative line to that of bold revisionism. But regardless of their ideological stance, most of these historians shared a common conceptual framework: they either marginalized or ignored the theme of organized religion.

This neglect is widespread. For example, four recent compilations of essays on western history—*A Society to Match the Scenery* (1991), *A New Significance: Re-envisioning the History of the American West* (1996), *Many Wests: Place, Culture, and Regional Identity* (1997), and *Over the Edge: Remapping the American West* (1999)—pay virtually no attention to the world of organized faith.[1] Even Quintard Taylor's excellent overview of African Americans in the West, which does acknowledge the central role played by the black church in the nineteenth century, drops the theme in its analysis of the twentieth.[2]

Two well-written recent surveys by journalists, Timothy Egan's *Lasso the Wind: Away to the New West* (1998) and Robert D. Kaplan's *An Empire Wilderness: Travels into America's Future* (1998), fall into the same camp. The contemporary West that so fascinates Egan and Kaplan is almost completely secular.[3] The somewhat quirky *Atlas of the New West* (1997) provides the best example of this recent trend. The *Atlas* devotes more text to the themes of "Jet-setting in the West" and "Guest Houses" than it does to religion, which is represented by two pages on the New Age movement.[4] A person who reads only recent works might well conclude that the modern American West has evolved into a thoroughly secular society.

Yet this is decidedly off the mark. Orthodox theologian Alexander Schmemann once termed secularity "a lie about the world."[5] Similarly, I believe that a completely secular interpretation of regional history is a lie about the West. Such a view not only slights some of the chief institutions of the region, it also ignores a central component of the human experience, the historical locus of both personal and social vision. It has always been a puzzle to me why so many modern historians have downplayed the religious history of the West. On a local level, Catholic schools, Jewish hospitals, Protestant social programs, and Mormon group projects continue to play vital roles. The various western "new religions" have garnered an enormous amount of publicity. All the national polls show that Americans remain one of the most religious peoples of the industrialized world. Why, then, have historians been so reluctant to explore this theme?

The answer is complex, but perhaps one can point to four probable causes. First would be the constitutional separation of church and state, which seems to thrust "politics" to the center of common concerns and confine "religion" to the private sphere. The multiplicity of religious groups in the West—several hundred organizations—points to yet another factor. The presence of such pluralism makes it difficult to construct a single, all-encompassing narrative line as one might for, say, the "evangelical South." As a result, most western religious history has been written with either a local, state, or denominational focus, all of which considerably restrict readership.

The largely "indifferent" nature of the contemporary Academy suggests a third cause. From Frederick Jackson Turner forward, most western historians have simply looked elsewhere for their historical explanations.[6] The "New Western Historians," for example, have placed most of their emphasis on the themes of race, class, and gender. Yet I think the most probable reason for this relative neglect lies with the fact that a religious template realigns all the traditional categories used to understand the western past: ethnic, political, economic, social, the traditional westward expansion, and the new triad of race-class-

German Reformed Church, Dempster, South Dakota. This handsome building on the northern Great Plains reflects the important role that the church played in holding the European ethnic communities together.

gender. The religious history of the modern American West introduces a new cast of characters and often forges its own boundaries.

In the pages that follow I will attempt to establish these boundaries by discussing religion in the modern West through three overlapping periods. Part I covers the era from the 1890s to the 1920s. During this time the forces of organized religion drew upon traditional sectarian rivalry and shared biblical metaphors to lay down much of the institutional infrastructure of western life: hospitals, schools, orphanages, and the local welfare system. In most areas, the three historical faiths—Protestantism, Catholicism, Judaism—coexisted with relative equanimity as they tried to serve their congregations, elevate the moral tone of their communities, and (they hoped) shape their regions for the foreseeable future. In Utah and surrounding regions, the fourth major faith, Mormonism, continued to hold cultural dominance even as it slowly modified its earlier positions. On the Great Plains and elsewhere, the churches and synagogues served as the primary "ethnic glue" that held the immigrant populations together, from German Lutherans in Nebraska to Russian-German Mennonite communities in Kansas to Ukrainian Orthodox churches in North Dakota.

Part II covers the years from around 1920 to 1960. In the immediate post–World War I decade, the major western religious forces clashed in what might be termed "round one" of the twentieth-century cultural wars. During the Great Depression of the 1930s, however, organized religion dropped this noisy quarrel to concentrate primarily on economic survival, simultaneously inaugurating a variety of social welfare programs. This period also witnessed the emergence of two themes that would have long-term regional consequences. During the late 1930s, the Latter-day Saints introduced their innovative social welfare system, and the distinctive Pentecostal subculture that had emerged in the Texas-Oklahoma-Arkansas region during the 1920s began to move en masse to California and the Pacific Northwest. The aftermath of World War II witnessed a major western church/synagogue building program plus the essential "mainstreaming" of all four religious groups. In addition, in 1952 the Southern Baptist Convention voted to inaugurate the serious evangelization of the Far West, a decision that would have considerable impact on that historically "semisecular" region.

Part III covers the years from around 1960 to 1999. During this tumultuous era, western Native American faiths received their first popular sympathetic hearing from non-Native groups. The 1990 federal Native American Graves Protection and Repatriation Act involved the highly publicized return of human remains and sacred objects stored in museums to their respective tribes for ceremonial reburial. At the same time, Native spiritual leaders watched in dismay as various New Age leaders borrowed and distorted traditional Indian teachings, leading one multitribal group to issue a "Declaration of War Against Exploiters of Lakota Spirituality" in 1993.[7]

Behind this overall framework rests a number of assumptions, all of which may safely be asserted but none of which can be absolutely proven. Still, they probably should be laid on the table at the onset. By "American West" I mean the area extending from roughly the 100th meridian to the Pacific Coast. The 100th meridian, which divides the Dakotas, Nebraska, Kansas, Oklahoma, and Texas, marks the region of about 20 inches of annual rainfall, the infamous line of aridity that still determines the contours of regional existence. Except in the Pacific Northwest, the issue of water has dominated western life in a way that the rest of the nation simply cannot fathom. As the old adage phrased it, in western towns whiskey was for drinking and water was for fighting. This lack of water restructured settlement patterns to turn the West into an "urban oasis" while also making available to experimental religious groups vast areas of "vacant" land.

Second, although the twentieth century has often been viewed as an age of impersonal institutions, I believe that human activity lies at the heart of any meaningful historical narrative. Thus, the last chapter of each of the three sections profiles some of the more important western religious figures of that era. The careers of Rev. Judson Boone, Rabbi William Friedman, and Catholic bishop Leroy T. Mattheisen deserve to be better known. The more recognized names, such as evangelist Aimee Semple McPherson, health reformer Ellen Gould White (the founder of Loma Linda University), and media personality Robert Schuller, can best be understood by placing them in a western context.

Third, I confess at the onset that limitations of time and space have forced me to slight numerous groups and individuals who rightly deserve much more attention. My criteria for inclusion rest largely with my assessment of the centrality of the group for modern western history and the narrative impact of the group's story. English historian Thomas B. Macaulay once wrote in his journal that his goal was to skip as quickly as possible over the dull and dwell as long as he could on the significant and the dramatic.[8] I still find that an admirable goal for historians.

My overall thesis may be phrased as follows: although the modern American West participated in all national religious trends, westerners generally bent these trends along their own trajectories. Thus, the social gospel emphasis of Denver, San Francisco, and El Paso was not identical with that of Chicago. Similarly, the mild anti-evolution agitation of the 1920s West could never be confused with the media hoopla that surrounded the 1925 Scopes Trial in Dayton, Tennessee. The religious response to the Great Depression and World War II proved equally distinctive, as did the building program and new evangelism of the 1950s. With the onset of the interstate highway system and the ongoing media revolution, one might expect that the religious history of the West would become more like that of the rest of the nation. In fact, almost the opposite has occurred. Cities like San Francisco, Seattle, Los Angeles, and Denver became homes to a variety of new religions that cast but faint shadows back east.

During this same period, the mainline denominations slowly lost their cultural hegemony over national mores. Pushed from mainline to sideline, the more established churches watched in dismay as neo-evangelicalism, a rising spiritual individualism, increased secularism, and a wave of new religions usurped their historic role as shapers of culture. During this time, the activities of the often extreme new religions brought religion in the West into the national media spotlight through a variety of bizarre controversies. In addition, the western clash between religious liberals and religious conservatives over evolution, homosexuality, and a variety of other issues—round two of the national cultural wars—introduced a dimension of religious acrimony into regional life that shows little sign of fading. Similarly, smaller communities such as Santa Fe, New Mexico, and Sedona, Arizona, emerged as magnets for the New Age movement. The most vocal anti-nuclear Roman Catholic bishops hailed from the West for the very good reason that their dioceses contained large nuclear installations. Similarly, the renewed respect for Native American spirituality had a western focus because that is where most of the reservations are. As a final example, the longest-lasting religiocultural tension in western life has never been Jewish-Christian or Protestant-Catholic; rather, it remains Mormon-Gentile (i.e., non-Mormon). In Mormon country today, a person's primary identity is still cast in those terms, just as it has been for the last 150 years. Moreover, although certain subregions might reflect the cultural hegemony of a specific faith, taken as a whole, the American West has never produced any religious mainstream. With few exceptions, the celebrated individualism of western life has remained preeminent. Consequently, the American West may well have set the stage for national religious life in the twenty-first century.

Acknowledgments

I would like to thank Gerald D. Nash for inviting me to participate in this series and Richard W. Etulain for his continued encouragement along the way. Thanks, too, to Joanne O'Hare at the University of Arizona Press for her support. Stanley Hordes, Noel Pugach, and Henry Tobias were most helpful in expanding my understanding of Jewish history. Michael Engh, S.J., and Steve Arvella, S.J., were equally gracious in providing information on western Catholicism. Thomas Alexander did the same for Latter-day Saint history, and Richard Etulain added considerably to my understanding of evangelical culture. Special thanks are also due to the two anonymous readers for the University of Arizona Press (one of whom, I deduced, was Martin Marty). Their critiques were both invaluable.

Much of the research for this study emerged from the cutting files held by regional public libraries and state historical societies. The extensive collections in every city library I visited clearly revealed the importance of churches and synagogues at a local level.

This research always proved interesting. In several archives, the file folder "Churches, Evangelical" was followed by "Churches, Jewish." When I sought information on western religion in the Panhandle-Plains Historical Museum in Canyon, Texas, the archivist suggested I look under "P." Why "P"? I inquired. "Why, for 'Preachers,' of course," he replied. These archivists are vital to any historian's effort, and overall I am much in debt to the following: Lee Mortensen of the Nevada Historical Society; the staffs of the public libraries in Reno, Amarillo, Albuquerque, Santa Fe, Roswell (New Mexico), Carlsbad (New Mexico), El Paso, Boise, Lincoln (Nebraska), and Price (Utah); the Menaul Historical Library, Albuquerque; the Arizona Historical Society; the Las Vegas, Nevada, Historical Library; the Nebraska Historical Society; the Kansas Historical Society; Thomas Jaehn and William Tydeman, formerly of the Idaho Historical Society in Boise; Eleanor Gehres, director of the Western Room, Denver Public Library; the Panhandle-Plains Historical Museum, Canyon, Texas; and, of course, the staff of the Zimmerman Library of the University of New Mexico. Once again, I would like to credit the typing skills of Penelope P. Katson. Most of all, however, I want to thank Margaret Connell Szasz for sharing this historical journey with me.

PART I

The 1890s to the 1920s

Chapter 1

The Western "Gospel in the World"

From the mid-nineteenth century forward, the American West has meant more than simply a geographical region. It has always loomed in the American imagination as semisacred space, different in character from both North and South, perhaps less bound by traditional mores and conventions.

In 1906 playwright William Vaughan Moody captured this sentiment in his play *The Great Divide,* a Broadway sensation that was praised at the time as the "Great American play."[1] *The Great Divide,* which was based on a real incident, tells the tale of an impoverished New England middle-class woman, Ruth Jordan, who moves to Arizona. There she meets a rough entrepreneur, Stephen Ghent, who threatens to sexually assault her, but she negotiates a "marriage" with him instead. Over the course of two acts, one set in Arizona and the other in Massachusetts, Ghent reforms and saves the Jordan family fortunes, and the couple live happily ever after. *The Great Divide* obviously echoed on several levels for Moody's audiences: Victorian mores versus "Arizona" behavior, men versus women, and, especially, the East versus the West. The audience members eventually realized that Moody's American West represented a very different world indeed.

The religious statistics of the day reflected many of those differences. In 1890 the Bureau of the Census collected the first reliable figures pertaining to church membership, number of clerics, value of edifices, and so on. In 1906 the Census Bureau again sent out a two-part questionnaire to organized religious bodies across the land. It repeated the process in 1916 and 1926. The 1926 census has been widely praised as one of the best of its time.[2]

In 1912 H. K. Carroll, religious editor of the Boston-based *Independent,* tried to evaluate the 1890 and 1906 figures. Carroll marveled at the infinite variety of religions in the United States, a diversity that included 143 denominations divided into a variety of "families," including six Adventist, seven Catholic, twelve Mennonite, twelve Presbyterian, thirteen Baptist, sixteen Lutheran, and seventeen Methodist denominations, "the why of which must forever remain an inscrutable mystery to the mass of mankind." Carroll also discovered that about one in twelve Americans was either an active or passive *opponent* of any organized religion. Although he praised the Catholic Church as being as American as the Lutheran, he also claimed that "evangelical Christianity" was the dominant religious force in the United States and that "in its various forms it shapes the religious character of the American people."[3]

Carroll's observation may have been more-or-less true for America east of the 100th meridian, but it did not provide an accurate portrait of the American West. In this area evangelical Christianity did not shape the "religious character" of the region. In fact, in many places it found itself a decided minority.

A few examples. A 1900 Arizona estimate placed the Catholic population at around 40,000, including virtually all the Hispanic citizens, the majority of churchgoers. Second place went to the Mormons at 7,000; the Presbyterians and Methodists came in third and fourth, with about half as many members each. Taos, New Mexico, during the same era contained about 8,000 Catholics. The 317 Protestants in Taos composed about 4 percent of the population.[4]

In Utah in 1906 the Mormons held 87.4 percent of the church membership, with the Catholics second at 5.3 percent. Third place went to "others" at 3.4 percent; the largest evangelical Protestant group, the Presbyterians, came in a distant fourth at 1.1 percent.[5] The Mormons similarly dominated neighboring Idaho, with a majority that ranked slightly under half of all church membership. Catholics were second in Idaho, and both Mormons and Catholics were each approximately as large as all other Protestant groups taken together. The regional center of Boise contained about 6,000 people in 1898, of whom 716 (about 12 percent) claimed membership in *any* organized church.[6]

In 1909 a *World's Work* tabulation of religious statistics concluded that Catholics maintained the largest percentage of church members in sixteen states and territories, half of which lay in the West: New

Mexico, 88.7 percent; Montana, 73.1 percent; Nevada, 66.7 percent; Arizona, 66.2 percent; California, 58 percent. The Catholics also held the largest proportion, although not a majority, in Washington, Wyoming, and Colorado.[7]

Carroll's state-by-state pie charts show the religious uniqueness of the turn-of-the-century West. In North and South Dakota, Catholics and Lutherans were approximately equal, each larger than all other Protestant denominations combined. Only Kansas, Texas, Oklahoma, and to some extent Nebraska boasted significant mainline Protestant numbers.[8] *Outlook* religious writer E. H. Abbott added his personal observations to these figures. He once described Kansas as filled with Yankees—"a combination of Puritanism and the prairie." Abbott credited the Yankee influence for the state's Sabbatarianism, moral earnestness, and vigorous prohibitionist sentiment, concerns he did not find elsewhere in the region.[9]

The weakness of western mainline Protestant denominations could be seen in the larger West Coast cities as well. Although evangelical Protestantism had established a firm presence in Seattle, Portland, San Francisco, and Los Angeles, it hardly shaped the cultures of those cities. A 1902 Northern Baptist publication spoke of the "religious destitution" of western Washington.[10] San Francisco formed a Catholic-Jewish enclave, with only about 15 percent of the city claiming membership in Protestant churches. In 1915 the Episcopal Church boasted 1,010,874 members, but only a little over 50,000 lived between the Mississippi River and the Pacific Coast. The bishop of Oklahoma complained that most citizens of his state knew "absolutely nothing of that strange body with its queer ways of Prayer-Book services and vested ministers—the Episcopal Church."[11] The missionary bishop of West Texas had another observation. As he noted in 1890, "the condition of things in the East and the Southwest is in marked contrast. In the one, our people are almost universally found among the most prosperous class. In the other, they are rarely ever so."[12] Consequently, the religious denominations west of the 100th meridian often moved on different trajectories from their counterparts east of the Mississippi. This proved especially true in the regional response to the premier national concern of the day: the "social question."

It is not surprising that numerous western faiths manifested a strong concern for the Gospel-in-the-world during these years. Drawing on Pope Leo XIII's 1891 encyclical, *Rerum Novarum,* Baptist theologian Walter Rauschenbusch's books, and the traditional Jewish concern for the social order, Catholics, Protestants, and Jews all across the land had begun to deepen their understanding of the biblical message.[13] Rauschenbusch, for example, argued that the idea of sin extended far beyond the individual. The social order itself, he suggested, could also embody sin. Like the individual, society stood in need of God's grace. Rauschenbusch argued for a revived twentieth-century evangelism that would introduce an "applied Christianity" to the country. A nation manifesting an unjust social order, he declared, was an offense to God. Popular author Winston Churchill conveyed this sentiment to a wider audience in many of his novels. Sin, he wrote in 1914, was simply a rejection of service to others.[14]

With some exceptions, this concern for the social order crossed denominational lines with relative ease. It also briefly bridged the nascent Fundamentalist-modernist split that would so disrupt the mainline Protestant churches two decades later. Initially, few fin de siècle contemporaries saw much conflict between traditional evangelistic crusades and the newer, liberal emphasis on church social services. In fact, they were often seen as two sides of the same coin. Charles A. Tindley's most famous gospel hymn, "We Are Often Tossed and Driven" ("We'll understand it better by and by"), written in 1906, deals not simply with otherworldly hopes but reflects social concerns as well. The ecumenism of this position was succinctly phrased by *Outlook* editor Lyman Abbott: "My Roman Catholic brother, and my Jewish brother, and my agnostic brother and I, an evangelical minister, have started in various quarters, and are going in different directions, but we are all aiming for the same place [the Kingdom of God]."[15]

During the fin de siècle years, the ideas of the social gospel moved into most denominations. As historian C. Howard Hopkins has observed, however, the social gospel never really became an organized "movement."[16] Instead, the men and women who shared its basic theological underpinnings utilized the existing denominational frameworks to enact their social reform programs. Because of this flexible structure, the clerics varied their social emphasis from region to region.

In the urban Northeast the churches directed most of their social gospel efforts toward resolving the problems of the growing immigrant slum areas. They emphasized public health measures, free legal aid, employment assistance, and other social services. When the southern churches became involved with social concerns, they expressed a slightly different focus. The southern clergy stressed the issues of anti—child labor legislation, prison reform, Sabbath observance, temperance, and Appalachian mountain work. Ironically, even as the nation's religious groups increased their concern for such issues, the major responsibility for securing a just social order was shifting steadily to the secular political institutions.[17]

Since the social gospel proved to be more an attitude than a set of prescriptions, regional clergymen could adjust it to suit the problems at hand. Western priests, ministers, and rabbis responded accordingly. In western urban areas that duplicated eastern slum conditions, the clerics introduced similar social service programs. Others in the polyglot mining areas followed suit.

Such social gospel activities in the West, however, did not represent much of a shift from traditional church efforts. From the Spanish *entrada* of the 1540s through the onrush of Anglo-American settlement after the Civil War, western churches had always been concerned with the social order. The (largely southern) idea that the clergyman's role was simply to "preach the old Gospel" had rarely been accepted in the Victorian West. Faced with the virtual absence of *any* social institutions, pioneer ministers, priests, and rabbis all became "social gospelers" well before the term was created. From the onset, western clerics established schools, orphanages, and hospitals; denounced alcohol, lawlessness, and Sabbath breaking; fulminated against prostitution and corrupt elected officials; and tried to locate themselves in the very heart of their communities.[18] Thus, the western social gospel efforts from the 1890s to the 1920s reflected less a revived emphasis on renewed moral custodianship than a simple extension of traditional western religious practices.

The unique situations in which many western clerics found themselves, however, required equally unique applications of the social gospel emphasis. Major western social concerns included increased urban social work; the founding of orphanages; missions to immigrant Mexicans, Chinese, and Native Americans; improved health care; and, especially, the establishment of a variety of schools, ranging from kindergartens to universities.

The Gospel-in-the-world ethic formed a prominent aspect of turn-

of-the-century western religious life. From 1890 to 1920 the major urban centers in the region—Denver, Los Angeles, Portland, San Francisco, and Seattle—shared many of the same social problems of New
York or Chicago. Indeed, the term "skid row," which became a syn-
onym for urban slum, originated in Seattle. San Francisco's infamous
"Barbary Coast" also entered the language. Consequently, these Pacific coastal cities all produced prominent clerical social gospel cru-
saders. Every western Progressive Era campaign for clean government
had its clerical spokesmen. In Seattle Presbyterian Mark A. Matthews
denounced bootleggers, corrupt politicians, and social dislocation in
many a sermon and pamphlet. In San Francisco Catholic priest Peter
Christopher Yorke championed the nascent labor union movement.
Neither man, incidentally, remained a social gospeler for long. After
World War I, Matthews became a prominent Fundamentalist and Yorke
a militant Irish nationalist.[19]

The dominant city of the interior West, Denver, exhibited a variety
of social gospel activities. A community of 213,000 in 1910, Denver
had wrestled with skid row problems ever since gold rush days, when
unemployed miners would often drift into the city to pass the winter.
During the fin de siècle years, however, clerics from all faiths worked
with local lay officials to try to ameliorate social problems.

In Thomas ("Parson Tom") Uzzell and Myron Reed, turn-of-the-century Denver produced two highly articulate clerical spokesmen for
social justice. In 1885, after leaving his pastorate in Leadville, Uzzell
took over Denver's Methodist "People's Tabernacle." He remained there
until his death in 1910. In addition to his regular ministry, Uzzell established a free dispensary, with three physicians on duty, and founded
a free second-hand store in the church's basement. He also began an
employment bureau. Through his connections with the railroads,
Uzzell secured half-price rail transportation to any point in the nation
for people in distress.

Uzzell had numerous friends among the city's elite, and he worked
with them to establish several municipal welfare programs. The
People's Tabernacle regularly arranged free summer camp excursions
to the mountains. His church was one of the first to establish night
schools and kindergartens, and it also taught sewing, cooking, and
English to immigrants. Later, Uzzell organized an annual rabbit hunt
in Lamar, in the southeastern part of the state. After the rabbits had
been dispatched, the hunters shipped the meat to Denver to be given

to the poor. When Uzzell died, he was one of the most deeply mourned citizens of Denver.[20]

His fellow pastor, Myron W. Reed, achieved a similar local reputation. Called to Denver's First Congregational Church in 1884, Reed remained a prominent public figure until his death in 1899. He always considered the church as a key agent in the molding of humankind into a cooperative moral community. His sympathy lay largely with the working class of the region, and he became one of the Mountain West's most articulate spokesmen for the cause of labor. He advocated improved safety devices for the mines and steel mills and worked hard for the enactment of a workmen's compensation law. He also attacked sweatshops and child labor. His sympathy for working men eventually got him in trouble with his fashionable, middle-class congregation. During a bitter 1893 labor strike at Cripple Creek, Colorado, he confessed to his church that his heart lay with the miners ensconced on Bull Hill. Shortly thereafter, he broke with the Congregationalists and founded a popular nondenominational church that lasted until his death.[21]

Baptist Jim Goodheart and Methodist Francesco P. Salmonetti inherited Denver's social gospel mantle from Reed and Uzzell. A former gambler and reformed alcoholic, Goodheart was close to suicide when he was converted in Denver's Sunshine Mission in 1904. In 1908 he returned to Denver to head the mission and later, although he had no formal training, was ordained a Baptist minister.

Goodheart made the Sunshine Mission into a major Denver institution. His church provided an employment bureau, offered free food and lodging for transients, took in orphans, and assisted a segment of the population that few churches were able to reach. In 1918 the mayor of Denver created the position of city chaplain (really the director of public welfare) for Goodheart. The local chief of police said that if it were not for Goodheart, he would have to add thirty men to his police force.[22]

In 1910 the Methodists established the Holy Trinity Italian Evangelical Institutional Church. Francesco Salmonetti's sermons in Italian were supplemented with free medical treatment and free legal advice. In addition, the church opened an evening school to teach English. In 1915 the Methodists also established a Spanish Methodist church that specialized in bilingual classes in sewing and cooking and also sponsored noonday luncheons for undernourished children.

This church had a library, with a regular story hour, and taught both music and handiwork. It administered to about a thousand Spanish-speaking residents.[23]

Denver's social gospel emphasis crossed denominational lines. Rabbis, Catholic priests, and Protestant clergymen all worked together for a common goal. In both Portland and Denver such ecumenical cooperation helped establish the cities' first organized charity systems. Myron Reed described the situation: "I saw a Jewish rabbi, a Catholic priest, an Episcopalian rector and a Congregational parson in one carriage going to the burial of a newspaperman who belonged to no church." It was a good sign, Reed noted, when the representatives of the different faiths could appear together on a platform not to dispute but to agree on a public concern.[24]

Excluding the coastal areas and Denver, however, the fin de siècle West contained few areas that might be described as genuinely urban. The populations of Salt Lake City, Topeka, and Lincoln were around 50,000, but after that the figures fell rapidly: Colorado Springs, 21,000; El Paso, 16,000; Oklahoma City, 10,000; Tucson, 8,000; Tulsa, 1,390; Albuquerque, 7,000; Boise, 6,000; and Missoula, 4,000. As Episcopal home missionary Hugh L. Burleson observed in 1918, the Intermountain West has "no city problem in the ordinary sense of the term."[25]

Although the clergy in these medium-sized cities never confronted the same degree of social dislocation as the West Coast, they also introduced their own version of the social gospel. Salt Lake City and Topeka could hardly be considered major urban areas, but the clerical leaders in each town founded the same types of institutional churches and social outreach programs that were located in Denver or Seattle.

In 1915 the Utah Methodists invited an Italian minister from Butte to help establish a mission in the heart of Salt Lake City. Working with a community of about two thousand Italians, he inaugurated a series of social programs: immigrant clubs, English language classes, and several mothers clubs. Volunteers from the church also helped run the city library.[26]

In Topeka, Congregationalist minister Charles M. Sheldon launched a number of similar Gospel-in-the-world ventures, including his one-week stint as editor of the local newspaper (in which he printed only "proper" news). He is still fondly remembered as the author of the best-selling classic novel *In His Steps* (1896 and still in print), which asked readers to consider, "What would Jesus do" in any situation?[27]

Even the clergymen who served in the isolated western plains drew from the concept of the social gospel. In Hankinson, North Dakota, for example, a Congregational minister organized a gymnasium for the young men in the region. The church in the mining community of Rock Springs, Wyoming, proved even more imaginative. Rock Springs contained forty-seven different ethnic groups and claimed that it was a "New York in miniature." From 1907 to 1912 the local Methodist church functioned as if it had been located in the lower East Side of New York City. It organized night schools, reading rooms, and various educational courses. Two women church workers arrived from the East, and at one time they boasted six different classes in operation.[28] Similarly, numerous ministers in El Paso began settlement houses for Mexican immigrants. Thus, the western clergy adopted the framework of the social gospel for a variety of communities, ranging in size from Seattle and Salt Lake City down to Rock Springs and Hankinson.

The numerous denominational missions to the Native Americans could be included under the Gospel-in-the-world umbrella. The Catholics, Methodists, Episcopalians, and Christian Reformed all established missions on the sprawling Navajo Reservation. The Presbyterians were active on the Nez Perce Reservation in Idaho and among the Pima in Arizona. The Dutch Reformed maintained a visible presence among the major Apache groups in New Mexico. All of these denominations emphasized the education of Native American children.

In several cases local church workers defended Native rights against a hostile white majority. For example, in 1905 Catholic priest Joseph Schell accused the merchants of northeastern Nebraska of defrauding the Winnebago Indians. Later Schell was mysteriously beaten and removed from his post against his will. In 1902 Baptist missionary Lillie Corwin moved to Reno, Nevada, to found, among other organizations, the Nevada Indian Association. By 1916 Corwin had become the driving force in establishing Nevada's "Indian Colonies" (small reservations) scattered in a dozen towns throughout the state, thus assuring Native Americans at least a modest land base. The Washoe tribe today officially commemorates her efforts in their museum. Wealthy Philadelphian Mother Katharine Drexel spent her life and her considerable fortune financing Indian Catholic education in Wyoming, New Mexico, Idaho, Montana, California, and Oklahoma.[29] The list could be extended.

Concern over immigration had always lain at the heart of fin de siècle social reform efforts. Immigrants came from every corner of the globe (Chicago's Hull House once counted thirty-two different national groups in the area), but the West harbored one ethnic community, the Chinese, that remained largely limited to the region.

As late as 1905 Chinese miners in Silverton, Colorado, were still being loaded onto box cars and sent to Durango with orders not to return. In 1910 an aristocratic Chinese visitor observed that no Chinese gentleman would dare send his son to study or travel in America. The son would surely be lumped with the Cantonese coolies and be either scorned or persecuted.[30] Virtually the only groups that tried to ameliorate this situation were the churches. Numerous clerics all through the West organized Chinese schools or special missions as part of their church enterprise. While these efforts were scattered and often short-lived, they should not be discounted. Dealing with the "Chinese problem" formed an important aspect of the western social gospel program.

The Chinese schools rose and fell as the need dictated. In 1895 the Baptists established a Chinese mission in El Paso. Denver's First Baptist Church provided weekly English instruction during the early 1890s for about sixty-five Chinese students. The class was "doing an imperishable work for a greatly neglected and pitiable class," the official booklet noted, "a class whom the Master loved and saved." The Chinese school of Central Presbyterian Church in Denver lasted well into the twentieth century.[31]

Teaching English and the rudiments of Christianity to this group was not easy. The Chinese population fluctuated constantly. Everyone hoped to strike it rich and then return home. Several of the men resisted the introduction of Christianity and spoke ill of "American religion." One observer felt that the Chinese attended the English classes in spite of the religious dimension rather than because of it. Some of the laborers went to both Protestant and Catholic missions, seemingly without distinction. When the Silverton, Colorado, Congregational church began a Chinese Christian Endeavor Society in 1891, the Silverton Standard cynically noted that its goal was "to convert the Chinese and induce them to handle soiled linen and red checks with more Christian charity."[32]

Chinese and English, of course, share no cognates, and it is unlikely that many of the teachers were familiar with the Chinese language. Moreover, they had access to few teaching aids. Isolated hymn books or missionary tracts with parallel columns of text were all that were available. Thus, the Chinese men often sat down to face the beginning McGuffey readers. One Denver Presbyterian layman journeyed to Shanghai for a full year of language study. One can imagine his reaction when he returned to discover that the language of North China, which he had learned, was totally unintelligible to the Canton peasants in his classes.[33]

In spite of the difficulties, however, many Asians learned English, and, along the way, several converted to Christianity. One estimate suggests that perhaps 50,000 Chinese had joined American churches by 1910. Several converts became ministers. Christian evangelist Lum Foon pastored up and down the West Coast, while Sia Sek Ong, Gee Gam, and Le Tong Hay (Methodists); Ton Keet Hing and Fung Chak (Baptists); and a Reverend Wong (Presbyterian) were also active. Naturally, both the Protestants and Catholics established the majority of their Chinese missions on the West Coast. There was even a short-lived journal entitled the *Chinese Episcopalian.*

It is difficult to assess the effectiveness of these sporadic church efforts. For those Chinese who remained, the language training must have been invaluable. Most returned to Asia, however, and gradually the letters to their former teachers dwindled. Some, such as Charlie Wann, a product of the Congregational Chinese School in Prescott, maintained their contacts. Wann returned to China and became a millionaire merchant. Later he established a Christian hospital in Hong Kong, and he always provided considerable support for Chinese missionaries.[34] Through these Chinese schools, the western churches established their own version of practical Christianity.

———

Medical care formed another crucial aspect of the western Gospel-in-the-world. From 1865 forward, virtually all western hospitals and orphanages, large or small, had roots in some religious organization. The makeshift hospital in Price, Utah, an overwhelmingly Catholic mining town, drew its funds from a compulsory donation from every miner. The nursing nuns left only when the ores played out. The same plan prevailed for Saint Louisa's Hospital in Virginia City, Nevada. For years the sole health care facility for all of eastern New Mexico came from the Southern Baptist hospital in Clovis. It closed in 1939 upon completion of a county-run building.[35] In a similar fashion, the Episcopal Church established a small hospital in Indian Territory to aid Natives, miners, and railroad men and a larger one on the Navajo Reservation in Arizona. The Methodists alone set up nine hospitals in Montana.

These church-run hospitals and orphanages in rural or mining areas functioned on a very modest scale, and eventually most of them disappeared. The religious organizations in the larger cities, however, had both a stronger financial base and a larger mass of people. In these cities, many church-founded institutions remain active almost a century later. In 1901, for example, the Sisters of Charity began Saint Anthony's Hospital in Amarillo, still a major health care provider. Saint Luke's (Episcopal) and Saint Alphonsus (Roman Catholic) hospitals continue to dominate the Boise medical world today. So, too, does Saint Elizabeth's in Lincoln, Nebraska. On the northern Great Plains, the Grey Nuns, the Presentation Sisters, the Benedictine Sisters, and the Sisters of Mercy were all active in the field of health care. On the West Coast, the Sisters of Mercy established at least three hospitals in southern California, as well as many other institutions. When Mother Mary Baptist Russell died in San Francisco, the newspaper described her as "the best known charitable worker" on the Pacific Coast.[36]

Although they treated all the illnesses of the day, a surprising number of these early-twentieth-century institutions had some link with tuberculosis (TB). In 1900 the "White Plague," as it was termed, claimed over 150,000 people a year. It was easily the nation's leading killer, far ahead of cancer and heart disease. No cure existed; treatment included rest and a high, dry climate. Colorado, New Mexico, Arizona, and West Texas were all highly praised in this regard. In the early years of the century the National Tuberculosis Association estimated that perhaps seven thousand people with TB moved to the Southwest every year. By 1920 perhaps 10 percent of New Mexico's population consisted of health seekers.[37]

Disciples of Christ minister Harold Bell Wright was one of these health seekers. When Wright settled in Redlands, California, in 1907 he was already a celebrity for his religious novels, especially *That Printer of Udell's* (1903), which had earlier been entitled *Practical Christianity*. After moving to Redlands, Wright continued his sermonic storytelling in several other best-sellers that made him one of the most popular novelists of his day.

Wright's novels portrayed simple moral truths in lively prose. They took the side of the western "little people" against cruel, impersonal Eastern antagonists. Wright's *The Eyes of the World* was even filmed (1916) as a ten-reel morality play. Wright had considerable influence on his generation (later President Ronald Reagan was one of his greatest fans) as he preached ethics, religion, and the American West in roughly equal combinations.[38]

While a number of smaller southwestern communities, such as Carlsbad, New Mexico, actively recruited health seekers, others, such as Phoenix and Tucson, tried to discourage them. The reasons were economic. Many tuberculars arrived in the Southwest so ill that they could not work and thus became public charges. The Phoenix and Salt River Valley Immigration Commission warned that people "should arrive with sufficient money to pay all living expenses for at least one year." New Mexico and Arizona spokesmen had to appeal formally to eastern physicians not to send them tubercular patients who could not support themselves.[39]

A surprising number of clerics first came West because either they or their families were trying to "chase the cure." These included Albuquerque Congregationalist Jacob Mills Ashley, who moved to New Mexico chiefly because his son had TB, and Baptist Bruce Kinney, who accepted an offer to pastor Albuquerque's First Baptist Church because of his ill wife. The files of Episcopal missionary bishop J. Mills Kendrick are full of requests from seriously ill clergymen seeking a position in the Southwest.

Numerous private sanatoria had been built to meet the health seeker demand, but their fees restricted them to the wealthy. According to the National Tuberculosis Association, over half of those who arrived in the Southwest were on the verge of poverty. Moreover, as the contagious nature of the disease became known, southwestern sentiment began to cool toward the new immigrants. The New Mexico territorial legislature forbade consumptives from entering the teaching profession. Arizona ranchers and businessmen often refused to hire TB sufferers, and western landlords increasingly hesitated to rent to them.[40] Thus, many immigrants lived in hastily constructed tent cities, partly to be outdoors, but partly because they could afford nothing better. "If there is one above another deserving our sympathy," noted a southwestern Presbyterian observer, "is it not that one who is afflicted with tuberculosis, poor in this world's goods, a thousand miles or more from home and friends, regarded with fear, and excluded from honest hotels."[41]

The western clergy viewed the dilemma of the health seekers as a legitimate area of religious concern. This proved to be a unique aspect of the western social gospel, and it spread across all denominations. In 1902 the Catholic Sisters of Saint Joseph began a hospital in Albuquerque for victims of lung disease. In 1904 the Baptists sent a trained nurse to the city to help the growing public health program. Two years later, Presbyterian minister Hugh A. Cooper (who had himself arrived with TB) opened a five-room cottage for indigent health seekers that grew to become the Presbyterian Hospital of Albuquerque. In 1912 the Methodists established a TB sanatorium in the Manzano Mountains east of Albuquerque. The Episcopalians set up Saint Luke's Hospital for TB patients in Phoenix, and the Methodists briefly ran a similar institution in Tucson. Saint Joseph's (Catholic) sanatorium in San Diego also began as an attempt to aid TB sufferers. The main accomplishment of Rabbi William S. Friedman (to be discussed in chapter 3) was the establishment of the National Jewish Hospital in Denver. It complemented the city's (Episcopal) Saint Luke's. The Baptists established TB hospitals in both El Paso and Tucson, and the Methodists set up what is now Good Samaritan in Phoenix.[42]

At the turn of the century, the cure for TB lay far in the future. No cure was found until the World War II years. Hence, these sanatoria remained a western social gospel concern for almost half a century. They were widely praised at the time for combining the resources of modern science with the ancient wisdom of Scripture. "Is this not an appealing work?" asked a writer in the Presbyterian magazine *La Aurora* in 1913. "Is it not a humanitarian undertaking? And more, is it not Christian?"[43]

In the area of education, the western religious groups also had few rivals. Unlike ecumenical social work, missions to the Chinese, or the establishment of local hospitals and orphanages, the erection of school systems contained potential for sectarian conflict. Roman Catholic doctrine of the day, which considered parochial education essential for the formation of religious character, voiced considerable suspicion of state-supported schools. Catholics argued, not without reason, that these schools were either aggressively secular or largely Protestant in tone.

Much of the same argument prevailed among the Lutheran Church, Missouri Synod, the largest body of Lutherans of the region and the denomination with the strictest doctrinal position. Virtually from the onset, the Missouri Synod established a system of Lutheran parochial schools. Initially, these schools were formed to protect German children from being "Americanized," but over the years they assumed the task of also protecting Lutheran children from the rationalism/liberalism that church leaders found rampant in the public school system. Modeled on the German *gymnasium,* the Missouri Synod Lutheran school system began with the lower grades, moved on to the high school level, and culminated (for elite students) in a bachelor of divinity degree from the Concordia Theological Seminary in Saint Louis.

The Roman Catholic parochial school system in the major cities of California had roots that stretched back to the gold rush days. Virtually all the early California towns of any size boasted Catholic schools. Since these were often the only schools available, they educated numerous non-Catholics as well, thus allowing the Church to become "catholic" in the original sense of the term. Jewish immigrant and later famed stage impresario David Belasco was a product of these schools. So grateful was he for his Catholic education that he often wore a clerical collar and termed himself "The Bishop of Broadway."

The parochial school systems of San Francisco and Los Angeles functioned with exceptional smoothness. By 1920 these schools educated about a third of San Francisco's youth and over 15 percent of the children in Los Angeles. As one spokesman phrased it, "The schools were the pearl of Los Angeles Catholicism." Not only did the Catholic Church run an elaborate private school system, by 1915 the Sisters of the Holy Family (founded in 1872 in San Francisco) also enrolled almost eight thousand children in a regional Catholic Sunday school program. The result was to turn certain sections of Los Angeles and virtually the entire San Francisco Bay Area into Roman Catholic enclaves. So marginalized were the Protestant immigrants to San Francisco that many felt they lived in a "different cultural world."[44]

The capstone of the church-sponsored school systems involved the creation of denominational colleges. Here one finds sectarian rivalry at its sharpest. Western Episcopal clerics argued that since eastern rectors generally failed in the West, the success of their church depended on establishing regional denominational colleges, for they alone could train up local residents. Outside of Texas, however, Episcopal ventures into higher education remained limited to a few female academies.

The historical model for this college rivalry lay on the midwestern, antebellum frontier, where the various denominations raced to claim the area via their denominational schools. Victorian Ohioans boasted that while France had one university and England two, Ohio had fifty-two. From Notre Dame to Knox, from Ohio Wesleyan to Otterbein, from Butler to Saint Olaf's, from Carleton to DePaul, the denominations established their universities all through the Midwest during the mid-nineteenth century.

The same rivalry occurred west of the Mississippi after the Civil War. Methodists set up Southern Methodist University in Fort Worth and Nebraska Wesleyan (initially called Northern Methodist) in Lincoln. In the Pacific Northwest the denominational schools of Willamette (Methodist), Whitman (Congregational), Whitworth (Presbyterian), Linfield (Baptist), Gonzaga (Catholic), and Pacific Lutheran dominated regional higher education until the era of World War I.

The Latter-day Saints established Brigham Young College in Logan and Brigham Young University (BYU; it assumed university status in 1903) in Provo. Although the former eventually merged with the state agricultural college, BYU remains today the nation's premier Mormon educational institution. The Presbyterians responded with Hastings College in Hastings, Nebraska, and Occidental College in Los Angeles. Virtually every college in the West traced its origin to some religious denomination.

In the Panhandle region of Texas, this sectarian rivalry proved exceptionally vigorous, but here it was fought out on an academy or high school level. When Catholics set up an academy in the railroad town of Clarendon, the Disciples of Christ followed with one in nearby Hereford and the Baptists with another in Canyon. Modest though they might have been, the presence of such schools allowed the various towns to term themselves the "Athens" of West Texas or Indian Territory.

In the borderlands area of the Southwest and in Utah, establishment of these schools served as a surrogate for the social tensions of the region. By 1900 the Catholics of New Mexico had established over twenty schools plus a college run by the Christian Brothers in Santa Fe. The Presbyterians, Methodists, and Congregationalists also established parochial school systems throughout the Southwest. In 1908 over a third of New Mexico children were enrolled in some form of parochial education, although this figure dropped sharply once the state-supported system finally took hold.[45] Although the religious groups occasionally exchanged harsh words, the Protestant and Catholic school systems eventually worked in parallel with each other rather than as rivals. The fact that most of the mission teachers were women probably helped dampen the potential for violence.[46]

In a similar fashion, the various denominations also established theological seminaries, often linked to their chief denominational colleges. Methodists set up Iliff in Denver and the Perkins School of Theology in Dallas; the Disciples set up the Berkeley Bible Seminary in California and the Brite Divinity School in Abilene. The Episcopalians established the Church Divinity School of the Pacific in Berkeley, while the Baptists established numerous Texas seminaries. Presbyterians founded the San Francisco Theological Seminary in 1891, which later moved to Marin County to become one of the key institutions of the region. In 1915 the Pacific Theological Seminary (Congregational) in Berkeley became interdenominational and changed its name to the Pacific School of Religion. The Catholics also established numerous western seminaries, scattered from Seattle to San Diego.

Although many of these denominational schools have achieved fine regional reputations (Hastings College, Denver University, Westminster College in Salt Lake City, among them), it seems safe to say that they have never played the same role in the education of the West that Harvard and Yale did for New England or Notre Dame and Ohio Wesleyan did for the Midwest. So intense was the western rivalry that many denominations overextended their resources. The Interior West not only contains numerous "ghost towns," it is also littered with "ghost colleges." Who has heard of Della Plain Male and Female Institute (Texas), Central Plains College (Texas), Gooding College (Idaho), Sedalia University (Kansas), Presbyterian College of the Southwest (Colorado),

Montezuma Baptist College (New Mexico), the College of the Sisters of Bethany (Kansas), Artesia College (New Mexico), Saint Vincent's College (California), or Goodnight Baptist College (Texas)? These are just a few of the denominational schools that died along the way for lack of funds and too few coreligionists. In the first fifty years of Oklahoma history, the Presbyterians lost four schools and the Methodists eight of nine. Most of these denominational dreams, like that of Rev. D. J. Pierce, who wanted to build a great Baptist University in the midst of Yellowstone Park, quietly fell by the wayside.[47]

———

By the era of World War II, the large state universities, with some exceptions, had emerged as the premier educational institutions of the West. The University of Wyoming, the University of Idaho, the University of New Mexico, the University of Colorado, and the University of Nebraska have few regional rivals. But there are three subregions of the West where denominational schools still retain much of their previous cultural hegemony: Utah, the Pacific Coast, and Texas/Oklahoma.

Mormon Utah ever remains the great exception in western religious history. During his brief life, prophet Joseph Smith, Jr., made numerous statements regarding the importance of education. Thus, when modern Mormon leaders began to focus on erecting their system of schools, they could draw on the prophet's words. With the University of Utah, Weber State, Southern Utah State, and Utah State, the state boasts one of the highest university ratios per capita. BYU (the "Y") and the nearby Mormon junior colleges remain an essential part of this educational complex.

The Catholic colleges and universities of the Pacific Coast have retained a similar regional influence. By 1900 California Catholics had established flagship schools in every major coastal city: the University of San Diego, Loyola of Los Angeles, the University of Santa Clara, the University of Portland, the University of San Francisco, Seattle University, and the premier Benedictine school, Saint Martin's in Lacey, Washington.[48] In addition, religious orders of women established seven colleges in California and twelve in Oregon. Many of the Catholic schools were run by Jesuits. By around 1930 Jesuit emphasis on philosophy and religion had produced a theological sophistication among their graduates that few Protestant schools could match.[49] On the Pacific Coast, the Catholic institutions easily outdistanced their smaller

Protestant rivals. In fact, by the early years of the century most of the California Protestant schools had dropped their denominational affiliations to become nonsectarian. The California Catholic schools, however, still continue to hold their own with the state institutions.

In Texas and Oklahoma, the situation was reversed. Here the Catholic colleges remained small while the major Protestant universities created a cultural hegemony all their own. Oklahoma Baptist University, the University of Tulsa, Southern Methodist University, Texas Christian University, Trinity University, and Abilene Christian University all contributed to this atmosphere. The Episcopal Church—related black schools, Wiley in Marshall and Texas College in Tyler, deserve mention here as well.

———

Although the western clerics borrowed from the national Gospel-in-the-world idea, their concerns often proved quite distinct from other regions. Unlike their northern or southern counterparts, from the 1890s to the World War I era the forces of organized religion in the West essentially created the institutional infrastructure for their subregions. This was especially true in the areas of health care and education. During this period, clerics from all faiths were viewed as civic leaders. They drew upon common social concerns and a shared Judeo-Christian scriptural rhetoric to introduce their programs of civic betterment. As a Denver observer noted in 1902, "If a new hospital is wanted or a new college is wanted, it is the church people of the locality who are called upon to meet the expense of it."[50] Thus, the "great divide" between East and West proved to be an important part of fin de siècle American religious life.

Chapter 2

Religious Life in the Urban and Rural West

Citizens of turn-of-the-century America were well aware that they were living through an Age of Doubt. In many regions a variety of new theologies challenged the inherited Judeo-Christian institutions, and increasing gaps between rich and poor challenged the very social order itself. Both eastern and western observers were unsettled by this situation.

For example, when journalist Ray Stannard Baker covered the 1893–94 Jacob Coxey March, a demand for mass employment on public works, from the Pacific Northwest to Washington, D.C., he found the crowd filled with faith healers, hypnotists, "mind cure specialists," and spiritualists. He entitled his account of the nation's religious life *The Spiritual Unrest* (1910). In 1917 George T. Bushnell of Pacific Grove University summed up the movements of the day as follows: "organized philanthropy, social service, laymen's missionary movements, Sunday School Reform, psychical research, spiritualism, Christian Science, New Thought, Theosophy, gifts of tongues, psychical therapeutics—their number is without end." Writing in 1912, Gaius Glenn Atkins suggested that one would have to return to the first three hundred years of the Christian era to find a comparable creative period in religious life such as America had undergone since 1880.[1] The traditional British jibe that the United States was a "vast commonwealth of sects" and the French sneer that America had "fifty-two religions but only two sauces" were exceptionally applicable at the dawn of the twentieth century. Such groups were so prevalent that the Equitable Life Insurance Company could run a 1910 advert that proclaimed, "Old Fashioned Life insurance—like old fashioned religion—is what is needed today in this age of 'isms' in theology and fads and schemes in life insurance."[2]

The American West of this era housed a variety of these new religious movements, a surprising number of which involved spiritual healing. For example, in 1895 thousands of people in New Mexico and Colorado stood in lines to be touched by an immigrant German spiritual healer, Francis Schlatter. Surviving photographs show that Schlatter bore an uncommon resemblance to the traditional portrayals of Jesus. Many visitors walked away from the experience professing themselves cured. A decade later, a Mexican immigrant healer, Teresa Urrea, astounded Tucson and San Diego with similar spiritual cures. Although the *curandera* tradition had long been a part of borderlands Hispanic culture, Schlatter's and Urrea's healing reached both Hispanic and Anglo-American households. The major New Thought movements, which also advocated spiritual healing (Unity of Kansas City, Divine Science of Denver, and Religious Science of Los Angeles), all established themselves in western locales.

The turn-of-the-century West also provided a home to a variety of communal experiments. The Puget Sound region of the Pacific Northwest hosted at least six such ventures, most of which were aggressively secular, although a few were based on a vague "brotherhood of man." The vast expanse of the Great Plains beckoned to other communitarians. As the name suggests, Liberal, Kansas, began as a colony of aggressive rationalists. In the late 1890s the Salvation Army sponsored three holiness "Prairie Homes for City Poor" on the plains of eastern Colorado. The Land of Shalam, a Faithist community near present-day Las Cruces, New Mexico, collapsed around 1909 after a two-decade experiment in social reconstruction. Life in Shalam revolved around the message found in *Oahspe, a New Bible,* a book "dictated" by spirits to wealthy Bostonian John Balleau Newborough. Although less well known than *The Book of Mormon, Oahspe* is America's second indigenous scripture.[3]

The state of California had long beckoned to such social visionaries. As historian Robert V. Hine has shown, by 1920 California boasted a larger number of utopian colonies than any other state. These ranged widely in scope, from the short-lived "Holy City of Perfect Christian Divine Way," founded in 1918 in the Santa Cruz Mountains, to the substantial community of Theosophists at Point Loma, founded in 1897. At Point Loma, long-term leader Katherine A. W. Tingley, the "Purple Mother," proclaimed her community to be "a practical illustration of the possibility of developing a higher type of humanity."[4] The Point

Loma Theosophists introduced the ideas of karma and reincarnation to a growing audience of recently arrived immigrants to southern California. The majority of these newcomers hailed originally from the East or Midwest, and when they reached the golden shores of the Pacific they seemed to discard the conventions of their inherited (often Protestant) faith. But their search for a personal faith and a shared religious community continued afresh. For example, when Abdul Baba, a Baha'i prophet, brought his message of "a new day for Universal Brotherhood, International Peace, and Religious Unity" to Stanford University in 1912, it commanded front-page attention.[5]

The majority of the religious seekers seemed to gravitate to southern California. A 1920s survey found that San Francisco church life was dominated by Catholics, Protestants, and Jews, but when the survey team reached Los Angeles, they counted 147 Roman Catholic churches, 816 Protestant churches, and 860 that they labeled "other."

In spite of this religious ferment, the nation's inherited Judeo-Christian framework remained essentially in place during the fin de siècle decades. In fact, biblical metaphors proved so pervasive that numerous groups drew upon them to articulate their points of view. It was not just the churches and synagogues that utilized biblical imagery during these years. So too did the critics of religion. Socialist orators argued that people should be "born again" to a new view of society. The lyrics from many radical Industrial Workers of the World (IWW) songs were often matched to old Methodist hymn tunes. "There Is a Power in the Union," for example, was but an IWW revision of "There Is a Power in the Blood [of Christ]." Other radicals spoke of mankind being "crucified" between businessmen and bankers. When eccentric socialist S. P. Dinsmore founded a "Garden of Eden" in Lucas, Kansas, to extol the virtue of the workers, he filled it with crude statues of Adam, Cain and his wife, Noah, and Christ. The writings and speeches of Oklahoma's most notorious socialist, Thomas W. Woodrow (active 1914–1919), were replete with biblical references.[6]

A number of fin de siècle clerics moved leftward to adopt some form of socialism during this era. A few, such as Presbyterian Norman Thomas, discarded the church entirely for the Socialist party, but most liberal clerics remained firmly linked to some form of organized faith. In Berkeley, Congregational Church pastor J. Still ran for mayor on the Socialist ticket. Radical Denver Congregationalist Myron Reed was twice nominated for the U.S. Congress. Another California Congregationalist established a liberal church in Los Angeles that preached a strong socialist message. Similarly, a surprising number of western Episcopal bishops proclaimed that they were "Christian Socialists."

Thus, the socialist/religious rhetoric of fin de siècle America overlapped in a variety of western areas. Nebraskan William Jennings Bryan electrified the 1896 Democratic convention with his "Cross of Gold" speech, perhaps the most famous oration of its day. Observers of the Populist movement have often likened it to a religious revival. Historian Peter Argersinger has described Kansas Populism as "a movement of religious people and a religious movement of the people."[7] Two decades later, Oklahoma harbored both a strong socialist movement and a strong evangelical religious upsurge. Thus, much of the social ferment of the fin de siècle West operated under an umbrella of Judeo-Christian rhetoric and scriptural allusions. The boundaries between the biblical kingdom of God and various versions of economic justice often overlapped in western America.

By the onset of the twentieth century, most of the mainline religious groups had established themselves in all the major western cities. The bird's-eye city maps so popular during this era clearly reflect this presence. Before the skyscraper phase of American urban life, large churches and synagogues invariably dominated the western urban skylines.

The lofty spires of these western religious buildings, often constructed at great expense, did more than simply provide the people with places of worship. As the embodiment of the sacred, they had symbolic functions as well. Local city officials welcomed churches and synagogues as signs of "respectability." The various denominations also used their architecture as a means of announcing their presence. Thus the fin de siècle western urban church buildings often functioned as distinct cultural statements.

Virtually every Roman Catholic bishop dreamed of erecting a cathedral in his city. When Salt Lake City's Saint Mary's Cathedral was finally dedicated in 1909, it represented forty years of effort by Utah bishop Lawrence Scanlon. The *Interdenominational Catholic* termed Saint Mary's "an architectural achievement worthy of the Ages of Faith."[8] But Saint Mary's served another role as well. It firmly announced the Roman Catholic presence in the Latter-day Saints' City of Zion.

Saint Mary's Catholic Cathedral and pastor's residence, Cheyenne, Wyoming. Dedicated in 1909, this modified English Gothic church became the center of Wyoming Catholicism.

This also proved true in other western cities. The Cathedral of the Blessed Sacrament dominated the skyline of Sacramento, as did the English Gothic Saint Mary's in Cheyenne, Wyoming. Until gutted by fire in the 1906 earthquake, the cathedral in San Francisco was the largest church building on the Pacific Coast. Denver's cathedral was dedicated in 1912, and two years later Catholics in the "Gateway to the West" put the finishing touches on their majestic Saint Louis Cathedral, probably the most important symbol of the influence of Catholicism in the trans-Mississippi West.

The mainline Protestants tried to follow suit. First Presbyterian Church of El Paso erected a forty-thousand-dollar building in 1907. In Montana the Presbyterians of Helena and Bozeman rivaled one another for the most elegant Protestant churches on the northern Plains. In 1931 the First Congregational Church of Lincoln erected a "singing tower" of forty-eight carillon bells to echo (architecturally) the lofty spire of the state capitol only a few blocks away. The brownstone exterior and lofty spire of Denver's Trinity Methodist—the "Cathedral of Methodism"—still epitomizes downtown Denver for many visitors.

Holy Family Roman Catholic Cathedral, rectory, and school, Tulsa, Oklahoma. Built between 1912 and 1919, this modified Gothic cathedral reflects the strength of "Bible Belt" Catholicism.

Historian Lyle Dorsett has compared Denver's fascination with erecting large downtown churches in this era with the building of cathedrals in the Middle Ages.[9]

The Episcopal Church probably erected the most impressive western Protestant religious buildings. Heir to the English cathedral tradition and the best funded of all the Protestant denominations, the Episcopal Church tried to erect its churches and cathedrals in cities that were expected to prosper. Idaho Episcopalians finished their Boise Cathedral in 1889, locating it in the shadow of the Idaho state capitol in hopes of influencing political life. El Paso's Saint Clement's Episcopal Church was completed in 1908 at a cost of $80,000. When Wyoming Episcopalians constructed Saint Matthew's Cathedral in 1896, they proudly termed it "one of the handsomest church buildings in the West."[10] Denver's first Episcopal Cathedral was modeled on the Jesuit Church in Montreal, and its second, built in 1911, cost over

$400,000, an expense only slightly less than that of the National Cathedral in Washington, D.C. These cathedrals served a variety of functions, of course, but sectarian rivalry was never far from the forefront. The National Cathedral was needed, one rector wrote to Bishop J. Mills Kendrick, to counter the Catholic Church, which was "concentrating its efforts to make Romanism the dominating religious influence in the Capital of the United States."[11]

The Jewish community also entered this architectural competition to produce synagogues that rivaled any western Christian building. Portland's Beth Israel temple (1889) contained two large Byzantine towers and became a widely recognized regional landmark. B'nai Israel (1891), with its Byzantine style and large dome, also ranked as one of Salt Lake City's prominent religious structures.[12] Denver's Temple Emanuel (1889) similarly boasted three impressive towers, while Temple Israel in Omaha (1908) reflected both lofty towers and classical themes. In 1890s San Francisco the Jews had established six synagogues, for their four thousand members had made them the second largest religious group in the city.[13] The impressive Temple Emanu-El (dedicated in 1866) thrust two Gothic-Byzantine towers into the San Francisco sky. A representation of the Tablets of the Law was carved between the towers, which also carried numerous stars of David and other Hebraic emblems. One observer remarked that Emanu-El "arrests the eye before all the Christian churches." "In point of wealth and grandeur," another noted, it "might be taken for Solomon's Temple." When a new Temple Emanu-El was constructed after the 1906 earthquake, the Hebraic designs were considerably subdued; when the last version (1923) was built, it resembled the Palace of Liberal Arts at the 1915 San Francisco Panama-Pacific Exposition more than any other building. A cross between Spanish Revival and public architecture, this last version of Emanu-El proclaimed the synagogue as genuinely "Californian." It similarly reflected the concept that the Jews were one of the many groups that had helped pioneer the state. The dedication of these synagogues invariably became a civic occasion. Virtually every ceremony involved participation by politicians and clerics of other faiths.[14]

———

By consensus, the most impressive early-twentieth-century structure between Chicago and the Pacific Coast—secular or religious—was the

Mormon Temple in Salt Lake City. Dedicated on April 6, 1893, the building—Utah's fourth temple—took over forty years to complete.[15]

Unlike Catholic or Protestant cathedrals, Mormon temples are not used chiefly as places of general worship. Rather, they are reserved for special ceremonies for those members deemed especially worthy. Mormons maintain that temples not only fulfill biblical prophecy (Micah 4:1 speaks of the House of the Lord being built on the tops of the mountains), they are also essential to the salvation of believers. Mormon theology maintains that the Gospel of Jesus Christ consists of two parts. The first involves righteous living; the second demands proper observance of certain ordinances, such as baptism, confirmation, the Lord's Supper, and ordination to the priesthood. Some LDS observances, however, are so sacred that they can be performed only in temples specifically built for this purpose. Foremost among these are marriage ceremonies that not only bind husband and wife for both "time and eternity" but also "seal" their children to them as well. Temple marriage, as Elder Mark E. Petersen of the Church Council of Twelve explained in 1978, "is a means of uniting entire families forever."[16] The other major function of the temples is for vicarious baptisms, the living being baptized for the dead to insure their salvation. The emphasis on building LDS temples has stimulated the genealogical activity for which the Saints have long been famous.

The design of the Salt Lake Temple may be traced to Brigham Young's missionary tour to Britain in the early 1840s. During his stay, Young toured a number of English cathedrals and returned with a great admiration for these buildings. But the early Mormons did not simply copy English church architecture. Since LDS converts came from every European nation, the architects modified all historic traditions to the purpose at hand. As a result, Utah today boasts some of the most unique religious buildings in the nation.

"The centerpiece of Zion," as the Salt Lake temple has been termed, remains the premier building in all of Utah. The exterior is replete with LDS symbolism. The slightly taller eastern spires represent the presidencies of the Melchizedek, or higher, priesthood (which is also the governing First Presidency), while those on the west represent the Aaronic, or lower, priesthood. The twelve-and-a-half-foot golden Angel Moroni, with his six-foot trumpet calling all people to hear the new Gospel, sits astride the top-most pinnacle. Mormons believe that the Angel Moroni led prophet Joseph Smith, Jr., to uncover golden

Temple Square, Salt Lake City, Utah. Home of the centerpiece of Mormon architecture, Temple Square ranks among the top five most visited sites in the United States.

plates buried on Hill Cumorah in upstate New York and that Smith translated these plates to produce *The Book of Mormon* (1830). The temple facades show the Big Dipper pointing to the North Star, a symbol of the lost finding themselves in the priesthood, and the all-seeing eye of God, symbolizing God's omnipresence and divine protection. Other LDS symbols such as earthstones, moonstones, starstones, and sunstones reflect the purpose of the temple as a location where heaven and earth intermingle, as well as various degrees of glory in the Mormon afterlife.[17] The temple reflects Mormon folk history as well, for tradition credits Brigham Young with instructing the architects to leave empty shafts running the height of the twin towers. Later these shafts became homes for elevators. No structure symbolizes Salt Lake City better than the LDS temple.

Non-Mormons are allowed to tour LDS temples only before dedication, and six hundred toured the Salt Lake structure in the spring of 1893. A Tennessee reporter at the scene was most impressed. "I have been through the palace of the Duke of Westminster near Chester, England, which is said to be the finest in England," he remarked, "and in many royal palaces on the continent of Europe, but never have I seen such magnificence as this temple of the Latter-day Saints which was dedicated today."[18]

Others must have felt so, too, even though visitors are today restricted to viewing the temple from the outside. In 1993 Temple Square (which includes the Visitors Center and Tabernacle, both open to the public) ranked among the top tourist attractions in the world. It is surpassed in America only by Disneyworld, Disneyland, the Smithsonian Institution, and the Great Smoky Mountains. Temple Square draws about five million visitors every year.[19]

―――――――

In addition to being architectural statements, the impressive church buildings pointed to the religious equality of much of the urban West. San Francisco cathedrals reflected the Catholic domination of San Francisco religious life, at least until the 1960s. Elaborate synagogues attest to the role Jews have played in the building of San Francisco, Portland, Omaha, Los Angeles, and other western cities. The numerous religious buildings in Lincoln, Nebraska, even caused it to be termed locally the "city of churches" (less fondly, the "holy city").[20]

Religious plurality, rather than uniformity, has long been deemed a civic virtue. Consequently, the various western communities invariably have pointed with pride to the variety of their church/synagogue buildings. Even size didn't seem to matter. The Amarillo Christian Science Reading Room was termed "an oasis in the desert," while the modest College View Seventh-Day Adventist Church of Lincoln (built in 1894) was lauded as the "most impressive wood frame building west of the Mississippi." Similarly, the *Denver Republican* praised the newly erected African Methodist Episcopal Church (1890) as a fine building "that reflects great credit upon the colored people of Denver who are not wealthy as the world goes."[21]

Viewed from the outside, these buildings embodied the arrival of the major faiths in the western cities. Viewed from the inside, however, they also functioned as the staging grounds for numerous religious quarrels. Although outsiders might lump the various groups together as Catholic, Protestant, or Jewish, each faith experienced a variety of internal disputes. Most were (more or less) resolved, but a number simmered for decades as unresolved tensions.

The concerns, naturally, varied from faith to faith. For the western

The Boston Avenue United Methodist Church, Tulsa, Oklahoma. Dedicated in 1929, this Art Deco structure combined local motifs (coreopsis and tritoma) with traditional Methodist imagery. Designer Adah Robinson once said, "Every line expresses a thought. Look for it."

Catholic bishops, the most perplexing issues were three: lack of finances, shortage of western nuns and priests, and (especially) ongoing conflicts over ethnicity. The Catholic Church has long been termed a "church of the immigrants." Every western Catholic bishop had to resolve competing claims among his Irish, Italian, Mexican, German, Portuguese, Czech, and other parishioners. Each group, naturally, hoped to have a priest of its own. The issue of Mexican immigration to the borderlands (to be discussed in chapter 5) proved especially perplexing.

But Judaism in the American West was equally a faith of immigrants and thus reflected similar ethnic tensions. These were complicated by theological/ritual disagreements stemming from differences among the three major branches of Judaism: Reform, Conservative, and Orthodox. In Seattle in 1910, for example, the more acculturated

Temple Mt. Sinai, El Paso, Texas, with the Star of David, menorah, and inscription, "This is none other than the House of God," on the facade. Completed in 1910, this building reflects the integral role that Judaism played in the American Southwest.

Ashkenazim scorned the recently arrived Sephardim. As late as the 1940s, marriage between the two groups "was looked upon as if it were an intermarriage."[22] In Portland the tension lay largely between German and Polish Jews. The records of Denver's Temple Emanuel noted that their Reform rabbi was officially cautioned in 1884 to cease ridiculing the Orthodox faith.[23] During the 1930s, Zionist versus anti-Zionist arguments plagued all Reform congregations, especially those in Denver, Omaha, Portland, and Los Angeles. Los Angeles Judaism was further divided along economic lines—the wealthy Wiltshire Boulevard congregation versus the poorer garment district groups.[24] The establishment of ethnic synagogues, the secession of Conservative or Orthodox groups, and, eventually, the economic success of the poorer congregations all helped mitigate these internal conflicts, but they did not really disappear until after World War II. (Protestant quarrels will be discussed in chapter 4.)

In all areas of the West, the churches and synagogues served to an-
nounce the presence of specific ethnic, theological, and social groups.
But there existed a major difference between the urban and rural regions. In urban areas, newly arrived Americans could visit ethnic bak-
eries, restaurants, and fraternal organizations or mutual aid societies
as well as attend ethnic churches or synagogues. They could smell the
smells and hear the language of the old country and survive, if necessary, with only a smattering of English. Safe within an ethnic enclave,
the immigrants could let "the other America" go its own way. In the
more sparsely settled rural West, however, especially the Great Plains,
the situation proved quite different. Here the rural churches and synagogues had to assume all of these ethnic functions by themselves.

Although Texas historian Walter Prescott Webb wrote his classic
account *The Great Plains* (1931) with scarcely a mention of ethnicity,
a glance at the census figures for 1890–1930 reveals quite another picture. In 1900, for example, 35 percent of the population of North Dakota was foreign born. If one includes the immigrants and their American-born children, the percentages increase dramatically: by this count,
North Dakota ranked at 71.3 percent, the highest in the nation. South
Dakota, Nebraska, Montana, Wyoming, Colorado, Utah, Nevada, Washington, and California also ranked above the national average.[25]

Memoirs from this era, such as those by Elinore Pruitt Stewart,
Sophia Trupin, and Willa Cather, all recall the ethnic dimension of
life on the Great Plains. Some Nebraska and North Dakota counties
were virtually 100 percent ethnic. The southwestern corner of the Great
Plains remained heavily Hispanic. African Americans approached 40
percent of several Oklahoma counties, and the percentage of Native
Americans in the heart of Cherokee country was over 90. As geographer James R. Shortridge observed of the Dakotas, an older Yankee
culture might have named the counties and towns, but by 1910 it no
longer controlled the social order.[26]

Most immigrants to the Plains and Intermountain West came from
European peasant backgrounds. Consequently, they viewed land as
the ultimate symbol of social stability. As best they could, they hoped
to re-create the European peasant village in the heart of the American
West. At the core of the old village lay the religious building, which
the immigrants often built along familiar architectural lines. For example, the Hellenic Orthodox church, the Assumption, in Price, Utah
(1916), reflected Byzantine design, with a dome resting on a square

supported by four pillars and the nave in the form of a cross. The interior was filled with painted icons, the "Bible of the unlettered." This little church formed the heart of the Greek community for all of central Utah.[27] Similarly, the onion-domed Saint Joseph Ukrainian Church in Gorham, North Dakota, would have fit perfectly on the steppes of Russia.

Consequently, the churches and synagogues in the rural West often provided the core of ethnic identity. Religion and nationality overlapped extensively, producing what might be termed two "Bible belts" for the region. On the northern Plains, one found an ethnic Bible belt that revolved largely around Catholicism and Lutheranism. On the southern Plains, there existed a similar Bible belt that centered on different versions of evangelical Protestantism. The vast spaces of this region helped create places where every group could maintain its special identity.[28]

When immigrants (such as the Jews) lacked the "critical mass" necessary to re-create a religious core, they felt the loss considerably. Although there were about forty experiments in establishing agricultural colonies for immigrant Jews from 1851 to 1930, none really succeeded.[29] Isolated settlers carried on ceremonial functions as best they could, but individual Jewish immigrant farmers of the rural West felt the loss of their Old World community with special poignancy.[30] North Dakota immigrant Sophia Trupin once described each isolated Jewish settler as a "Moses," lamenting that the settlers had "no synagogue, no rabbi, no kosher butcher, and no *Cheder* for their children."[31]

One of the first structures built by immigrant farmers in the rural West was the church. In many areas people initially created "union churches" because of the heterogeneity of the population. The Episcopal missionary bishop of North Dakota described his 1895 congregation as consisting of "barefooted boys, colored people, Indians, large numbers of the class of men denominated 'tramps,' unbelievers, and agnostics." Colorado pastor Frank Bayley observed that his small congregation came from twenty different denominations and described it as "the miniature of the Kingdom of God on earth."[32] Frontier Jews occasionally attended Unitarian services for lack of an alternative. These union churches, however, seldom lasted long. They usually broke into denominational components within a generation.

In the central and northern Plains the immigrant groups rarely bothered to form a union church because their churches reflected a specific ethnic identity from the start. Norwegian Evangelical Lutherans, Icelandic Lutherans, German Catholics, and others all viewed the union idea with suspicion. Sermons generally remained in the native language until the World War I era. Only after World War II would these churches, often with great reluctance, combine with other groups. When no minister was present, local men and women usually led the services. Women were especially important here. While the father brought the farm tools to America, the old adage had it, the mother packed the Bible, hymnbook, and sermons. Everywhere these churches served as the social center for rural immigrant life.

———

In addition to the larger immigrant groups, the Mennonites and Hutterites added a unique ethnoreligious mixture to life on the northern Plains. These Anabaptists, whose roots dated from Reformation times, arrived from Russia in the late nineteenth century to settle the plains of Nebraska, Kansas, the Dakotas, Montana, and the prairie provinces of Canada. The Hutterites, the only Reformation group to fully adapt communtarianism, found that a combination of Reformation faith and communal life proved ideal when tackling the rigors of life on the Great Plains. Their faith rested on their ideal of submission to the will of God (*gelassenheit,* literally "giving-up-ness") and to the will of the community. Unlike their better-known theological "cousins," the Amish, the Hutterites' willingness to utilize the latest farm machinery made them a potent regional economic force. The Amish farmers who ventured onto the Great Plains usually failed; their small-scale traditional agriculture worked far better in the fertile soil of Pennsylvania and the Midwest than it did elsewhere. The Mennonites and Hutterites, however, prospered virtually everywhere.

Initially, both the American and Canadian governments welcomed the Hutterites. When a colony applied to be admitted to the prairie provinces in 1899, the Canadian authorities consented, terming them "a most desirable class of settlers" and granting them numerous privileges, including freedom from military service.[33] But the Hutterites did not wish to participate in any aspect of regional western life: they eschewed political office and refused to take oaths or pay taxes if these would be used for military purposes.[34] Consequently, provincial governments soon began to view them with some displeasure, although the Hutterite colonies never rankled Canadian authorities as did the

Russian "Old Believers." During both world wars, American authorities also viewed the Hutterites with suspicion. In the Cold War era, when they were accused of being Communists, a number of Hutterites fled across the border to Canada, which proved more tolerant in this regard. Northern Plains small farmers also resented the Hutterites' highly capitalized operations, which enabled them to purchase nearby land and the latest machinery.

Unlike the Hutterites, the various bands of Mennonites have been more willing to compromise with "the world." Also driven to America by czarist persecution in the 1870s, many Mennonites settled in Nebraska, Kansas, and Dakota, where their agricultural skills proved much in demand. Local legend phrased it thus: where they had no water, they irrigated; where they had no wood, they planted trees. Kansas folklore also credits them with revolutionizing Great Plains life by introducing the famed Turkey Red winter wheat into the region's agricultural base. The story of Anna Barkman, the little Mennonite girl who allegedly selected from a Russian granary 250,000 of the best Turkey Red wheat seeds to plant in her new Kansas home, has evolved into local legend.[35]

The Mennonites proved fractious, however, splintering into seventeen separate branches by the era of World War I. Some were communal, some were individualistic; some flirted with the emerging Fundamentalist movement, while others avoided it. Some utilized modern technology such as telephones and automobiles, while others did not. Some compromised in the 1920s by allowing automobiles as long as they had black bumpers, deemed necessary as a mark of humility. Modern observers tend to smile at such fancy footwork, but the issue involved was a serious one. Where does one draw the line between the church and the world?[36] Over the years, the various branches of Mennonites have retained similar beliefs, but their customs differ considerably.

Unlike the Amish or Hutterites, the Mennonites produced a liberal wing that worked more or less comfortably within the world. The larger Mennonite groups accepted the social gospel program but rejected the liberal theology that frequently went along with it. Mennonites founded hospitals and foreign mission stations and also established colleges such as South Dakota Mennonite College (founded in 1900) and Tabor College (1908) and Hesston College (1909), both in Kansas.

Although the larger Mennonite groups found themselves in agreement with many Fundamentalist positions, the outbreak of World War I ended any possibility of a merger with this branch of American Protestantism. The reasons were ethnic, for during the conflict extreme patriotic groups turned on all things German. Vandals hurled rocks through windows of German-American homes, and arsonists set the main building of Tabor College ablaze in 1918. Historian Frederick Luebke has argued that during World War I the Mennonites were the most seriously abused of any American cultural group.[37]

The war also provided a renewed sense of mission for the Mennonite denominational family. After the war church leaders focused on the traditional themes of pacifism and service such as disaster relief as their main message to the world. These remain prominent Mennonite concerns today.

If the central and northern Great Plains reflected an ethnic biblical culture, the southern Plains earned the reputation as a Protestant Bible belt, with certain towns—Tulsa, Oklahoma City, Abilene, Lubbock—all variously labeled the "buckle." While this is more or less accurate, one should also note that the southern Plains served as home for a variety of ethnic groups as well.

When he arrived in the Texas Panhandle in 1911, for example, Rev. Gustav Wiencke sought out the Russian-German colony of Lipscomb to organize the Peace Lutheran Church in Kiowan, the first in the region. A few years later, Rev. D. J. Werner served seventeen separate Lutheran congregations at the same time, stretching from Amarillo to Tulia to Pampa to Plainview. A similarly named Peace Evangelical Lutheran Church near Clinton, Oklahoma, long considered itself a spiritual leader for its community of Russian-German farmers.[38] When the first twelve African-American families moved to Amarillo in 1909, the first organization they formed was a church, "without any thought for organization of denomination." This grew into Mt. Zion Baptist Church, the acknowledged mother church of the entire Plains black community.[39] As historian Harry S. Stout has noted, ethnicity has long been the vital center of religion in America.[40]

Whereas ethnic distinctions usually dominated the religious divisions of the northern Plains, denominational distinctions served the same purpose farther south. In the Panhandle region, lines that had often blurred elsewhere still remained quite distinct. When the Society of Friends (Quakers) established a successful colony at Estacado, Texas, Methodist Rev. Horatio Graves was motivated to plant a Methodist colony in nearby Clarendon. Another Methodist cleric, Lewis H. Carhart, envisioned this region as the center of Panhandle Methodism and promoted the town during the 1890s as a place of "no whiskey forever." Whether a person belonged to the Disciples, Church of Christ, Methodists, Church of God, Baptists, Lutherans, Quakers, or Roman Catholics meant a great deal in terms of personal identity on the Great Plains. Given this situation, sectarian clashes proved inevitable. Catholic-Lutheran tension usually manifested itself in aloof behavior toward the other side. A Catholic priest in Kadoka, South Dakota, used the columns of the local paper in 1908 to denounce the "faithless" Lutherans. But those attacked were less his contemporary neighbors than their ancestors who had separated from the Catholic Church at the time of the Reformation.

Overall, however, general cooperation rather than conflict characterized religious life on the Plains. Bishop John Ireland of Saint Paul gave practical advice to the founders of the Jewish colonies at Painted Woods and Devil's Lake, North Dakota. North Dakota farmers who put up Jewish peddlers for the night usually fixed them eggs as a courtesy rather than the customary salt pork.[41] The Lutherans and Catholics in Olpe, Kansas, each of which comprised half the population, eventually learned to get along. In White Deer, Texas, Presbyterians, Methodists, and Baptists rotated services in an (officially) Presbyterian church until 1922.[42] The first Jews of Amarillo (three families by 1909) used the rooms of the Central Presbyterian Church and the annex of the Episcopal church for their initial services. (The first rabbi arrived in 1926, and the first temple was not dedicated until 1929.) A Jewish firm put on a Christmas celebration, with one partner dressed up as Santa Claus, for the entire town of Carlsbad, New Mexico, in the 1920s. Church records show that local Jewish merchant Joseph Wertheim donated to several Catholic churches in the lower Pecos Valley. In Deming, New Mexico, the lone Jewish merchant contributed his share to the sole (Episcopal) clergyman's salary. These acts of cooperation would not likely have been duplicated east of the Mississippi. Perhaps the most lasting example of this interaction is reflected in Archbishop Jean Baptiste Lamy's Catholic cathedral in Santa Fe, New Mexico. One can still see the Hebrew letter for God at the top of the main archway, a donation from the Spiegelbergs, a prominent local family with whom Lamy had forged an enduring friendship.

Church ethnicity persisted in a variety of forms for the entire twentieth century. The 1940 history of Saint Paul's Evangelical Lutheran Church of Lincoln, Nebraska, was written partly in German. The 1994 history of the Buegeros and Gallegos Catholic Church of eastern New Mexico was written mostly in Spanish. The German Catholic groups of Ellis County, Kansas, have retained their self-identity until the present.[43] The German settlers of Fredericksburg and New Braunfels, Texas, even created a distinct form of architecture—"Sunday Houses" in town—where they could stay overnight to avoid a long drive home. The Umbarger, Texas, German Catholic church of Saint Mary's continues to celebrate a gigantic sausage festival to this day.[44]

━━━━━━━

In addition to holding the community together on ethnic or denominational lines, the western rural churches often served as a major source of culture and entertainment. Due to the isolated nature of ranching and farming, genuine frontier conditions persisted among the rural western churches long after they had disappeared from other regions. Because of this "scatteration," as one cleric phrased it, the local church often became a key center of fun and fellowship for the region. Outside the railroad, individual travel remained horse and buggy well into the late 1930s. With a few movies and only local radio, the men and women of the rural West had to create their own entertainment until well after World War II.

The churches invariably lay at the heart of this social world. In 1891, for example, the Presbyterian ladies of Laramie, Wyoming, invited the entire town to their "pink tea" supper festival. In 1902 the Phoenix Presbyterian church boasted only sixteen members, but it still staged a monthly social event for the entire community. The Phoenix "Ladies Cultural Society" took their charge seriously. The Presbyterian women of Kadoka, South Dakota, sold dinners to the public on both Circus Day and Election Day. Their counterparts in Oklahoma City provided meals at the state fair. In Amarillo the First Presbyterian Church staged a fully costumed production of *The Mikado*. Other churches staged Shakespeare readings. In 1902 Catholic priest J. Donnell borrowed the Clarenden, Texas, courthouse to deliver a lecture series on the nature of Catholicism for the benefit of non-Catholics.[45] In the early 1920s in Rawlins, Wyoming, Presbyterian Rev. James Fraser, described as a "regular fellow," donned boxing gloves and fought with the rector of the Episcopal church as entertainment for the Rawlins Lions Club.[46]

Church dances, cake sales, Christmas celebrations, and church suppers that often served such exotic foods as oysters and ice cream both raised money and supplied fellowship. "Everyone had a good time and the church fund was swelled somewhat," reads a typical account.[47]

These gatherings often proved quite inventive. Rawlins women put on "Apple Polly" socials and Halloween socials. Several churches held box socials where men bid to purchase a lunch as well as the company of the lunch maker. A common prank involved "bidding up" a box in order to annoy a husband or boyfriend. The Kadoka, South Dakota, Presbyterians held a "poverty social," where everybody dressed in rags, and an "experience social," where everyone had to raise a dollar and then explain how he or she did so. Other churches sold baked goods and staged a fish pond in which people "fished" for prizes from behind a blanket.[48] Methodists of the Reno area held a 1920s "jitney dinner," a progressive meal where people traveled to different homes for various courses. The Hebrew Ladies Aid Society of Tucson staged a bazaar and ice cream festival to raise money for worthy causes.[49] Black churches frequently commemorated Juneteenth—the end of slavery—with a similar celebration.

Part of regional entertainment for this era derived from public debates over theological and/or social issues. Although such disputes had generally died out east of the Mississippi (sociologists Robert and Helen Lynd found that no one argued theology in Muncie, Indiana, in the 1920s), this did not hold true for the southern Plains. There, public theological disputes remained prominent until after World War II. Without microphones, these debates often descended into shouting matches.

For some reason, Disciples of Christ ministers positively relished public theological disputations. Disciples leader Joe S. Warlick virtually made a career out of attacking all other faiths in a series of public lectures and/or pamphlets. His *Some Baptist Blunders* reached three editions by 1923.[50] Universalists who proclaimed that all would be saved were criticized by (literally) everyone. As a southern Plains

Quaker said to a Universalist minister who had offered to preach in his neighborhood: "If thy doctrine be true we do not need thee; and if thy doctrine be false we do not want thee."[51]

In most cases, however, these church-sponsored events served as "civilizing" functions for their regions. Western life often had a rough edge to it. When a Reverend Griff arrived in Farmington, New Mexico, in 1885, local cowboys shot holes in the floor around his feet when he refused to drink alcohol with them. Shortly afterward, they broke up the area's first stereopticon picture show in the schoolhouse by shooting at the canvas.[52] Rowdies sometimes interrupted sermons with cries of "gospel grease" or "chin music." The day prohibition was enacted in Flagstaff, Arizona, cowboys spat at local women on the street, saying, "Damn the women. They are the cause of this."[53] "Lent does not seem to make any difference in Tonopah," wryly observed Episcopal bishop Franklin Spalding in 1905.[54]

In the following cowboy ballad (supposedly based on a real incident), "Silver Jack," who had not always "used the Lord exactly right," attacked a rationalist coworker for maligning the faith of his mother. The last four verses read:

But at last Jack got him under
And slugged him once or twice
And Bob straightway acknowledged
The Divinity of Christ

But Jack kept reasoning with him
Till the poor cuss gave a yell
And allowed he'd been mistaken
In his views concerning hell.

So the fierce discussion ended
And they got up from the ground
Then someone fetched a bottle out
And kindly passed it 'round.

And we drank to Jack's religion
In a solemn sort of way
And the spread of infidelity
Was checked in camp that day.

Similarly, "A Christian Cowboy's Creed" reduced the faith to bare essentials: "All the creed I try to practice / Is the old time Golden Rule."[55]

The southern Plains churches also tried to smooth various rough edges during the union Sunday schools (really Bible study classes), which directed their message to adults much more than children. One recurring theme was self-control. A. C. Stewart, colporteur for the American Sunday School Society in Arizona from 1917 to 1931, considered this one of his central duties. Although he fulminated against gambling, dancing, Mormons, and Mexicans (both of whom loved to dance), he saw his chief enemies as "false seductive doctrine" and general indifference.[56] Colorado Sunday school colporteur W. H. Schureman concentrated on reaching ranch children. He was confident that if he could win the hearts of the children, he could more easily convince their parents to participate in church life. Accordingly, whenever he stopped at a wayside home he left cards and pamphlets for the children. Sometimes he even carried small presents—dolls, picture books, balls, and pocket knives. Schureman believed that if he could gather these somewhat rough-hewn youth into Sunday schools, their parents would found a church to create "moral and Christian influences that eventually [would change] the entire character of the community."[57]

The goal of fostering individual self-control through God's grace formed a large part of the southern Great Plains cowboy camp meetings. The most famous of these was the Bloys Camp Meeting, begun in 1890 in the Fort Davis Mountains of West Texas. It has remained an important part of the isolated trans-Pecos ranch world of West Texas/ New Mexico to the present day. In 1890 William D. Bloys, a U.S. Army chaplain at Fort Davis who had come west for his health, introduced a regular cowboy camp meeting. Bloys had helped establish Presbyterian churches in nearby Fort Davis, Alpine, and Marfa in West Texas and had also provided regular services for interested ranchers. One of these men, John Means, suggested that Bloys preach at Skillman Grove, a high-mountain pasture located about nineteen miles from Fort Davis. The first meeting there began a tradition. By 1900 the gathering had become interdenominational and had taken on the name Bloys Camp Meeting. Bloys knew his audience well. He never tried to force a man to accept a faith he did not feel he needed. Bloys held up Jesus as an ideal on which a person could pattern his life. The essence of his message was that God was there for all who would have Him and that a person was not a sissy to declare a faith and live by it.

In 1990 the Bloys Camp Meeting celebrated its centenary. Over the years, many of the famous Protestant clerics of the region have preached there. The tabernacle that was built there still seats about one thousand people. An original Bloys rule—that nothing be bought or sold within camp grounds—remains in effect. The rule originally applied to horse and cattle trading, which had to be carried on outside the fence. In 1986 the Texas State Historical Society erected an official marker at the "Spiritual Hitchin' Post of West Texas," as it was termed. Current residents note that the Bloys message has not changed much in a century. A local adage has it that no boy ever "raised up at Bloys ever landed in Jeff Davis County Jail." Western writer Joe M. Evans described the Bloys Camp Meeting as the greatest thing that ever happened to West Texas. As C. Kenneth Smith recalled, frontier women and W. B. Bloys provided the main forces for stability on the West Texas frontier.[58]

———

Finally, religious life on the Great Plains was partly shaped by the relentless sun, the endless horizon, the steady winds, and the unpredictable, often violent weather. This ever-present awareness of climate has led to an attitude that might easily be termed "spiritual." On the Great Plains, one confronts a society of extreme weather patterns that even late-twentieth-century technology has been unable to tame. When a "Blue Norther" cold front moves south from Canada, it can cause temperatures to fall thirty degrees in an hour. Similarly, a Chinook wind rushing down the eastern slope of the Rocky Mountains can melt six inches of snow in an afternoon. The infamous "Tornado Alley," where continental cold fronts mix with moisture-laden gulf air, has made uncertainty a central part of Oklahoma/Texas life. Similarly, a contemporary North Dakota bumper sticker reads: "-43° Keeps out the Riff Raff." Living amidst such extreme weather leads quickly to the realization that a person is never completely in control of his or her life. Although ranchers might scorn regular church attendance, few could be classified as atheists.

This theme may be clearly seen in writer S. Omar Barker's 1950 "A Cowboy's Christmas Prayer." Born in 1894, Barker grew up herding

cattle on his father's New Mexico homestead. He belonged to no denomination and never attended church, but he reflected a general version of Plains Christianity when he wrote:

I ain't much good at prayin', and You
may not know me, Lord—
I ain't much seen in churches
Where they preach Thy Holy Word,
But You may have observed me out
here on the lonely plains,
A-lookin' after cattle,
feelin' thankful when it rains. . . .

Don't let no hearts be bitter, Lord.
Don't let no child be cold.
Make easy beds for them that's sick
and them that's weak and old.
Let kindness bless the trail we ride,
no matter what we're after.
And sorter keep us on Your Side, in
tears as well as laughter.
I've seen ol' cows a-starvin', and it
ain't no happy sight:
Please don't leave no one hungry,
Lord, on Thy good Christmas night. . . .

We speak of Merry Christmas, Lord
—I reckon You'll agree
There ain't no Merry Christmas for
nobody that ain't free.
So one thing more I'll ask You Lord:
just help us what You can
To save some seeds of freedom for
the future sons of man![59]

The religious life in the urban and rural West during the turn-of-
the-century years proved multifaceted. In terms of architecture, the
dramatic West Coast synagogues and Catholic and Episcopal cathedrals ranked with any east of the Mississippi, but the even more im-

pressive Mormon temples stood as solemn reminders that the West formed a unique religious environment.

In both urban and rural areas, the churches lay at the heart of the immigrant experience. Turn-of-the-century Denver, for example, contained German Catholic, Irish Catholic, and Spanish Catholic churches, all within three blocks of each other.[60] On the Great Plains, membership in the churches and synagogues provided the primary means of self-identity. In truth, ethnicity in that region remained in place longer than in urban areas, which all offered easy access to schools. As late as the 1930s one could encounter American-born children on the Plains who spoke only minimal English. The national religious ferment reverberated with its own echoes in many areas of the American West.

Chapter 3

Varieties of Religious Leadership

There is an old saying that the reputation of a clergyman seldom extends beyond one generation. Certainly that proved true for much of the late-nineteenth- and early-twentieth-century West. Although the stained-glass image of Methodist John L. Dyer is found in the capitol in Denver and a statue of Unitarian Starr King is in the California section of Statuary Hall in the U.S. Capitol in Washington, D.C., few today can recall why. Similarly, the Jesuits who played such important roles in Pacific Northwest history—Anthony Ravalli, Pierre de Smet, and Joseph Cataldo—are virtually forgotten. Although their names survive on the land (Priest Lake, Idaho; Priest River, Idaho; Ravalli County, Montana; DeSmet, Idaho; and Cataldo Mission, Idaho), their accomplishments have faded with their generation. These turn-of-the-century clerics have had great difficulty in entering the myth of the American West.[1]

The reason for this may lie with the transience of so many of them. A perusal of the 50th or 100th anniversary of any church history reveals that the early clerics rarely remained more than one or two years. Their transience often mirrored that of their parishioners. The Depression of the 1890s, the relentless search for economic opportunities, the playing out of mining areas, the boom of the 1920s, and the Great Depression of the 1930s kept many western churchgoers on the move, all seeking their own "angle of repose."

But those clerics who remained in one location for their lifetimes had the type of opportunity that knocks but once. They became "builders," and in many cases their institutions still survive. Situated in the midst of growing regions, these clerics were able to wield influence (however measured) for a generation. As Arizona Sunday school missionary A. C. Stewart recalled, such influence was crucial to overall church success: "I have learned that if a community gets well started on its way to the Devil when it is first organized it is almost impossible to reclaim it after a series of years have been spent in godless living, in which feuds and quarrels have embittered families and caused enmity where friendship might have as easily reigned had they started out right."[2]

The period from 1890 to 1925 also found the clerics at the height of their social powers. Ironically, it similarly introduced them to an enemy that would steadily chip away at their prestige over the course of the century. This foe was seldom science or the marked agnosticism of the day.[3] Rather, as Lyman Abbott noted in his *Reminiscences* (1915), "the greatest foe to spiritual religion is neither heresy nor skepticism but thoughtless indifference."[4]

This chapter details the careers of four western clerics and three laypeople who fought this indifference with one hand and built up their local religious communities with the other. Although largely forgotten today, they were regional household names during their lifetimes.

Episcopal bishop of South Dakota for most of his career, William Hobart Hare (1838–1909) not only supervised church activities for the region, he also became a strong national voice for the Native American cause. On numerous occasions he stated that the United States had wronged the Indians more than any other people. Appalled by the rough-hewn tone of his congregations ("there was not one cultivated, refined face to be seen," he once wrote), Hare ever insisted upon the use of the dignified Episcopal ritual amidst the crudest of surroundings. He also placed his emphasis on youth, establishing four Indian boarding schools as well as the All Saints School for Girls in Sioux Falls in 1885. A firm believer in the evolutionary anthropology of his day, Hare saw the reservation system for Native people as only temporary. He believed that the Sioux were steadily climbing the "ladder of civilization," terming the Ghost Dance religious upsurge of 1890 "heathenism grown desperate." When Hare died in 1909, about 10,000 of the estimated 20,000 Sioux in South Dakota were baptized members of the Episcopal Church. Hare personally confirmed about 7,000.[5] Several prominent Sioux spokesmen of the post–World War II years such as the Deloria family have roots based in this religious heritage.

As Hare left his impress upon South Dakota, so did Methodist itinerant William Wesley Van Orsdel (Brother Van, active 1872–1919) influence Montana. From 1872 until his death, Brother Van traversed the state with his evangelical message, conversing with miners, ranchers, homesteaders, politicians, and Native Americans. Once when Van was preaching to a band of Blackfeet, a group of horse thieves disrupted his sermon with a raid. Van helped retrieve the stolen animals and, when all was again in order, finished his sermon. Afterward, Little Plume, a Piegan chief, invited him on a buffalo hunt and gave him the honor of bringing down the lead buffalo. Famed Montana artist Charles M. Russell depicted this classic event in a 1919 painting.[6]

Hare, Van, Ravalli, Cataldo, and other western clerics spent endless hours in community service. Rabbi David Lesk of Fargo, North Dakota, assumed yet another duty. When a parishioner lacked sufficient funds or credit, the local banks asked the rabbi to cosign or otherwise endorse the note.[7] Through countless means, these fin de siècle clerics tried to get their small communities properly situated.

The foremost female religious figures of the day were probably the various orders of Catholic sisters, Seventh-Day Adventist writer Ellen G. White, the advocates of New Thought, and the Protestant missionary teachers who staffed the Sunday schools and various parochial school systems. Although virtually all local church histories give great praise to the women, their story still remains to be told.

Some western female religious leaders, however, achieved fame (or notoriety) during their lifetimes. The three most prominent were Alma White, Donaldina Cameron, and Aimee Semple McPherson (who will be discussed in chapter 6).

Born in Kentucky, Alma White (1862–1946) and her Methodist minister husband, Kent White, moved to Colorado in the late 1880s. Encouraged to exhort by her friends, she experienced a "second blessing" (entire sanctification) and in December 1891 organized the Pentecostal Union Church (later the Pillar of Fire) in Denver. The following year she published the first of what would become an enormous amount of autobiographical, inspirational, and polemical literature, culminating in the four-volume work *The Story of My Life* (1916–1935). Because of her output, Alma White ranks as one of the most prolific religious writers of her day, not only for the West but for the entire nation. Only Adventist leader Ellen G. White, who authored over thirty books, approached her in this regard.

Alma White had many enemies whom she denounced with regularity. She attacked the Pentecostal movement as "one of the great counterfeits of the age"; the Christian Scientists for misleading people and "blast[ing] their hope of heaven"; and the Nazarenes for practicing "counterfeit holiness."[8] But Alma White built institutions as well: a children's home and a Bible school in Denver, numerous mission churches in neighboring states as well as overseas, a radio station, and eventually her headquarters in Zarephath, New Jersey, where she moved in 1908. During the 1920s she gained notoriety for defending the Ku Klux Klan as fulfilling biblical prophecy. Although controversial from the onset, her message reached an audience that the more established churches seldom touched. Clearly, the less structured religious atmosphere of Colorado allowed her to present her message with only a minimum of resistance.

Daughter of Scots immigrants to New Zealand, Donaldina Cameron (1869–1968) moved with her parents to the San Joaquin Valley of California in 1871. After teacher training and a broken engagement, she began home mission work in 1895 with the Presbyterian-run Chinese Mission Home at 920 Sacramento Street on the edge of San Francisco's Chinatown.

The "rescue home," as it was termed, existed largely to shelter young Chinese women who had been lured to the United States to work as prostitutes. The presence of organized Chinese gangs (tongs), the unbalanced gender ratio in Chinatown, the exclusion laws of 1882 that allowed only wives of American-born Chinese to emigrate, and the corrupt San Francisco politicians of the day (who were paid kickbacks from the more prosperous brothels) all allowed this trade to flourish.

By 1900 Cameron had assumed the position of superintendent of "920," as it was called, and she remained there until her retirement in 1934. Her daring raids into Chinatown, often in disguise, to rescue her "girls" made for colorful and exaggerated newspaper coverage. Several photographs show her in the actual act of rescuing Chinese prostitutes, although the events were surely staged by local newspapers. The tongs frequently threatened the "Jesus woman" (one even placed dynamite at the door of 920), but she doggedly continued her efforts. The last Chinese slave girl entered 920 in 1938.[9]

Once the women were inside the Mission Home, Cameron and her staff tried to instruct them in cooking, sewing, the English language, and other useful skills. She also oversaw a number of marriages, many of which later established middle-class, Chinese-American families in several California cities. As historian Peggy Pascoe has noted, however, the Chinese women who entered 920 were real people rather than simply missionary images. Many of them utilized the mission for their own purposes. A few entered to secure better treatment from their husbands. Several ran away.[10]

Considered a living legend during her lifetime, Cameron reluctantly consented to have the mission renamed "The Donaldina Cameron House" in 1942. Upon Cameron's death at age ninety-eight, a Chinese-American assemblywoman praised her in a memorial to the California Legislature as a "distinguished state citizen." Recent studies by Pascoe and Laurene Wu McClain, however, have been more critical.[11] They have stressed Cameron's rigid Victorian moralism, her refusal to learn Chinese, her reluctance to include any Confucian philosophy in her program to help rehabilitate the women, and her overall disdain for Chinese culture. Still, most San Franciscans of her day were in awe of the Carrie Nation tactics of "Chinatown's Angry Angel."[12]

Virtually all the mainline western clerics of this era became involved in some form of education. One of the most prominent of these was Presbyterian William Judson Boone (1860–1937) of Caldwell, Idaho, whose long career helped shape the contours of the Boise Valley.

Born in Pennsylvania in 1860, Boone often boasted of a family link with the legendary Daniel. Judson Boone earned his undergraduate degree at Wooster College in Ohio and, after an interim career, attended Western Theological Seminary in Pittsburgh. In 1887 he was ordained a Presbyterian minister. The same year he married Annie E. Jamison of Pittsburgh and accepted his first pastorate in Caldwell, Idaho. The fledgling church there had its origin in a group of women who had been dismissed from another, stricter denomination for unspecified violations of social norms. Thus, the Caldwell Presbyterian Church, with its roots in the Ladies Aid Society, was one of the first Presbyterian churches to be founded entirely by women.

For six years Boone both pastored the Caldwell church and served several outlying rural districts. He often drove his horse and buggy to such places as the Stackpole homestead cabin, which functioned as one of the few churches for the lower Boise Valley. After the services, he would invariably share Sunday dinner with the various member families. During these occasions, the farm wives almost always served chicken—the "Sunday bird"—to their clerical guests. Local folklore suggested that the chickens ran in terror whenever a visiting pastor drove onto their farm.

Boone had few clerical rivals in the region for several years, and he performed a number of religious services. In the mid-1930s C. Ben Ross, then governor of Idaho, recalled that William Judson Boone had not only married everyone in that area, he was called on to serve at funerals as well. During his career, Boone earned the reputation of having married and buried more Idahoans than any other minister of his generation.[13]

During this period, Mrs. Annie Boone assumed all the duties expected of a minister's wife. She managed the household, essentially raised their four children, taught Sunday school, helped establish the Caldwell public library, and remained active in a number of College of Idaho clubs. To improve her education, she enrolled in the Chautauqua Reading Circle program—actually a literary correspondence course—and graduated with the diploma. As a reporter later phrased it, "she was adverse to public gaze, but nevertheless exerted a public influence."[14]

In 1893 Judson Boone relinquished his pastorate to devote full time to managing the College of Idaho. He had begun laying plans for a Presbyterian college in 1889–90, and in the fall of 1891 the school opened with "two trembling candidates for higher education," Lillian Potter and Minnie Reed. The first building, a frame house with a hipped roof, was dedicated the next year. The initial faculty numbered eight, but it included several men who later went on to fame in Idaho politics: John C. Rise, who served on the Idaho Supreme Court, and John F. Morrison and Frank Steunenberg, both of whom became governors. Miss Potter and Miss Reed both graduated in 1894, but the school functioned for years more as an academy than a genuine college. It was not until 1906 that the first authentic college freshman class began. This class graduated in 1911, and from that year forward the College of Idaho lived up to its name. In such rural regions, schools had to build up their own educational infrastructures before they could become true colleges.

As president of a shoestring educational operation, Boone found himself wearing many hats. During his vacations, he often visited wealthy Presbyterian churches in the East, begging for funds and recruiting for what he proudly termed "the first college in the Boise Basin." During the winter, he taught Latin and all of the science classes: botany, zoology, chemistry, physics, and geology. As the number of students increased, Boone dropped Latin and gradually relinquished the sciences, one by one, to new instructors, but he always claimed the field of botany as his own.

In fact, Boone achieved a modest reputation in national botanical circles. Answering an advert in *Century Magazine,* he planted the first tea roses in Caldwell, descendants of which still adorn many a Boise Basin garden. He devoted many hours to his roses and later became Idaho vice-president of the American Rose Society. He corresponded for years with a number of Los Angeles hybridizers, and they eventually named one hybrid "Doctor Boone" in his honor.

The College of Idaho ever remained the central focus of his career. No athlete himself, he attended virtually every athletic contest that the college staged. Since he had excellent facility with names, he could recall almost all the students who had passed through the College of Idaho doors. From Miss Potter and Miss Reed and eight faculty members in 1891, the school grew to five hundred students and forty faculty in 1937, with five buildings on a twenty-five-acre campus. At the end of his career, Boone was America's longest running college president. His alma mater, Wooster, awarded him a D.D. in 1903 and an LL.D. in 1934. "It is not too much to say," noted W. H. Miller on Boone's death, "that in a real sense he was the College of Idaho."[15]

Boone's final legacy may be seen in his enormous diary. Begun in 1891 and typed by devoted disciples, the extensive Boone diary today rests with the Idaho Historical Society. Boone seldom skipped a day, and his entries reflect the religious divide between East and West of this era. For example, in July 1925 eastern religious circles were fascinated by the Scopes Trial in Dayton, Tennessee. The national papers were filled with statements by William Jennings Bryan, Clarence Darrow, and others on the truth or falsity of the theory of evolution. But Boone's diary entries reflect far different concerns. In July 1925 he wrote of thunderstorms, planting beans, attending Kiwanis meetings, and going fishing.[16]

Born in Chicago of German immigrant parents, William S. Friedman (1869–1941) grew to maturity largely in Jewish orphanages. He graduated from the University of Cincinnati in 1889, the same year he simultaneously graduated from nearby Hebrew Union College. Founded by the foremost nineteenth-century American rabbi, Isaac M. Wise, Cincinnati's Hebrew Union sent out a steady stream of Reform rabbis to many a western community.

In 1890 Friedman accepted his first job at Temple Emanuel, Denver, where he presided over about fifty German-Jewish families. Although he received periodic calls from Boston, Portland, and Chicago, Friedman remained in the Queen City for over four decades.[17] The Friedman scrapbook, now held by the Western Room of the Denver Public Library (incidentally, it opens from left to right), is probably the most extensive scrapbook left by an American rabbi. It is no exaggeration to say that Friedman became the foremost western rabbi of his day.

Life in 1890s Denver proved challenging. Then, as now, the central city of the Intermountain West, Denver experienced its own economic dislocation well before the onset of the 1893 depression. A few months before Friedman arrived, Denverites had established the Tabor House as a boys and girls home and an employment association. The goal of the Tabor House was "to raise up these homeless waifs from their degraded condition and surround them with a purer atmosphere and make them citizens who will be a credit to society."[18] The city also teemed with unemployed laborers and a variety of health seekers.

The religious situation proved equally unsettled. In Denver no single denomination could claim cultural preeminence (as, say, the Congregationalists could in Washington, New Hampshire, the Catholics in Baltimore, Maryland, or the Episcopalians in Richmond, Virginia). Thus, all the religious groups began on roughly the same footing. Moreover, a number of very talented young clerics arrived in Denver at approximately the same time. Samuel Elliot, son of Harvard president Charles Elliot, pastored the city's Unitarian Church; British-born H. Martyn Hart served as dean of Saint John's Episcopal Cathedral; Irish-born William O'Ryan pastored Saint Leo's Roman Catholic Church; and social gospel advocate Myron W. Reed served the city's First Congregational Church. Friedman immediately joined the circle as the Jew-

Rabbi William S. Friedman of Denver, founder of the National Jewish Hospital in Denver in 1899. Rabbi Friedman played an important role in Colorado civic affairs for forty years.

ish representative. Within months, the group decided to try to standardize the city's chaotic welfare situation. After several meetings, these young clerics centralized and rationalized Denver's charity system (which later became the United Way), forming lifelong friendships along the way. "We organized the charitable effort of the city but we kept ourselves free of professionalism [i.e., sectarianism]," Friedman recalled many years later. "We worked together under the banner of one God as brothers and sisters."[19]

The next year Friedman turned his attention to Denver's health seekers. Working with a wealthy Mrs. Frances Jacobs, he laid plans for a Jewish tuberculosis hospital and oversaw the erection of a small wooden building by late 1892. But the financial panic of 1893 placed this project on hold. Finally, in 1899 B'nai B'rith came to the rescue, and the National Jewish Hospital officially opened for thirty-five patients. In an unprecedented gesture, the hospital charged no fees for TB sufferers. "We did not ask of what nationality or faith they were," said Friedman, "only that they be sick and unable to pay."[20]

Almost from the day of his arrival, Rabbi Friedman established a high public profile. His darkly handsome visage and insightful Friday night sermons soon drew large crowds. A number of Gentiles attended on a regular basis as well. Denver reporters began to print his sermons in the *Republic* and *Rocky Mountain News.* As one reporter noted, Rabbi Friedman "does not limit his sermons to biblical themes but branches out upon all subjects of public, charitable, economic and educational interest. He stands on the broad ground that whatever benefits and elevates the people is not too profane for a pulpit."[21] Friedman occasionally exchanged pulpits with the Unitarian minister, Charles Elliot, and beginning in 1908, when Denver inaugurated its tradition of staging a multireligious Thanksgiving dinner, he always represented the Jews. Over the years he presented the "Jewish view" on such items as Sunday concerts in the parks, the proposed James G. Blaine Amendment, patriotism in World War I, Denver's Ku Klux Klan, and so on. Reporters also sought his views on international Jewish issues, such as the Russian pogroms that plagued the early twentieth century.

During his four decades in Denver, Rabbi Friedman assumed the mantle of a "cultural broker." Through literally thousands of speeches, articles, and sermons, Friedman took on the role of John Bunyan's "Interpreter" to bridge the gap between Jews and Christians. Every October he explained Yom Kippur in the papers, and every December he did the same for Hanukkah. In the spring he would similarly explain Passover. Although Denver had both Conservative and Orthodox congregations, Friedman's Reform Judaism held dominance as the American Jewish view on most matters.

Friedman ever kept an eye out for issues that might defame his people. When various "converted rabbis" arrived in Denver in 1890 and 1896 to solicit funds from the churches to send missionaries to the Jews, he denounced them as frauds and charlatans.[22] Most Jews were hard-working, thrifty individuals, he repeatedly told Denver audiences. One should not judge the Russian Jewish immigrants by the conditions in the eastern tenement houses. Give young Jews access to tools and education, and they will aid mankind.[23] He demanded that public school teachers excuse Jewish students from writing December essays on Jesus or Christmas, and he soundly denounced the czar for his treatment of Russian Jews. Over the years he spearheaded a variety of relief efforts on their behalf. In 1905, after two boys stoned some Jewish cart peddlers on Capitol Hill, Friedman spoke to the mayor and police chief to demand that such persecution cease. Although he agreed that America displayed relatively little anti-Jewish sentiment, he believed that American anti-Semitism manifested itself largely through ostracism by a group he termed the "snobocracy."[24] During the 1920s, he denounced both Henry Ford and the KKK. He lived long enough to speak out against the Nazis as well.

A number of Friedman's crusades raised local Christian hackles. After he spoke before the Ministerial Alliance in 1892 on the Christianity of Judaism, in which he told evangelists to leave his people alone, the Alliance held a discussion. "Parson Tom" Uzzell opened the discussion with a good-natured invitation: "Now, gentlemen, pitch into the rabbi's theology. I know it don't suit a whole lot of you."[25] In 1905 Friedman caused an even larger stir when he gave a public lecture on Christian prejudice against Jews, in which he stated that Sunday schools taught hatred of the Jewish people. This accusation caused much discussion among Denver church people and brought forth vigorous newspaper denials. Where did Rabbi Friedman get his information, the Denver clerics asked? The Congregational minister said he knew a great deal more about the Sunday schools than Friedman did, and he vigorously denied that such a position was ever taught there.[26]

In one of his most interesting crusades, Friedman began in 1907 to attack vaudeville's portrayal of the "stage Jew." Here he borrowed techniques from the Ancient Order of Hibernians and from various German-American groups who had tried to eliminate the "stage Irishman" and the "stage German" from vaudeville as well. Friedman minced no words: "The ridiculous and contemptible stage Jew must go." He urged his congregation and, through the newspapers, other Denverites to complain to vaudeville managers (many of whom were Jewish themselves). If that didn't work, he said, patrons should boycott the theater. The pulpit was ill equipped to stop such performances, he confessed, because those who attended such theaters seldom attended religious services.[27] After a number of protests, the various managers capitulated. "Stage Jew Driven out of Denver," read the headlines of the May 1, 1908, *Jewish Independent.*

Throughout his career, Friedman presented Jews as simply "Americans with a difference." True to the Reform position, he denounced Zionism and stated that America itself had become "God's Israel."

Within a short time, this "brilliant young Jewish teacher" had become a household word in Denver. When he journeyed to New Orleans in 1903 to marry Juliet Freyham, a reporter termed him "one of the best known and most talented ministers in the West."[28] In 1901 the

University of Colorado in Boulder hired him to head its Hebrew Department. Five years later, the university awarded him an honorary LL.D., noting that his influence had been a mighty force for good in the region. Two years later, Temple Emanuel offered him the position of rabbi for life, which he accepted.

Friedman fit well into the social gospel era of turn-of-the-century Denver. A genuine liberal, he maintained that service would prove the only measure of a "true aristocracy." In that regard, he always presented Judaism as the "religion of humanity."

Where the church had once been largely theological, he urged it to become more sociological. All people have a spark of the divine within them, he maintained, and the goal of all faith is to teach parishioners to become "temples of humanity." He argued that proper theological education would serve as the great remedy of misunderstanding, for "no error is ever exposed by science." The crime of the age, he said in 1910, was "to treat the Jews *en masse* instead of as individuals."[29]

During his career in Denver, William S. Friedman became a model of the urban and urbane civic-minded clergyman. Not only did he attend to the needs of his largely German-Jewish congregation, he also supervised new building projects as his congregation outgrew two old temples. But he reached out to greater Denver and to the state as well. For years he served as vice-president of the Denver Public Library Commission and for twenty-two years as president of the State Board of Charities. He remained active in the Big Brother Movement and for a quarter of a century served on the board of the National Jewish Hospital. He retired in 1930. In 1938 he had a stroke, from which he never fully recovered, and when he died on April 26, 1941, in California, the family brought his body back for burial in Denver. His wife lived until 1956.

Friedman's central role in fin de siècle Denver reflected, in miniature, the basic mainstreaming of western Judaism. Jewish pioneers held a number of elected offices in the West long before they did in eastern or midwestern states such as New York or Illinois. Jewish politicians served as early mayors of Albuquerque and Salt Lake City and as governors of Utah, New Mexico, and Idaho. In 1913 San Francisco mayor "Sunny Jim" Rolph extended the same recognition to Rosh Hashanah and Yom Kippur as had been traditionally accorded to Good Friday, the first western mayor to do so.[30] In Denver Rabbi Friedman personified this mainstream position with exceptional skill.

Early-twentieth-century California boasted a variety of prominent Roman Catholic figures. From Archbishop Joseph Sadoc Alemany (1814–84) through Cardinal James Francis McIntyre, to the present-day historian Francis J. Weber, the California Catholic Church has produced a number of articulate spokesmen. Ironically, however, the person who did the most to highlight the early-twentieth-century California Catholic world was the son of a Massachusetts clergyman, Charles Fletcher Lummis.

Born in 1859 in Lynn, Massachusetts, Lummis, whose father was both a minister and a teacher, grew up in a religious home. Thus, the white clapboard architecture of New England Congregational churches fronting village greens formed a key part of his early life. Lummis carried this architectural memory with him through his dramatic 3,307-mile walk across the country to Los Angeles in 1884–85. There he worked first as city editor of the *Los Angeles Times* and then as editor of *Land of Sunshine*, later *Out West*, which presented the story of western life to largely eastern audiences.

When Lummis arrived in California, the twenty-one Franciscan missions that stretched from San Diego to San Francisco lay largely in ruins. California architects of the day had begun to draw on Spanish Revival themes, but this emphasis remained limited chiefly to hotels, railroads, and restaurants. The red tile roofs and white plastered walls represented a different, exotic culture that made California "romantically Spanish" or, in another variation, "Italy-on-the-Pacific."[31] In either version, however, California remained in the Roman Catholic camp. Yet the largest number of immigrants to the southern part of the state were midwestern Protestants, many of whom still harbored a lingering suspicion of Roman Catholicism. These newcomers to California needed a shared past that would tie them to their new surroundings. As a result, a number of people began to "manufacture" a history of the Hispanic past that placed the twenty-one Franciscan missions at its very center. A variety of individuals joined to foster this "crusade": popular author Helen Hunt Jackson, defrocked cleric George Wharton James, converted Catholic playwright John Steven McGroatry, and others. But Charles Fletcher Lummis probably remained foremost in this invention of "ecumenical" Franciscan Catholicism.

In essay after essay, Lummis argued that one need not be either

Catholic or Hispanic to appreciate the Franciscan eighteenth-century missions. Like the clapboard churches of New England, the old missions retained a symbolic grandeur of their own. Although the Association for the Preservation of Missions (founded in 1888) began the process of renewal, Lummis, founder of the Landmarks Club with the same goal, became the driving force behind the enterprise.[32] Gifted with a journalist's eye for a phrase, he used *Out West* and other outlets to push his cause. Consequently, turn-of-the-century Californians consulted old Spanish architectural and documentary records to restore (more or less accurately) both missions and the historic Camino Real that had once linked them together. By about 1906 the California missions had achieved a national reputation. They symbolized "California" to the rest of the nation. In 1916 Lummis boasted that more postcards were sold of the missions than any other California landmark. "The old missions," Lummis wrote in 1918, "are worth more money to southern California than our oil, our oranges, even our climate."[33]

With this revival, the Catholic Church in California utilized these missions for its own purposes. When a young man entered the Franciscan Order, he prepared at Mission Santa Barbara, completed his novitiate at Mission San Miguel, studied philosophy at Mission San Luis Rey, and was finally ordained at Mission Santa Barbara.[34] Simultaneously, historian Zephyrn Englehardt, O.F.M., published numerous accounts of the missions, including four large volumes, *The Missions and Missionaries of California* (1908–16). By the end of World War I, the romance of the Franciscan missions had become a leading motif of California life. Rather than being Catholic, however, the missions had assumed a nondenominational, virtually ecumenical position. (The Native American voice had yet to be heard on the matter.)

The Spanish mission restoration idea soon spread to neighboring borderland areas as well. During the same time, Henry Granjon, the Catholic bishop of Tucson, began a restoration campaign to refurbish Mission San Xavier del Bac, just south of Tucson. Founded in 1783 by Jesuit Eusebio Kino, San Xavier served the southern Arizona Pima and Papago. Granjon bypassed the original coloring, which was probably either brick or a tannish lime plaster, to cover the extensive mission facade with white paint. (This was eventually replaced in a 1990–91 restoration by a softer, cream-colored lime plaster.) Still, by 1915 the "White Dove of the Desert" had emerged as the most striking building of the entire borderlands region.[35] It still holds this position today.

A similar romantic impulse swept through Texas. Around the same time, reformers began to refurbish their "Franciscan Gothic" structures in San Antonio (including the Alamo) and in nearby regions. The state of New Mexico also laid plans to restore the over forty Franciscan missions within its boundaries. Although some of them had fallen into disrepair, many New Mexico missions, such as those at Isleta, Acoma, Trampas, Chimayo, Zuni, San Felipe, and elsewhere still functioned as parish churches. These New Mexico churches housed a syncretic Native American/Catholic faith. Ironically, the low, narrow, brown mission churches of New Mexico, with an "authentic" past firmly in place, have never been as easy to romanticize as the restored missions of California, Arizona, or Texas.

The early twentieth century also witnessed a similar attempt by Catholics in the Pacific Northwest to restore some of their early missions. Joseph Cataldo returned to Idaho in 1915 and watched over Saint Joseph's Mission until his death in 1928. Idaho's Greek revival Coeur d'Alene Mission of the Sacred Heart (the Cataldo Mission) was similarly restored during this time.[36] Ignatius Mission on the Flathead Reservation in the beautiful Mission Valley of western Montana is now a national historic site. But none of the Northwest missions ever achieved the fame of those in California.

———

The person who had perhaps the strongest impact on religion in the West was someone whose connection with organized faith remained ever tenuous. Yet the "religion of Nature" that John Muir (1838–1914) helped found today boasts thousands of followers. Indeed, when combined with Native American spirituality regarding the natural world, it may rank as one of the nation's most rapidly growing contemporary faith perspectives. To a large extent, this view had its roots in the American West.

As historian Catherine Albanese has shown, Nature religion in America evolved from numerous origins.[37] Foremost among these, however, were the various Native American faiths. Native American religion today is widely acknowledged as a complex philosophical worldview. Since each of the roughly five hundred Indian nations has its own sophisticated belief system, one can never refer to a single "Native religion." What the faiths share in common, however, is a deep reverence for the forces of Nature, an awareness of the interconnect-

edness of life, and a special relationship to the land itself. Generaliza-
tion in this area is difficult. Contrary to prevailing opinion, Native
Americans utilize their reservation lands for many purposes: farming,
harvesting timber, mining, oil production, and, more recently, soccer
fields and casinos. All one can safely say is that Native peoples generally manifest a *different* relationship to their natural environment from
that of most Euro-Americans.[38] This, of course, was little understood
at the turn of the century save by a small cadre of anthropologists.

In 1900 the largest, most powerful Indian groups all lived in the
American West. Throughout the region, they had designated certain
areas as "sacred space": for the Navajo, the four sacred mountains that
surround their homeland; for Taos Pueblo, Blue Lake in the nearby
Sangre de Cristo Mountains of New Mexico; for the Lower Colorado
river tribes, Spirit Mountain in southern Nevada; for the Yakama, Mount
Adams in Washington. The list could easily be extended.[39]

Euro-Americans held a much more constructed view of sacred space,
limiting it to a graveyard, a church or synagogue interior, or an altar.
Although both Judaism and Christianity share the concept of the stewardship of land, this view was marginalized at the dawn of the twentieth century. Perhaps John Muir's greatest contribution was to broadcast this concept of stewardship to the country at large.

Born in 1838, Muir spent his first eleven years in the tiny town of
Dunbar, Scotland. There, he tells us in *The Story of My Boyhood and
Youth,* he became "fond of everything that was wild."[40] And Muir found
wildness everywhere: by the river banks, in Dunbar Castle grounds,
and especially by the shores of the North Sea. In addition, the schools
of his day thoroughly indoctrinated him in Latin, French, and English
grammar, along with thrilling tales of William Wallace and Robert the
Bruce, "with which every breath of Scotch air is saturated." For Muir
the saga of biblical history was mingled with that of Scottish history.
Young John had to memorize all of the New Testament and three quarters of the Old by age eleven. The punishment for failing to do so, he
dutifully recorded, was a sound whipping.

Muir eventually moved to California, where in 1880 he married
Louise Wanda Strentzel. Thanks largely to her inherited farm, he was
able to devote the rest of his life to natural history. Gifted with a facile
pen, Muir literally created the genre of "wildness journalism."[41] Moreover, he had a marvelous eye for the precise phrase. Sheep he once
described as "hoofed locusts." In 1871, while hiking in the Sierra, he

stumbled upon "a living glacier." Of cities he observed, "All are more or less sick; there is not a perfectly sane man in San Francisco." Of wilderness he said, "Man needs beauty as well as bread." In the midst of a fight to dam the Hetch Hetchy Valley to create a water supply for San Francisco, he argued: "Dam Hetch Hetchy! [You might] as well dam for water-tanks, the people's cathedrals and churches, for no holier temple has ever been consecrated by the heart of man." Perhaps his most famous aphorism was his invitation to the American public: "Come to the mountains and see."[42]

At the core of Muir's environmental accomplishments lay his vision of the interconnectedness of all life. Growing to maturity in a world of Darwinian materialism and rapacious utilization of natural resources, Muir's forging of a new relationship between humankind and Nature represented a genuine intellectual breakthrough for the Euro-American mainstream.

Muir's "Religion of Nature" put its emphasis on the majesty of creation with little or no concern for a redeemer. Through his writings, Muir advocated a oneness with both the animal and natural kingdoms. Although he occasionally hunted as a young adult, he later gained fame for his renunciation of hunting and his advocacy of the rights of animals. He spent much effort in devising new concepts of community and harmony that would include all living things. As he wrote in 1872, "[Robert] Burns may step outside the selfish circle of his species with sympathy for a suffering daisy or to claim the mousie as a fellow mortal but in the smug highwalled realms of the civilized such souls are rare."[43] Because the natural world revealed the handiwork of the Creator, Muir argued that Nature was holy in and of itself. Thus, one should always treat it with awe and reverence.

Historians have spent considerable time in trying to discover the exact sources of Muir's Nature ethic. Some credit his reading of the Transcendentalists while at the University of Wisconsin. Others see its origin in his childhood familiarity with Scottish ghillies and their land and game management techniques. But the most common position is to place Muir's new vision of man and Nature as a reaction against the strict Presbyterian doctrine of his Dunbar youth and the religious rigidity of his father Daniel's faith, usually termed "dour Calvinism."[44]

But historian Mark Stoll suggests that to interpret Muir's conservation ethic simply in terms of a rejection of Calvinistic Christianity is far too simplistic. Mainstream Judeo-Christian thought speaks of a human-Nature dualism, to be sure, Stoll notes, but it also contains a respect toward Nature as well. Even the dualistic idea that human-kind should "dominate" Nature and the natural world has always put forth a corollary: dominate not for the individual pursuit of wealth but for the common good (the Kingdom of God). Herein lies the biblical concept of the stewardship of resources. Even more significantly, from Neoplatonist times forward, Christian thought has contained a romantic mysticism wherein Nature reveals the hand of God in sublime form. Thus, when one is close to Nature, one is close to God as well.[45]

Since Muir's essays are replete with biblical metaphors and analogies, critics have found it difficult to link this "God language" with his "rejection" of Scotland's "dour Calvinism." But perhaps the critics have used the wrong model. Around 1848, Daniel Muir, who might be best described as a religious seeker, left the Presbyterians to join the Disciples of Christ in Dunbar. It was this conversion that drew him to the Wisconsin frontier. Indeed, the elder Muir often preached in Wisconsin for the Disciples. While John Muir's writings reveal dismay with his father's narrow, biblicist outlook, Muir the younger proved more indebted to the Disciples' point of view than he ever realized.

The denomination that came to be known as the Christians or the Disciples was founded in Kentucky, Ohio, and Pennsylvania in the early nineteenth century by the father-and-son team of Thomas and Alexander Campbell. Scotch-Irish graduates of the University of Glasgow, Thomas came to the states for his health around 1808, and Alexander followed soon after. The Campbells rejected their inherited Presbyterianism for a "restoration of the ancient order of things." They would discard all man-made church ordinances (synods, bishops, titles such as "reverend," conferences, missionary societies, lengthy creeds, etc.) to adopt the "watchword principle" forged by Thomas in 1809: "where the Scriptures speak, we speak; where they are silent, we are silent." Alexander Campbell proved an effective promoter of these new principles. He combined a stress on logic and reason on the one hand with a deep-seated emotionalism on the other. He also proved quite effective in debate. In truth, he loved nothing as much as a good theological argument.[46]

The Disciples faith that Daniel Muir adopted (and one that young

John must have heard endlessly discussed) was not dour Calvinism. Instead, it emphasized a New Testament biblical literalism; an Arminian (i.e., free will) position on salvation; a combination of simple rationalism and strong emotionalism; an "ecumenical" goal that only reluctantly evolved into another denomination; and a love of the art of debate. All these positions—save only the emphasis on biblical literalism—may be clearly seen in John Muir's later career.

Muir's ecumenical views moved quickly from the New Testament to the realm of Nature, but they remained no less all-inclusive for the shift. His appeal to "come to the mountains and see" echoed the altar call of the revivalist asking sinners to freely accept the offer of God's grace. One scholar has compared Muir's polemical writings to a Hebrew prophet's denunciation of wickedness in high places.[47] Muir himself drew on biblical phrases at virtually every turn. On one occasion he likened himself to John the Baptist: "Heaven knows John Baptist was not more eager to get his fellow sinners into the Jordan than I to baptize all of mine in the beauty of God's mountain."[48] After visiting Yosemite for the first time, he phrased the experience thusly: "We were new creatures, born again."[49] Thus, John Muir's "Nature ethic" probably derives less from a rejection of his Presbyterian youth than from his modification of his father's Disciples of Christ view of the world.

Founder of the environmental position of "Deep Ecology," John Muir called for awe and reverence in the face of Nature. A hundred years later, this movement, in various forms, has become one of the most powerful quasi-religious positions of the entire globe. In the 1990s the mainline Protestants, Evangelical Protestants, Mormons, and Catholics have all begun to rediscover a biblical basis for stewardship of the land. In 1995 the Eastern Orthodox churches formally acknowledged the concept of "sins against creation." To a large degree, the modern origins of this idea may be traced to California's most famous immigrant: John Muir. In a strange sense this renewed respect for the environment may be emerging as the most ecumenical position of the late twentieth century.

———

Although largely forgotten today, the turn-of-the-century clerics discussed here played multifaceted roles in their regions during their lifetimes. In many cases, the institutions they helped establish survive today. Still, it is intriguing that two nonclerical figures—Charles F. Lummis and John Muir—probably had more impact on the course of western religious history than all the others put together. The religious history of the early-twentieth-century West continued to march to its own drummer.

PART II

The 1920s to the 1960s

Chapter 4

Religion in the West
of the 1920s and 1930s

―――――

The First World War had a major impact on the world of organized faith. It took years for the mainline denominations to recover from the shock of the Great War, especially from the moral dilemmas raised by the new technologies: submarines, airplanes, machine guns, and poison gas. As a consequence, many clerics converted to pacifism, a position that remained popular in national religious circles until the late 1930s.

A second legacy of the war came with the "100 percent American" crusade that emerged after the United States entered the conflict in 1917. With the peace of November 1918, this superpatriotism became redirected toward national life. As it spread to the various states, America witnessed an extensive religio-cultural public controversy over "national values," the most intense discussion of this type since the era of the Civil War. As the 1960s would later demonstrate, this clash would not be the last of its kind. From the onset, religious themes were firmly embedded in the dispute. Nowhere is this more clearly seen than in the Fundamentalist-modernist controversy that sundered several of the mainline Protestant churches into liberal and conservative camps.

―――――

The Fundamentalist-modernist controversy proved a multifaceted phenomenon. By the first decade of the century, conservative Protestant spokesmen had already begun attacks on higher criticism of the Scriptures and the "new theology." In 1908 Seattle Presbyterian Mark A. Matthews attacked modernism as embracing "all phases of Higher Criticism, Evolution, Pantheism, Unitarianism, and all diluted forms of Christianity.'"[1] During the same era, Southern Baptist J. B. Gambrell fulminated against the biblical critics who wanted to modify old theological truths to "suit the age." He denounced liberal Baptists who claimed superiority in Baptist pulpits simply because they "[know] some things plain men don't know."[2] Only the outbreak of the Great War dampened this incipient quarrel.

Like the various disputes within Judaism and Catholicism, the Fundamentalist-modernist controversy began as an internal church problem. The issues varied from denomination to denomination but revolved around acceptance or rejection of the higher criticism of the Scriptures; the relationship between the social gospel and the need for a conversion experience; a fight over which group (conservative or liberal) should control the denomination's resources; and the truth or falsity of the theory of evolution.

Not all Protestant groups were affected to the same degree. Unitarians and Congregationalists generally avoided controversy because they had few conservatives in their ranks. Similarly, Missouri Synod Lutherans, Latter-day Saints, and Southern Baptists generally avoided controversy because they had few liberals in theirs. But all the groups in the "center"—Episcopalians, Methodists, Presbyterians, Disciples of Christ—experienced various degrees of difficulty. The controversy reached such acrimony that in 1921 the Presbyterian church in Amarillo advertised itself as a church that "makes no fight against any other church, desiring only to see the Kingdom of God established on earth."[3]

From the beginning, the religious forces of the West were much involved in this quarrel. In fact, two wealthy California oilmen, Lyman and Milton Stewart, served as the main financial backers for the Fundamentalist movement. Using the vast profits of their Union Oil Company, they bankrolled the publication from 1909 to 1914 of a series of pamphlets called *The Fundamentals*. These conservative booklets were mailed free of charge to every Protestant leader whose address the committee could discover. Over 100,000 people wrote in to request copies of issues they had missed.[4] Leaders from the newly founded Bible Institute of Los Angeles (BIOLA), also funded by the Stewart brothers, oversaw the distribution of the booklets.

Unlike the Catholic and Jewish internal quarrels, Fundamentalist-modernist controversy did not remain confined to denominational circles. Largely because of the issue of evolution, the clash spilled over into the public realm. It did so largely on the shoulders of three-time presidential candidate William Jennings Bryan, whose postwar anti-evolution addresses attracted widespread attention from the national press. By the early 1920s, the *New York Times* regularly carried front-page articles on this quarrel. The famed trial of John Thomas Scopes in Dayton, Tennessee, in July 1925 is usually seen as the most dramatic aspect of this clash.

The nonmainline Protestant areas of the West, such as Catholic/ Jewish San Francisco or Mormon Utah, showed little interest in the 1920s evolution fight. Largely Catholic New Mexico escaped as well. The *Albuquerque Journal* dismissed the whole Scopes Trial controversy as a "prejudice against the monkey tribe." Although it ran the story on the front page, it devoted equal attention to the Mary Pickford divorce trial.[5]

But the more heavily Protestant regions of the West were caught up in the controversy. The state of Oklahoma, for example, passed the nation's first anti-evolution law in March 1923, the only western state to do so.[6] In Tucson, Baptist minister R. S. Beale took issue with a 1924 statement by a University of Arizona astronomer that the purpose of faith was to provide young people with a "common sense religion." He inaugurated an attack on "infidelity" on the University of Arizona's campus, and this soon evolved into an intense public discussion, via the newspaper, on the issue of scientific evolution.[7] The Glendale, California, Presbyterian church argued that since the biblical origin of humankind was excluded from the schools, so too should all other origin theories. In Los Angeles, Methodist minister Robert ("Fighting Bob") Shuler denounced evolution along with films, jazz music, and political corruption in his attempt to save "the only Anglo-Saxon city of a million population left in America."[8] Such fulminations forced Pasadena scientist Robert Millikan to take to the lecture platform to deny that "real" science and religion could ever be in conflict. California avoided actual anti-evolution legislation because the California State Board of Education decided in 1925 to accept biology texts in which evolution was taught as "theory," not as "fact." Overall, however, the western states remained marginal to the 1920s fight over evolution. As will be discussed in chapter 8, their position would change considerably in the post–World War II era.

If the West largely avoided public controversy over evolution during the 1920s, it found itself in the center of the revived nativist sentiment. As historian Kenneth T. Jackson has shown, the Ku Klux Klan became active in a number of western states: Oklahoma, Utah, California, Colorado, Oregon, Washington, and West Texas. In fact, Klan agitation in El Paso soured Protestant-Catholic relations for over a decade.[9]

The religious forces of the West also lay at the center of *anti*-Klan activities. As early as 1914, the premier Catholic lay organization, the Knights of Columbus (K of C) created a commission on religious prejudice. In 1916 they published a pamphlet denouncing religious attacks as "hostile to the spirit of American liberty and contrary to God's law to love thy neighbor."[10]

Wherever the Klan began to attack western Catholicism, the K of C served as the main focus of opposition. In Carbon County, Utah, the Klan burned a cross on a hillside. In reply, the K of C led a group of Catholic and Orthodox miners who burned a circle on a hillside across the valley. All the ethnic groups in Utah—Greeks, Slavs, Italians, and Irish—banded together in this crusade. They viewed an attack on one as an attack on all. Usually they blamed the Mormons—a people the Greeks of Carbon County described as "without salt"—for the difficulty.[11] The Denver K of C led a similar protest against allowing the Klan to use public buildings for their inflammatory speakers. African-American churches in Oklahoma similarly helped organize the "Friends of Fair Play" to oppose local Klan attacks.[12]

Although the Klan proved especially strong in Texas and Colorado, its most spectacular success occurred in Oregon. There Klan members joined forces with numerous other antireligious groups to try to dismantle the state's Catholic parochial school system. This quarrel, which eventually reached the U.S. Supreme Court, marked the highlight of the West's religio-cultural tensions during the 1920s.

Oregon had always had a unique religious history. It proved home to a variety of Native faiths and welcomed the first Anglo-American settlers, who were largely Catholic fur traders and Methodist and Presbyterian missionaries. But Rationalist forces also proved strong, and Freethinkers organized a State Secular Union in 1889. Oregon's Secular Union listed a series of demands: all churches must pay taxes; U.S. chaplains should be dismissed and no public aid should be offered to support religious services or any sectarian charitable institution; an end to judicial oaths and religious holidays; no Bible reading in public schools; and an end to all laws fostering "Christian morality" rather than "natural morality." Portland organized a First Secular Church in

1893, complete with a secular Sunday school. Freethinkers even opened a Freethought Liberal University in 1899, but it lasted only two years.[13] Portland Freethinkers also produced an anarchist and sexually radical publication, *Firebrand,* during the mid-1890s.[14] Thus, organized "antireligion" had strong roots in the Pacific Northwest.

In the early 1920s, the various "anti's" joined forces. The Rationalists (who disliked all religious groups) linked with the Masons (who disliked Catholics) and the Klan (who disliked all nonconservative evangelical Protestants). This unusual alliance agreed on only one matter: Catholic parochial schools were "un-American." In 1923 the alliance led a successful initiative measure that required all Oregon children to attend public schools. This bill reflected a distinct regional nativist mood. The state of Nebraska had recently passed a similar measure that forbade the teaching of any foreign language (i.e., German) before the eighth grade. A Lutheran parochial school teacher challenged this measure, and it was eventually overturned by the U.S. Supreme Court.

Similarly, in late 1923 the Sisters of the Holy Name of Jesus and Mary challenged the Oregon law. Aided by the National Catholic Welfare Conference, the case of *Pierce vs. Society of Sisters* slowly made its way through the court system. The 1920s were decidedly a pre-ecumenical age, but *Pierce* brought together a significant number of religious denominations. Catholics, Presbyterians, Episcopalians, Lutherans, Seventh-Day Adventists, and the American Jewish Committee all filed *amicus curiae* briefs with the courts. In 1925 the United States Supreme Court declared the Oregon measure unconstitutional (as it had done earlier with the Nebraska measure), and with this the religio-cultural clash in the West began to fade. The defeat of the Oregon law was widely touted as a key victory for Catholic parochial education and for cultural pluralism in general.[15]

━━━━━━

If the cultural clash of the 1920s somewhat bypassed the world of western religion, the economic downturn of the Great Depression proved less discriminatory. Although national and local politicians offered a variety of political solutions to solve the Depression, unlike the Progressive crusade of the previous generation, few clerics played much of a role in the western reform measures.

Instead, the problems boiled down to one word: finances. All the churches, as institutions, suffered considerably during the economic downturn.[16] Demands for basic welfare services rose on the local level, and virtually every denomination increased its services to the poor. Church contributions to this realm of "hidden charity" can only be approximated.[17]

All groups were affected. The working-class Jews of Los Angeles joined the welfare rolls in proportionate numbers, and California Judaism found that it had to swallow its proud claims that the Jews "took care of their own." Because of the appeal of Communism to many California Jews, the community also battled increased anti-Semitism through the Depression years as well. In 1935 California Jewish organizations began to hire private investigators to shadow local Nazi groups.[18] This attempt to equate Jews with Communists was softened somewhat by speeches from liberal California Protestant clergymen and, especially, by the ecumenical activities of Reform rabbi Joseph Magnin.

Born into an acculturated San Francisco family, Magnin headed the Wilshire Boulevard Temple and achieved a reputation as "Rabbi to the Stars." An excellent speaker and organizer, Magnin also had links with the Gentile community. From the late 1920s forward, he spoke to service clubs, liberal organizations, and countless radio audiences. He also had his own newspaper column. In these presentations he emphasized the "Jewish contributions" to California and to the West. Like Rabbi Friedman before him, Magnin functioned as a "cultural broker" between the Jewish and Gentile communities in southern California.[19]

Because of their extensive social and educational responsibilities, western Catholic bishops of the Depression decade found themselves especially hard pressed. In the Pacific Northwest, the Saint Vincent de Paul Society functioned virtually as a Catholic Salvation Army and was always short of funds. In Sacramento Bishop Robert J. Armstrong worked closely with a volunteer Ladies Catholic Relief Society as he tried to professionalize Catholic Welfare Services.[20] The organizations established by Los Angeles bishop John J. Cantwell and the Confraternity of Christian Doctrine to aid Mexican immigrants were similarly overwhelmed. Perhaps 50 percent of the Los Angeles Bureau of Catholic Charities recipients hailed originally from Mexico, and while the Los Angeles diocese had established four settlement houses for Mexican immigrants, complete with English language classes and other services, the Church relied largely on the L.A. parochial school system as the primary means of "Americanization." Cuts in finances severely disrupted its efforts.

Part of the difficulty in this regard lay with the organizational structure of the American Catholic Church itself. The decision to utilize national missions to minister to the immigrant Mexicans, rather than establishing a local church with a resident priest, proved detrimental in the long run. It meant that priests could refer Mexicans in need to a national board, which ever remained short of funds, much to the detriment of local integrationist forces.

The Church made several attempts to acknowledge the unique Mexican minority. In 1939 California monsignor William E. Corr oversaw the erection of a shrine, the "Lourdes of the West," to satisfy Mexican devotion to Mary. But lack of access to farm workers and minimal integration of Mexican Catholics into the Euro-American urban mainstream continued to plague the California Church. Later critics charged the Church with a "history of neglect" of the Mexican-American minority.[21]

From the bishops' point of view, ministering to the Mexican immigrants of the southwestern borderlands proved problematic. Deeply Catholic though they were, the Mexicans carried a unique Catholicism with them to Texas, Arizona, and California, one interwoven with many pre-Christian, Native beliefs. Flowers, fiestas, a cult of mediation in which personal relationships with various saints remained crucial, healing shrines, God parenting, lay societies, belief in omens, fear of the evil eye, wariness of curses, faith in the healing power of *curanderas,* and, especially, devotion to the Virgin of Guadalupe characterized the immigrants' faith. This version of folk Catholicism proved a far cry from the Euro-American Catholicism shared by most western prelates.[22]

Other western Catholic bishops faced different problems during the Depression. The bishop of Oklahoma, Francis C. Kelley, lacked both priests and nuns to minister to his scattered and tiny flock (about 5 percent of the state). He once likened his situation to trying to make bricks without straw. In addition, Oklahoma abounded with anti-Catholic literature and fallen-away parishioners. "Some of our bitterest enemies have Catholic names," the bishop lamented. Kelley's response was to write books—eight before his death in 1948—and to buoy up his flock through inspirational addresses.[23] The bishop of Nebraska,

Louis Kucera (1930–57), similarly emphasized the overcoming of hardship by personal example. Although his flock lay scattered all through the state, he rarely missed a parish celebration or the chance to deliver an inspirational address.[24] The bishop of Tucson, Daniel J. Gercke, introduced the Catholic Church on Wheels, which took services to isolated districts in Arizona. Through actions like this, the Catholic Church in the West weathered the lean years of the 1930s.

The western Protestant churches also suffered extensively during the Depression. In Utah the Episcopal Church discontinued its mission work to the mining communities. First Congregational Church of Reno watched its various outreach organizations collapse one by one at the same time that church welfare demands increased. Ministerial salaries similarly declined.

In Las Vegas, Nevada, Congregational minister Albert C. Melton, who managed a grocery store to support his family, delivered wholesale groceries to the needy as his church became essentially a relief station to the tent-and-cardboard town that arose north of the city. "Only pastor Reynolds knows how many hundreds the church helped with food, clothes, and a word of faith," observed the official historian of the Las Vegas First Methodist Church, which introduced a similar relief program.[25]

On the Great Plains, which experienced fierce dust storms as well as severe population loss, the churches found themselves especially under siege. The Lutheran Church of Guymon, Oklahoma, had to be dug (literally) out of sand drifts in 1935. A member of the First Christian Church of Carlsbad, New Mexico, could not afford to pay his promised annual contribution of twenty-five cents.[26] Even formerly wealthy urban congregations, such as First Presbyterian of Tulsa, wrestled with problems of debt.

On the other hand, the collapse of the rural economy often made the churches more important as local gathering places. Church women staged numerous rummage sales, silver teas, town picnics, and food sales to raise funds. At times they reached for the exotic. The Catholic women of Milagra, New Mexico, not only sold enchiladas, tamales, and cakes to raise funds for a new church, they also held street dances and staged relay races. First Methodist of Carlsbad organized the region's first Rattlesnake Derby, complete with wagering. Handlers released the snakes inside a fenced-in area, and the first snake to pass under a numbered wicket won a prize for the person who held that wicket number.[27]

A few Protestant medical/social mission efforts survived the Depression, but they were usually one-woman operations. From 1932 to 1960, Methodist minister Ada Duhigg helped operate the Utah Protestant Mobile Mission and served the small community of Highland Boy in Bingham Canyon, Utah. As she noted in a 1980 interview, "Highland Boy House was interracial, international and interdenominational. Twenty-seven nationalities and fifteen denominations—Roman Catholics, Greek Orthodox, Mormon, and Protestant—worked together ecumenically before the word was used." Reverend Duhigg's duties proved varied. She not only pastored her mobile flock, she organized roller skating parties, basketball games, arts and crafts sessions, Bible study groups, Boy and Girl Scout gatherings, and well-baby clinics. She also spent much time transporting people to hospitals and offices in Salt Lake City. During the fire of 1932 and the snow slide of 1939, both of which wreaked havoc on the little community, she coordinated Red Cross and emergency relief efforts. The twenty-eight years of service of the "Angel of the Canyon" mixed both religious and social concerns.[28]

It took similar dedication to maintain the small Presbyterian mission hospital in Embudo (begun in 1916) in rural northern New Mexico. Early medical missionaries there battled TB, malaria, diphtheria, and typhoid. They even treated isolated cases of smallpox. Because of local cultural conventions (Hispanic males refused to allow male physicians to attend their wives during labor), the Presbyterians sent only female physicians to the region.

In 1932 Dr. Sarah Bowen, "La Doctora," arrived in Embudo, where she spent her next thirty-eight years. Later she was joined by Edith F. Millican (also "La Doctora") and Dr. Virginia Milner ("La Doctoracita"), who remained until after World War II. Conditions were as basic there as if the doctors had been stationed in a foreign land. In some operations, the cook administered the anesthetic. Payment came in the form of wood, hogs, timber, fruit, and vegetables. The Presbyterians ran the Embudo clinic until 1974, when they turned it over to a regional nonprofit organization; it is now the Embudo Valley Health Facility.[29]

Several unique aspects of western religious life in this era developed with the emergence of the nation's first mail-order religious faith (Psychiana), the rise of Nevada's "marriage mills," and the legalization of gambling.

Psychiana was the brainchild of English immigrant Frank Robinson, who arrived in Moscow, Idaho, in the late 1920s. The faith might best be described as a form of New Thought, that is, a metaphysical system of doctrine and practice that claims a person may control his or her destiny through cultivation of a "healthy-minded" attitude and through reliance on the "Christ spirit" within. Idaho's Psychiana had no official church structure. Instead, it distributed New Thought materials through a correspondence course, twenty dollars for twenty lessons, all mailed at two-week intervals.

Psychiana's upbeat approach fit well with the needs of Depression America. By the late 1930s, Robinson's staff mailed out 60,000 items daily, and the federal post office accorded tiny Moscow a first-class status. The movement lasted until 1953, five years after Robinson's death, but its success was not lost on Unity, of the Kansas City area, which distributes millions of similar items today.[30]

Simultaneously, Protestant Nevada launched its marriage mills. As Gretna Green, Scotland, was to Britain, so Reno (and to a lesser extent Las Vegas) was to America: the place for a quick divorce and/or marriage. In 1930 Nevada inaugurated a brief (six weeks) residency requirement for divorce. Since the nearby more heavily populated states of Oregon and California had much longer waiting periods, the new law insured a lively marriage and divorce trade all through the 1930s. Estimates ran to 1 to 5 million marriages and divorces annually, but these are just guesses; nobody knows for certain.[31] Divorces remained a civil matter, but marriages, which always outnumbered the former, usually called for clerical involvement. Consequently, Protestant clerics in Reno, then Nevada's largest city, spent much time marrying people they had never seen before.

A Reno Congregational minister, Reverend Case, whose church lay close to the county courthouse, had a full-time secretary to schedule these weddings. She let it be known that Case was available at any hour, and over the course of his career Case officiated at 10,000 wedding ceremonies, earning about double his salary by doing so. In one year (1952) his successor at First Congregational Church officiated at 358 weddings.[32] In 1947 the Reno First Methodist Church established a full-time pastor to perform these marriage ceremonies. This "minister of marriages" never charged a fee but accepted whatever the couple contributed.[33] Demands for quick marriages remained strong during the World War II years as well. By the late 1950s, however, gaudy wedding chapels had begun to compete with church involvement, and with the decline in church weddings went a significant portion of many a church budget.

Simultaneously, Nevada's religious forces had to confront the emergence of another unique western phenomenon: legalized gambling. In 1930 the Nevada Legislature legalized gaming, much to the churches' dismay, for religious groups had provided the bulwark for all previous state antigaming measures. With this, the Nevada Protestant religious and casino worlds began to move in virtually separate tracks. In 1954, for example, Harold's Club of Reno offered the First Congregational Church of Reno a monthly contribution of $4,200. But after extended discussion, the church rejected it. One member stated that if the church had to rely on contributions from gambling interests, it "had better dump the church into the Truckee River and start over again."[34] Consequently, organized Protestantism became marginal to the rapid postwar growth of Reno and Las Vegas. Catholics, Mormons, and Jews, for whom gaming had never been that important, retained their roles as Nevada's dominant faiths.

———

The rise of Pentecostalism in the subregion of Oklahoma/Arkansas/Texas and its subsequent spread to the West Coast provide yet another unique aspect of western religious life in the 1930s. In general, the mainline religious groups either held steady or declined somewhat during the Depression. The statistics for Oklahoma, for example, show that from 1926 to 1936 twenty-eight denominations suffered membership loss. Oklahoma Methodists led the decline, losing 293 churches and 13,512 members. Since the Baptists and Catholics each decided to consolidate their churches, they lost structures but held about even in terms of numbers. Still, stagnation affected Oklahoma's largest and wealthiest denominations.

But some groups prospered during the Depression years. Several smaller Pentecostal organizations combined to form larger churches. The Oklahoma Assemblies of God increased their number thirty-four times from 1916 to 1936, jumping almost four times during the latter decade to achieve membership of 11,428. The editor of the *Oklahoma Journal of Religion* believed that these numbers indicated a major shift in the state's religious make-up. He observed that "the churches with the better educated ministry are losing ground or at best standing still, and the ones with a comparatively uneducated ministry are moving forward."[35] Foremost among these gainers were the various branches of American Pentecostalism.

From its beginnings in the rural Midwest and South, the Pentecostals drew from several traditions: the Wesleyan Holiness movement, which stressed a "second blessing" that revealed God's entire sanctification of the individual; the dispensationalist, premillennial theology that saw all time divided into separate "dispensations," with a cosmic cataclysm ending each dispensation in conflagration; and turn-of-the-century ideas of "spiritual healing." The central concept behind the movement, *glossolalia,* or speaking in tongues, seems to have begun in a Topeka, Kansas, revival in 1900. Wesleyan revivalist Charles Fox Parham taught his students to expect this divine gift, and on January 1, 1901, Agnes N. Ozan became the first to do so.[36]

The Pentecostal movement as such, however, really traces its origin to the Azusa Street (Los Angeles) revival that lasted from 1906 to 1908. Located at 312 Azusa Street, the Apostolic Faith Mission ministered to a lower-class clientele in a city of about 100,000. The revival, which began under the auspices of black minister William Seymour, immediately evoked local press interest. Most reporters were appalled. They described how the "howlings of the worshipers" made the night "hideous."[37]

The Azusa Street Revival, where hundreds of people spoke in languages not their own, has produced a mythology all its own. The prevailing interpretation suggests that the Pentecostal movement began as an interethnic one. African Americans, Hispanics, and Euro-Americans all participated, and Seymour had visions of establishing a truly color-blind congregation. Indeed, during the first few years of the movement, Pentecostalism often crossed gender and color lines. In 1914, however, the primarily white Assemblies of God separated from the primarily black Church of God in Christ. The splintering has continued, and today twenty-one different groups are members of the umbrella organization, the Pentecostal Fellowship of North America.[38] There may be as many as three hundred separate groups in the States alone.

Historians and sociologists, many increasingly from Pentecostal backgrounds themselves, have tried to explain the success of the movement in the American West. There seems to be agreement that by the eve of the Second World War the Pentecostal movement had created a distinct regional subculture that lapped over into southern Missouri, Kansas, and Oklahoma, with branches in Oregon and Los Angeles. In part, these churches grew by separating themselves from the world. They professed a distinct theology, with equally distinctive behavior patterns: plain dress, no alcohol or tobacco, no card playing, no jewelry, and no movies. Indeed, the Pentecostal world as it emerged in the interwar years embodied a complete lifestyle. In the broadest sense, the descent of the Holy Ghost provided, to use a modern term, "empowerment" of the individual. Such divine gifts aided the weak and often despised person to confront a hostile and sorrowful world while simultaneously offering "service" to humanity. At the same time, the Pentecostal churches provided comfort if a person did *not* succeed according to the tenets of the world. The healing dimension of the Pentecostal faith also resonated with the various Native healing ceremonies, especially on the Navajo Reservation.

The social class from which the movement drew its strength may be seen in the initial leaders' attacks on the need for formal theological training. Rev. Charles Fox Parham, for example, once said that "D.D." stood for "dumb dogs" and that "seminaries" should be spelled "cemeteries." Another Pentecostal leader said of their church, "All were on a level. . . . We did not honor men for their advantage, in means or education, but rather for their God-given 'gifts.'"[39]

Although tinged with both exclusionism and anti-intellectualism, the interwar Pentecostal movement did not completely disregard higher education. The ministers and teachers inherited a substantial institutional legacy from the Holiness Bible Schools and Bible Institutes. Attendance at such schools provided an easy entry into the ministry. It was, moreover, a mark of considerable prestige for a young person to become a minister via this route.

Pentecostal worship services always involved much zeal and enthusiasm, including public display of emotions, a rhythmic response to music, often with stamping of feet and clapping of hands, and great use of Gospel singing. This emotional release, which became central to lower-class, urban religious services, proved of considerable value to transplanted rural people. It took them momentarily away from the pressures of business and the world of commerce. For middle-class churches, however, these vigorous toe-tapping, hand-clapping services were anathema.

The role of music loomed large in this world, and part of a successful Pentecostal service involved putting on a "good performance." Organists and piano players often had back-up guitar, banjo, or tambourine players, long before other denominations would have dreamed of using anything but an organ. The minister involved the people in the services through testimony, prayer, shouting, or hand clapping. Singing of traditional Gospel hymns—with an easily memorized chorus repeated many times—served to cement the theological message in the hearers' minds.

In addition to song, the Pentecostal subculture relied less on "theological logic" than on an oral tradition to spread its message. This proved true for both black and white worlds. During these first fifty years, Pentecostal ministers did not write many books or magazine articles. Rather, they relied on proverbs, jokes, personal testimonies, musical lyrics, and a wide variety of miracle stories, many of which involved spiritual healing. Given this situation, it is no accident that they were among the first to utilize radio and, three decades later, television. Both forms of electronic media provided ideal means to spread their message.[40] In so doing they created an emotional, distinct Pentecostal "style" of worship, one that would steadily expand into other groups.[41]

Probably the most famous western Pentecostal cleric of the twentieth century is Oral Roberts. Born into the Pentecostal Holiness subculture of southeastern Oklahoma in 1918, Roberts grew to maturity amidst agrarian poverty. His parents were both involved in preaching. In 1935 he contracted tuberculosis and began to fail in health. He then heard God clearly tell him: "Son, I am going to heal you and you are going to take my healing power to your generation."[42]

Oral Roberts followed the divine command. He utilized revivals, wrote articles for the *Oklahoma Holiness Advocate,* and from 1949 forward relied heavily upon radio to deliver his message. Moving to Tulsa, he soon became the city's most famous citizen via his *Healing Waters* magazine (begun in 1947) and his radio broadcasts.[43] By 1955 Roberts appeared on 250 radio outlets and had begun his first, tentative efforts on television. Claiming the whole earth as his pulpit, Roberts proudly drew on every promotional device he could think of to

Rev. Oral Roberts, c. 1965, praying for an ill child at one of his popular healing crusades.

"bring God to the masses."[44] He did so through radio, television, magazines, religious comic books, and, especially, through exhausting healing revivals held all across the nation. The brunt of his message stressed divine healing, but he took no personal credit for any cures. He emphasized that "God alone heals, whether it is through medicine, prayer, exercise or climate."[45]

In 1965 Oral Roberts opened the first accredited Pentecostal university, Oral Roberts University (ORU), in Tulsa. He did so to educate Pentecostal youth with what he hoped would be academic training superior to Bible colleges and equal to that found in any secular school. In 1978 ORU added a medical school after much opposition from local authorities. It planned to offer a combination of prayer and medicine in a "holistic approach to healing." In 1981 Roberts opened the even more controversial City of Faith Medical Center. Six years later he achieved his greatest notoriety when he announced, amidst grave financial difficulties, that God would "call him home" if he could not raise $8 million to keep his operations running. (The school reached its goal with a donation of $1.3 million from a dog track owner just

All Souls Unitarian Church, Tulsa, Oklahoma. Perhaps as a response to the evangelical culture of the region, this Unitarian church has become one of the largest in the West.

three hours before the announced deadline.) However, two years later the medical center had to close.[46] Roberts's recently published autobiography expresses his anguish at this disappointment.[47]

From the onset Roberts's flamboyant methods drew criticism. Ministers from the Oklahoma Churches of Christ called his claim that he could feel God's power surge through his right (healing) arm a "sham and hoax." They insisted that no man had divine healing powers. During his crusades in Phoenix, critics left printed cards on all nearby automobiles challenging Roberts to meet them in public debate. Local Tulsa ministerial and medical opposition has long been a thorn in Roberts's side. The fact that Tulsa houses All Souls Unitarian Church, one of the West's largest Unitarian churches with 1,300 members, may be directly traced to Roberts's influence. (The rationalistic Unitarians have often noted that their group serves as a refuge for those desiring to escape from a strict evangelical background.)

In spite of, or perhaps because of, the controversy that has dogged his career, Oral Roberts has had an incredible influence on American religious life. Not only is he Tulsa's most famous citizen, his biographer, David Edwin Harrell, Jr., has termed him one of the most significant religious figures of the entire twentieth century.[48]

The Pentecostal subculture was born in Los Angeles and matured in Missouri, Kansas, and Oklahoma during the 1920s. It moved to the Pacific Coast with the migrants during the Great Depression and World War II boom eras. It has found fertile soil in Los Angeles, the San Joaquin Valley, and in the agricultural areas of eastern Washington.

John Steinbeck's classic novel *The Grapes of Wrath* (1939) provides the best fictional account of this migration from Oklahoma to California. Steinbeck's book is replete with religious allusions. The title, the names of Rose of Sharon and Jim Casey (JC), plus the final scene of sacrifice all reflect this larger, biblical perspective. Still, the author's treatment of the migrants' actual faith is cynical. The only good preacher in the book is one who left the profession. Steinbeck looks toward New Deal government actions for secular, rather than religious, salvation of his people.

In *Rising in the West* (1993) the *Washington Post*'s Dan Morgan has traced the travels of an actual family migration from 1930s Oklahoma to California. Unlike the fictional Joads, the real-life Tathams first joined the Pentecostal Church in California, not a labor union. Although not without family difficulties, many individuals have prospered; some have become quite wealthy.[49] Morgan concludes that their traditional faith played no small role in this transformation.

Historian James N. Gregory's broader study of Dust Bowl migration to California has echoed Morgan's account. Rural evangelical Protestantism in a number of overlapping forms—Southern Baptist, Southern Methodist, Church of Christ, Disciples of Christ, Church of the Nazarene, and several versions of Pentecostalism—accompanied the Oklahoma and Arkansas migrants on their journeys westward. Upon arrival, many migrants found the established Baptist and Methodist churches too "brainy" and far less tolerant of their worship style. Sometimes the migrants switched denominations, but often they ended up swaying the local churches to their position. The Bakersfield, California, Presbyterian Church, the Congregational Church of Shafter, California, and the First Congregational Church of Wasco, California, all either left their parent denomination or became so evangelical that few would recognize their mainstream traditional affiliation.[50]

The Pacific Coast also proved receptive to this Oklahoma and Arkansas influx. California dairyman Demos Shakarian founded the Full Gospel Business Men's Fellowship International in 1951, and it soon spread across the region.[51] The faith perspectives that arrived on the Pacific Coast not only held the world at bay, they also infused the people with the self-confidence needed to master it as well.

During the last three decades of the twentieth century, the Pentecostals have grown, not only in the Pacific Coast states but also among Hispanic Americans of the Southwest and in Latin America. More Catholics are converting to Protestantism (often, but not always, a Pentecostal version) today than at any other time since the Reformation of the sixteenth century: 400 an hour by one count; 100,000 annually by another.[52] In 1989 Archbishop Pio Laghi, the Vatican's chief representative in the United States, described the annual loss of Spanish-speaking Catholics to these groups as "significantly—I would say disturbingly high." Sociologist-priest Andrew Greeley estimated in 1986 that about 23 percent of all Hispanic Americans had become Protestant. In 1990 the Catholic bishops of California and northwestern Mexico issued a statement denouncing the "unfair and coercive practices of these proselytizing sects." The pastoral statement, written by thirty bishops in Alta and Baja California, decried the systematic attacks on the Catholic Church and called on the proselytizers to allow "baptized Catholics to become better informed in their own faith rather than confuse them with alien, controversial ideas."[53]

Sociologists have come up with several theories to explain this situation. To a large extent, they argue, Hispanic Pentecostal churches have been able to re-create a traditional Roman Catholic peasant community in often harsh areas of the urban world. Second, the emphasis on conversion, an instant change to a better life, somehow resonates with the pace of the surrounding capitalist culture. Third, the miraculous healings that infused Hispanic/Mexican Catholicism are easier to replicate amidst Pentecostal circles than in the more staid, middle-class American Catholic churches. Perhaps the charismatic experience also offered a sense of mystery that people saw as disappearing with the end of the Latin Mass. Finally, the Hispanics seemed to be the only large Catholic immigrant group that somehow failed to bring their ethnic priests with them in any significant numbers.

The American Catholic Church has recently begun to fight back. For the Easter 1989 service, the cathedral in San Antonio borrowed from Pentecostal techniques to allow parishioners to come to a microphone and tell the Virgin Mary of their personal sufferings. Other churches have begun to include mariachi music. A few have instituted Spanish language services. A San Francisco priest confessed that he was not worried. "They'll be back," he said. "Catholicism is a religion for the long haul."[54]

The most creative western religious response to the Great Depression probably came from the Latter-day Saints of Utah: the church welfare system. The introduction of this unique welfare program has had numerous long-term effects. Modern statistics show, for example, that today the average Mormon family remains on church welfare for four months; the average Utah family remains on federal or state welfare for eighteen months; the nationwide average is thirty-six months.

The decision to construct their own welfare system during the Depression had deep roots in LDS history. In 1890 the governing body of the church, the First Presidency, issued a decision banning polygamy, and this paved the way for further accommodation with mainstream American culture. By this time, however, Mormon geographical expansion had largely reached its limits; any future expansion of the faith would occur by intermingling with Gentiles, not by converting them en masse.[55] Moreover, by this time the Gentiles had intruded into Zion via railroad towns, mining camps, the U.S. military, and numerous Gentile clergymen.[56]

In 1902 the Saints established a Bureau of Information and Church Literature in Salt Lake and began to station representatives at various LDS historic sites. The theology altered as well, as church leaders began to discourage spiritual healing, rationalize the church bureaucracy, and deemphasize the concept of the "Gathering" (i.e., immigration to Zion) that had initially brought so many immigrants to Utah. Henceforth, the church emphasized that Zion was less a place (Utah) than a location "where the people are."[57]

In spite of these changes, the religious history of Utah for most of the first half of the century might be termed a "cultural standoff." Secure as the dominant faith in the region, the Saints moved in a separate sphere from the Gentiles, one that overlapped only occasionally. This religio-cultural standoff was replicated in no other part of the nation.

The various religious groups all reached different forms of accommodation with the Saints. In general, the Catholics left them alone. Their hospitals, orphanages, and other institutions were largely intended for Gentiles. Episcopalians built similar civic institutions, but their bishops were much more willing to engage the Mormons in theological debate. The Episcopal bishop of Idaho declared in 1902 that the Saints were but "a passing feature in American social, political, and religious life."[58] Shortly afterward, Salt Lake City bishop Franklin Spencer Spalding launched an attack on LDS history with his *Joseph Smith, Jr. as a Translator*. This pamphlet utilized the scholarly methods of biblical criticism to fault Smith's translation of *The Book of Abraham* (1842) and imply that Smith's other translations in *The Book of Mormon* were equally wide of the mark. Only Spalding's death, Salt Lake City's first traffic fatality, in 1914 prevented him from continuing the attack.[59]

Of all the groups, the Jews, who do not proselytize, probably got along best in Zion. LDS–Jewish relationships have always been cordial, for both shared a similar concept of "peoplehood" and persecution. Brigham Young had great respect for the Jewish concept of Zion, and he proved quite helpful to the early Jewish community of Salt Lake City. He donated land for a cemetery, opened a ward house for their first (1854) services in Utah, and let the Jews use Seventies Hall on Temple Square for High Holy Day ceremonies. The LDS Assembly Hall, built in 1882, had a Star of David motif in its windows. B'nai Israel of Salt Lake City was organized in 1874 (reorganized in 1891) to become the state's leading Reform congregation. When the first Conservative synagogue was built in 1903, Joseph F. Smith, the first president of the church, laid the cornerstone.[60] Perhaps it is no accident that Simon Bamberger became governor of Utah in 1916, and Louis Marcus later served as mayor of Salt Lake City.

The more evangelical churches (Presbyterians, Methodists, Baptists, and Congregationalists), however, essentially declared open theological war on the Mormons. In 1915 the Protestant Churches established a comity agreement not to encroach on each other's territory. The American Baptist Home Missionary Society periodically sent professional evangelists to the region. Methodist minister E. E. Mork began his "Gospel Wagon and Tent" in 1907 and remained thirty-nine years in the Utah mission field. Ada Duhigg also took a Gospel wagon into isolated LDS strongholds.

The results of these evangelistic efforts were virtually nil. The Saints accepted the Protestant social services but treated evangelical doctrine in the same way as the evangelists had earlier treated Tom Paine's

Age of Reason or Robert G. Ingersoll's *The Mistakes of Moses*. The Saints already accepted Scripture as a source of revelation to which they added *The Book of Mormon* and Smith's other writings. Thus, the conservative evangelical appeals of sole reliance on Scripture seldom made headway.

Various statistical compilations reveal that Utah Gentile religious organizations grew steadily during the first part of the century, but only in proportion to immigration from the outside. In other words, virtually no Saints converted to Protestantism or Catholicism. The Mormons remained within their own religious structures; the few apostates were usually so bitter that they refused to join anything.[61]

By the 1920s the Presbyterians had assumed the role of the most vigorous opponents of the Saints. Although they had relinquished their parochial school system as soon as Utah developed its own public schools, Westminster College in Salt Lake City remained a fountain of opposition to the Mormons. A 1935 pamphlet admitted that Mormon converts were few and that tangible results from their efforts were negligible. Nevertheless, the Board of National Missions felt it essential to keep Presbyterian work alive in Zion. But the church leaders' goal shifted. They stated that they were less concerned with individual conversion than with shifting the entire LDS society toward a more mainstream "Christian" basis.[62]

As Mormon scholars have shown, this accommodation did, indeed, take place.[63] By 1920 Utah's public school system had produced a cadre of educated LDS youth who traveled east to study law and medicine. The Saints welcomed Protestant temperance advocates of the 1920s and generally gave them strong support. Protestants applauded the Saints' decision to intermingle traditional Christian hymns with Mormon hymn tunes and regularly reported that LDS worship services were increasingly drawing on scriptural references as well.[64] God has his own plan for Utah, Reverend Mork observed, and was working it out on a divine scale.[65] According to historian Kenneth Wynn, by the 1930s most Americans viewed the Saints in a positive light.[66] The Mormon response to the Great Depression certainly helped sway public opinion to the positive side of the ledger.

Like every other segment of the population, Mormons went on state and federal welfare during the early 1930s. But the conservative LDS leadership viewed this as close to a moral failing. Some leaders worried about the political implications. They maintained that no person could be politically free if he or she had to depend upon the state for sustenance. After 1935 this concern extended to Social Security as well. "Be independent," Elder Melvin J. Ballard of the Council of Twelve told members of a Salt Lake City Relief Society Conference in 1938. "Get along without all government assistance if possible and do not labor under the delusion that old-age assistance money is pension money to which all old people are entitled."[67]

Concern over federal involvement eventually drove the Saints to establish their own welfare system in 1936. Still largely a rural people, the church began to purchase family farms. They viewed this as a method of not only putting the unemployed to work but also as a chance to produce surplus agricultural goods. Simultaneously, church authorities worked with state and regional agricultural committees to combine subdivided farms into more productive units. They also began a program to find farming opportunities for those without land. On occasion, the church would buy a farm and the local stake would pay back the amount over the long term from farm revenues.

In 1938 church authorities also asked 750,000 faithful to fast twice a month and donate the cost of the missed meals to the needy. The first "fast day" program netted $431,000 but barely dented the church welfare outlay of $1,827,000 for that year.[68] The program continued into the post–World War II era. In 1947 the church asked for a December fast day, with the funds earmarked for the displaced peoples of Europe.[69]

All through the late 1930s, the church purchased farms, chiefly in Utah, Arizona, Idaho, and California. It also began to establish warehouses to store grains and other foodstuffs during fertile harvests for use in lean years. It became standard doctrine that all LDS households should maintain a year's supply of food and clothing.

The local bishops controlled the various storehouses, and no Saint went without, once his or her needs were known. By 1957 the church owned six hundred farms, thirty granaries, forty mills, a number of salvage shops, and even a coal mine. The day-to-day operation of this thirty-million-dollar "welfare business," headquartered in Welfare Square (a city block in downtown Salt Lake City), was run almost entirely by volunteers. The *Saturday Evening Post* praised the Saints for their efficient operation.[70] By 1990, incidentally, the church still owned about 160 welfare farms.[71]

In 1933 the First Presidency also began a recycling church security plan, later the church welfare plan, that was largely patterned after the Methodist-based Goodwill Industries. The first Deseret Industries plant opened in 1938, hiring people who wanted to work but were handicapped either physically or mentally. Managers assigned each one a task that fell within his or her capabilities. Within twenty-five years, Deseret plants and stores had been established in Logan, Ogden, Mesa, Arizona, Provo, Los Angeles, and elsewhere. The Saints insisted that no person, especially the elderly, should ever lack for food, clothing, or shelter. But they also insisted that such aid should come from the church or family members, not from the state or federal government.[72]

The Saints' church-run food and processing plants proved very successful. By 1977 the church owned 614 food production, processing, and canning operations. These included dairy farms, honey-processing plants, a corn cannery, and even a soap manufacturing project. The foodstuffs carried their own Deseret label. These goods were held in the various bishops' storehouses, and those in need had access to them. The only requirement was that all physically able-bodied people were expected to give back some service in return for the goods that they received. The alternative, the Saints argued, was loss of self-respect.[73]

Even critics of the Saints credited the LDS welfare plan as marvelously effective. Begun in 1936 to get the faithful through a bad year, it grew steadily. President J. Reuben Clark, Jr., gave a lengthy presentation on the program to a Citizens Conference on Government and Management in Estes Park, Colorado, in 1939. As Clark explained to the mostly non-LDS audience, the roots of their new welfare system, which all agreed was a major departure for the church, lay deep in Mormon history. Because of their unconventional beliefs, from the onset the church had been forced to rely on self-help. Indeed, persecution by local authorities left them no other choice. "No aid came from the outside," said Clark. "We never dreamed of asking for it." Prophet Brigham Young argued that all able-bodied poor should be set to work, for "to give to the idler is as wicked as anything else." The 1936 LDS view might be seen as a revived form of the Puritan work ethic. Clark actually termed the welfare system essentially one of spirituality rather than economics: "where the spirituality has been high, the plan has succeeded; where the spirituality is low, the plan has lagged."[74]

The fascination with the workings of the LDS welfare system has continued. In 1952 Adam S. Bennion of the Council of Twelve explained the plan to four hundred delegates from the Mountain States Conference of the American Public Welfare Program. He offered the church's plan as a means of ending idleness and the dole by instituting "industry, thrift, and self-respect."[75]

In 1979 President Jimmy Carter was similarly urged to look at the LDS welfare system as a model. In the 1990s, when U.S. senators began a major reform of the federal welfare system, they again sought advice from Mormon bishops. Presiding bishop Merrill Bateman explained the church's program to a Senate Finance Committee regarding the three-part plan of prevention, temporary assistance, and rehabilitation. He argued that the Saints overall encouraged independence, thrift, and self-reliance. He repeated the church's central position: "The dignity of a person is maintained when you help him take care of himself."[76]

Historian Jan Shipps has credited the LDS welfare plan as fundamental to the twentieth-century Mormon tradition. She argues that it became the church's means of refurbishing the Saints' sense of themselves as a corporate, separate people. The church plan has also helped draw a line between the Saints—widely acknowledged as a people who take care of their own—and the rest of the world.[77] Moreover, by so doing, it helped erode Gentile hostility toward the Saints.

———

The religious forces of the West were only modestly affected by the culture wars of the 1920s. Although Oregon and Nebraska enacted anti-immigrant laws, they were overturned by the U.S. Supreme Court. Except for Oklahoma and parts of California, anti-evolution agitation did not sink deep roots in the post–World War I West either. During the Great Depression, however, the western churches wrestled in a thousand ways with the economic downturn. Although the region experienced no revival, the local churches continued their role as centers of social activity. The creation of the LDS welfare system and the Pentecostal influx to California and the Pacific Northwest may loom as the most significant legacies of the Great Depression years. Each has become a permanent part of the modern western religious landscape.

Chapter 5

Western Religious Life
of the 1940s and 1950s

The outbreak of the Second World War inaugurated profound changes for the American West. Historian Gerald D. Nash has argued that World War II transformed the West from an economic colony of the East to an essential component of national economic life. Concentrating on California, Nash has also argued that the postwar West emerged as a "cultural pacesetter" for not only the nation but the entire globe.[1] Naturally, the onset of the war years affected the region's religious world as well.

Relatively ignored during the Depression, western clerics found themselves thrust into renewed positions of leadership after Pearl Harbor. The literature of the day reflects the extent to which the people fell back on church and synagogue for guidance. In retrospect, perhaps this is not that surprising. Unlike the Great War of 1917–18, which America fought largely as a moral crusade, the federal government presented the second conflict as more of a just, grim task that needed to be finished as soon as possible.

By the late 1930s, the prevailing pacifist sentiment of the interwar years had largely evaporated. Led by theologian Reinhold Niebuhr, the Protestant clergy reluctantly began to accept the legitimacy of armed resistance against the "intrusion of evil" into the international political realm.[2] Except for the historic peace churches, the attack on Pearl Harbor removed most clerical doubts about the just nature of the conflict. As a result, the clerics, rather than the U.S. government, often became key spokesmen for the moral issues of the war effort. Clerics were also among the first groups to publicly articulate the outlines of the hoped-for postwar world. Repetition of these overarching goals did much to merge the various faiths from their parallel tracks into a recognition of a common national purpose.

Western clerics played an important role in this transformation. In November 1943 a Denver Catholic priest and a Denver rabbi both signed a common declaration of Judeo-Christian forces, calling on the world leaders to establish a just society when the conflict ended. Such a society, they said, should preserve the rights of man and the dignity of the human spirit. They called on the victorious nations to guarantee the rights of minorities, control armaments, increase economic collaboration, and defend the integrity of international law.[3]

That same year, Salt Lake City Presbyterian Floyd W. Barr declared that Jesus was "the world's first democrat," arguing that he had long championed the downtrodden of all classes and races, Jews and Gentiles alike.[4] Like Barr, a surprising number of churches spoke out during the war on racial and ethnic matters. On Lincoln's birthday in 1944, the Congregational women of Oklahoma urged better race relations. They emphasized the fact that Hitler's primary strategy was to divide the United States by setting one race against another. Arguing that the war crisis had brought the status of African Americans into clearer focus, they declared that this issue "constitutes a moral challenge to the American tenets of democracy and Christian brotherhood."[5] In a similar fashion, the Episcopal bishop of Utah declared in 1946 the need for American Christians to understand other peoples and other faiths of the world. The bishop prophesied that the postwar world would not so much be an "atomic age" as one of "internationalism."[6] Likewise, the Presbyterian Synod of Nebraska asked its parishioners to accept the Japanese who had moved into the state after release from the wartime internment camps. More than any other event, the war awakened the western churches to the moral issues of ethnicity and race.

Virtually all of the religious organizations discussed their hopes that the churches would be leaders in the establishment of the postwar global world. Oklahoma Episcopalians introduced this concept to their parishioners only three months after Pearl Harbor.[7] The state's Congregationalists and the Presbyterian University of Tulsa joined in later. Everyone agreed that introducing justice into a postwar world would be a challenge. People responded automatically to the demands of Pearl Harbor, Stalingrad, and Dunkirk, the Episcopalians noted, but they reacted less spontaneously to the equally significant challenges presented by the conferences at Bretton Woods, Dumbarton Oaks, and San Francisco.[8]

From 1944 onward, the religious leaders of the American West began seriously to plan for the postwar world. That year, seven Catholic bishops of the Southwest met and concluded that they had little faith in war, politics, or state action to bring about economic justice and goodwill among nations. They argued that any reconstruction of human society required active involvement by "believers in the Word of God" and, especially, by cooperation among all religious bodies. Moreover, said the bishops, "we can co-operate in this work of reconstruction *without* in any way compromising our religious principles or diminishing our loyalty to discipline."[9] In 1944 Secretary of Agriculture Henry A. Wallace reiterated this position. He declared that the churches would bear the responsibility for the future of American freedom, science, and civilization.[10]

During the war years, western churches found themselves thrust into a variety of new roles. As in the Great War, when western women formed "Lick the Kaiser" clubs and packed kit bags for the soldiers, western women's church groups engaged in a variety of similar aid programs. They assisted the Red Cross and USO. Churches in Colorado founded "friendship classes" to help sustain the women while their husbands and brothers were away in the services.[11] On the 1944 anniversary of the fall of Bataan, the Carlsbad, New Mexico, Baptist Church held a special prayer for the young men of the region who had been captured in that battle.[12]

The Japanese internment camps, virtually all of which were located in the West, produced unique religious realignments. Several Catholic priests followed their parishioners into confinement. Numerous Protestant and Catholic churches sent gift boxes, especially for the children at holiday time. Quakers also did yeoman work in the camps. One camp created a unique Buddhist-Baptist alliance that lasted for the duration.[13]

Even the federal government acknowledged the importance of this revived religious sentiment. When the community of Grand Lake, Colorado, dedicated its community-built, pine-log church in 1942, it received a telegram of congratulations from President Franklin D. Roosevelt. The president spoke of the national need for strength that comes from "the reliance on the Most High" during times of conflict. In a similar fashion, the popular World War II magazine images of churches on village greens usually symbolized democracy or religious freedom.[14]

The Allied dropping of the atomic bombs in August 1945 and the subsequent disclosure of the Nazi extermination camps proved hard on the liberal moral imagination. They also cast grave doubts about the ability of churches and synagogues to reconstruct the postwar world. Still, virtually the only groups to immediately denounce the use of the bombs on Japan were religious ones: the Vatican, the liberal Protestant *Christian Century,* and the *Catholic Worker,* the voice of radical pacifist Dorothy Day.[15]

Thus faith in the rational nature of humankind and the inevitable progress of justice experienced hard sledding in the immediate postwar era. The war, indeed, proved the efficiency of technology, but that technology seemed to be morally neutral. The disclosure of the Holocaust revived the ancient doctrine of sinful human nature and the necessity to be on guard against any corporate evil. In the postwar era, Union Seminary theologian Reinhold Niebuhr emerged as one of the most respected public intellectuals of his day. His picture graced the cover of *Time,* and his counsel that only power could confront power influenced a generation of public officials from all political parties. As theologian Langdon Gilkey once observed, the consolidation of science and technology as the spiritual center of culture has had a hard time sustaining itself in times of deep national troubles.[16] Thus for the two decades after the end of the war, the nation's religious figures were once again accorded great respect from the culture at large.

━━━━━━━

Although most observers agreed that organized religion lay at the heart of national life in the 1940s and 1950s, considerable uncertainty existed as to the actual numbers of religious participants. At some time during the post—World War I years, people began to interpret the doctrine of the separation of church and state as prohibiting the government's compiling of *any* church-related data. Church response to the 1936 federal census was poor and in 1946 even poorer. None was attempted in 1956. But in 1950 the private National Council of Churches of Christ in the U.S.A. compiled extensive figures by requesting such data from the various national headquarters of participating bodies.[17] Edwin S. Gaustad drew from this compilation for his excellent *Historical Atlas of Religion in America* (1962; revised edition, 1976).[18]

Geographer Wilbur Zelinsky also examined the data and confessed that he found the West to be something of a statistical puzzle. Of the nine U.S. regions surveyed, "the western has the least recognizable personality." Migrants to the region during and after the war years meant that, excluding the Catholic sections of southern California and the Southwest, the West exhibited no clear pattern of dominance by any single religious group.

There were other discoveries as well. For unexplained reasons the Seventh-Day Adventists proved especially vigorous along the southern West Coast and in northern Oregon and southeastern Washington, especially in the vicinity of Walla Walla College. Catholicism remained strong throughout the region as El Paso and Albuquerque continued to rank in the top ten cities in terms of Catholic populations. By around 1952 Los Angeles had emerged as home of the third largest American Jewish community. Interestingly, none of the top ten Protestant cities lay in the West.

The 1950 census also confirmed the widespread rumor of the "heathen Northwest." Nationwide the reported church membership, as a percentage of total population, was 49 percent. Washington state, however, reported 30.5 percent, and Oregon trailed all forty-eight states with 23.7 percent. Even when California (40.7 percent) was added, the West came in last of all U.S. regions in terms of religious adherence.[19] The *Atlas of Oregon* (1976) revealed this trend on a county-by-county basis. Save for Alaska, Oregon ranked lowest—under one third—for total church affiliation. In addition, certain groups—Jews, Catholics, and Baptists—were decidedly underrepresented.[20]

Zelinsky puzzled over the meaning of these numbers, phrasing the issue in remarkable social science jargon: "It is unquestionable that individuals born within Catholic, Jewish, Mormon, Mennonite, or a number of other Protestant groups will inherit an ineradicable set of cultural differences from their families and co-religionists."[21] Few could argue with that. But what precisely did all of this mean in a region with no overall dominant religious trends and dotted with vast areas that could clearly be termed "unchurched"?

During the 1941–45 period, the national press placed a strong emphasis on the similarity of America's various regions and subcultures. This
focus on common themes extended well into the next decades. Thus,
the 1945–60 period produced no major ethnoreligious public quarrel
over values such as had characterized the 1920s. Instead, emphasis
lay with celebrating national commonalities, what historians have
termed "the culture of the whole."

In the world of religion, such emphasis upon "the culture of the
whole" meant a search for commonalities among the wide spectrum
of national faiths. Sometimes these commonalities proved hard to find.
Eventually they boiled down to restaurant placards suggesting grace
before meals or billboards that advised people to "attend the church
or synagogue of your choice." Religious attendance, it didn't seem to
matter where, also emerged as a mark of respectability in the postwar
West.

Since the Soviet Union was officially an atheistic state, the Cold
War helped Protestants, Catholics, and Jews in their quest for com-
mon ground. Photographs and memoirs from the Holocaust produced
a wave of sympathy for American Judaism. The rise of the state of
Israel, the concern for refugees, and the success of second-generation
Jewish children all helped bridge the various gaps within American
Judaism and those between the Jewish and Gentile worlds. "In just a
few short years," historian Leonard Dinnerstein has noted, "Adolf
Hitler's maniacal scheme to rid Europe of its Jews accomplished what
no Jew since Moses had done—practically unified world Jewry in ral-
lying to a common cause."[22]

In 1955 Will Herberg, a sociologist and disciple of Reinhold Niebuhr,
penned his *Protestant-Catholic-Jew*. The thesis of this seminal work
lay in the title. Herberg argued that the three great historic faiths had
become three different ways by which one became American. The
"mainstreaming" of the nation's three largest faiths served as a defin-
ing characteristic of the 1950s. Yet this postwar concept of mainstreaming was hardly new for the American West. In a number of areas—San
Francisco, Portland, Boise, Fargo, Denver, and so forth—the three historic faiths had long been viewed as roughly equal. Even more provincial regions such as Albuquerque, Salt Lake City, and Oklahoma City
had witnessed modest Protestant-Catholic-Jewish interaction.

Of course, some social anti-Semitism still existed in the postwar
West. In the late 1940s Screen Actors Guild president Ronald Reagan

resigned from the Lakeside Country Club because it refused to accept a Jewish applicant. The ethnic restrictions of Los Angeles' elite Hillcrest Country Club led to Groucho Marx's famous quip, "I wouldn't want to be a member of any club that would have me."[23] The Rosenberg atomic spy case of the 1950s kept this sentiment alive to some degree. So too did the congressional investigation of the Hollywood film industry.

Still, it was not long before such social restrictions virtually disappeared. The Holocaust caused the collapse of American anti-Semitism, even of the "genteel" variety. It was not long before overt anti-Semitism in the West had become virtually extinct, except within extreme African-American circles. By the onset of the 1970s, at the very latest, American Jews had been officially mainstreamed, but the West had long paved the way for this phenomenon.

The same mainstreaming could be seen in western Catholicism, but for far different reasons. With the growth of the postwar West, new states such as California began to assert increased political influence. Historically, Catholic missionaries and pioneers had formed the bedrock of Euro-American culture throughout this region. The early history of California, New Mexico, and Arizona essentially boiled down to the history of the Catholic Church. This was true elsewhere in the West as well.

Montana's Euro-American history largely began with the arrival of the Jesuits from St. Louis. The institutions founded by the Ursulines, the Daughters of Charity, and the Presentation Sisters dotted the entire northern Rocky Mountain region.[24] In Gilded Age Colorado, one third of all churches were Catholic, and the territory's first high school graduate matriculated from Saint Mary's Academy in Denver.[25] The list could be extended. Thus, the dominant post–World War II presence of New Mexico archbishop James Byrne or Los Angeles cardinal James Francis McIntyre, each of whom held more cultural power than any elected state official, is hardly surprising. Only Native faiths remained marginalized. But with the 1960s, that, too, was about to change.

―――――――

The heavy migration to West Coast industries and ports during the war placed severe demands on regional religious institutions. In the quarter century following the peace with Japan, western churches and synagogues tried their best to catch up. Every major subregion of the

West experienced a postwar boom of church, synagogue, and parochial school construction. Historian Steven Avella has argued that this
immigrant influx revolutionized the Catholicism of northern California, transforming Catholic life from a sleepy, rural identity to that of a
sophisticated, urban-centered culture.[26]

During this brick-and-mortar phase of construction, most western
groups built fewer "symbolic" church buildings and focused instead
on functional designs. It was not uncommon for the churches to add
ugly, boxlike "Christian education" buildings to their (usually) Gothic
structures. Thus, religious architecture of the day tended to expand
horizontally with the addition of meeting halls, rather than vertically
with towers or steeples.[27] A number of congregations, however, combined both. The First Christian Church of Tomorrow in Tulsa (dedicated in 1956 at a cost of $800,000) included a theater-in-the-round, a
youth center with tennis courts, a bell tower, and an educational building in one gigantic religious complex.[28]

Denver experienced a similar boom. A 1950 Denver survey discovered that the cost of recent church construction—thirty-five new buildings in five years—exceeded $1 million. From 1945 to 1957, Denver
officials issued 177 building permits for churches, church schools,
and other religious buildings, with a total valuation of over $10 mil-
lion.[29] The *Denver Post* noted in 1960 that over 250 new churches and
synagogues had been built in Denver at a cost of $25 million. Over
half of these were constructed in modern or contemporary design.[30]
Drawing upon the motto "recreation is re-creation," a number of mainstream denominations included gymnasiums, tennis courts, and other
play areas as a part of their church complexes. The Mormons excelled
in constructing such recreational centers.

Other western cities echoed Denver's postwar boom. Churches in
Lincoln expanded from 100 in 1910 to 123 in 1955. By 1960 Amarillo
had 140 churches, while Roswell, New Mexico, boasted 66. Lutheran
pastor Erick Hawkins, who served in Salt Lake City from 1950 to 1957,
put it succinctly: "Some pastors are called to teach and counsel; I have
been called to build churches."[31]

Since the presence of prominent religious buildings in a city still
denoted respectability, Las Vegas, Nevada, spokesmen were quick to
emphasize their postwar construction. Local church leaders periodically denied that Las Vegas deserved its "city of sin" reputation. One
reporter claimed that "Las Vegas is perhaps more spiritually minded

than most of the other cities in the country." In 1963 city officials boasted of their eighty different religious denominations serving 60,000 parishioners in the area.[32]

Since this construction boom occurred primarily in the suburbs, it had a major effect on the life of interior western cities. By 1961 over twenty Protestant churches had departed from downtown Denver.[33] Although several downtown churches found other uses, many fell to the wrecker's ball. Amarillo's Sacred Heart Cathedral was torn down, and even concerted action from the head of the Pillar of Fire denomination could not save its founding structure in Denver from demolition.

This move to the suburbs, however, isolated many postwar churches from the dilemmas of urban life. "It has become evident in our generation," a Lincoln, Nebraska, reporter wryly observed in 1968, "that God only speaks in the suburbs."[34] As Lutheran pastor Martin E. Marty noted, "I tell my congregation that their sin is not being middle class; their sin is not seeing through the limits of their class."[35]

Postwar church construction, however, was not limited to suburban church buildings. Shortly after the war, the Reformed Church in America, a relatively small body with a largely Dutch heritage, pioneered yet another innovation of religious architecture: the drive-in church. Other groups quickly borrowed the concept. Two drive-in churches opened in Denver in the fall of 1948. Housed in drive-in theaters, the services were advertised as nonsectarian. Mildly evangelical, they were also directed largely toward new groups: mothers with small children, invalids, and those about to explore the region's many natural wonders. [36]

The Denver drive-in churches survived for over a quarter century. Other Reformed churches instituted similar successful drive-ins in southern California and Arizona. By 1972 there were about eighteen, primarily in the West but also in Michigan and Florida. The pacesetter drive-in church has been the famous Garden Grove, California, Community Church (designed by architect Richard J. Neutra) begun in 1955 by Rev. Robert H. Schuller (to be discussed in more detail in chapter 9). Another walk-in/drive-in church in Long Beach, California, doubled its membership through this means, although the pastor worried that the people who remained in their cars never really became part of the church fellowship. It proved a real challenge, he discovered, to move the people from their vehicles to the pews. Still, the field director of the Reformed Church in the Western States attributed its rapid denominational growth largely to this innovation.[37]

Western Jews shared in the building boom as well. By 1952 Denver had nine synagogues that included close to 3,000 families and 15,000 members. All Jewish leaders agreed that the number of worshipers had increased, and they pointed with pride to the expansion of religious education programs for their young people. Jewish classes were usually held after public school. One group constructed a school building immediately adjacent to its synagogue. The 1951 dedication of Denver's new B'nai Israel synagogue was celebrated as a major local event. "The rise of the state of Israel is one of the important factors in the return to religion," observed Rabbi Joel Zion of Denver's Temple Emanuel in 1952. "By reflex action it's given Jews a deeper feeling of unity and charity. Furthermore, many people have been let down by their hope that science can salvage everything, and are returning to religious values."[38]

The horrors of the past war and the nuclear tensions of the Cold War also elevated traditional biblical teaching to a new level. A 1953 Denver Council of Churches pamphlet proclaimed that religion formed the bulwark for any moral society.[39] "What is a community without a church?" asked the Washington Peak, Colorado, Congregational Church in 1953. The pastor of Denver's All Souls Lutheran Church remarked that he believed his generation lived in constant, neurotic fear. Such spiritual uneasiness, he concluded, was the most difficult of all mental states.[40]

This observation proved commonplace in the 1950s, but it did inspire a number of western churches to spread their message as widely as possible. By the mid-1940s the Amarillo Ministerial Alliance had introduced Bible classes as credit courses in the local high schools and had established a Bible chair at Amarillo Junior College. In 1948 the Church of Christ helped fund a Bible chair at nearby West Texas State University in Canyon.[41] Perhaps the culmination of this effort came with the attempt to create a nondenominational chapel on the south rim of the Grand Canyon, built to reflect the universal theme of God working through Nature. Architects faced a genuine dilemma, however, for they could not build on the south rim, but neither could they exclude the majestic views. In 1970 their rather unimpressive chapel compromise was given over to the National Park Service to serve as a multi-use building.[42]

Western Catholic parochial education enjoyed a similar postwar construction boom. Catholic schools prospered everywhere. The Diocese of California doubled its school enrollment from 1940 to 1950. By the mid-1950s, approximately one-third of all youth in San Francisco attended Catholic school. In 1943 the California Legislature approved a "released time" (freeing public school students for religious education) measure that similarly increased religious instruction. By 1960 Los Angeles had over eighty parochial schools, almost one per parish. Tucson also approached the one-school-per-parish model. In Utah church parochial schools doubled (to thirteen), and Utah Catholics even established two small monasteries. The high point for many a western Catholic high school came in the early 1960s.[43] The bishops and laymen who oversaw this expansion have been termed "bricklayers for God."[44]

Such rapid "Catholic mobilization," as historian Jay P. Dolan has termed it, seldom looked much beyond its own parish boundaries. Catholic leaders were content to create "parallel institutions" to juxtapose against the mainstream culture.[45] For example, in the early 1950s the Church began its Fresno Academy of California Church history, dedicated to keeping alive the Catholic history of California.[46] The rise of new churches, new schools, and parallel organizations reflected contemporary Catholic emphasis on spiritual unity, morality, formal worship, and clerical authoritarianism as organizing principles. Historian Philip Gleason has viewed this 1950s concentration as setting the stage for the disintegration that followed the reforms of Vatican II.[47]

But such postwar expansion was not limited to the three historic faiths. Other groups, both large and small, participated as well. During the war, the "I Am" cult moved to southern Colorado and New Mexico. Later, a small band, the Brotherhood of the White Temple, began building a retreat in what they termed the Valley of Shamballa Ashrama, thirty-five miles southwest of Denver. The leader, Dr. M. Doreal, oversaw the construction of several large buildings there. A mystic who claimed that the Dalai Lama of Tibet had shown him a Great White Lodge seventy-five miles under the Himalayas, Doreal conceived of his retreat the day after he learned of the bombing of Hiroshima. His goal was to create a community to withstand atomic war, which he predicted with regularity until his death in 1963. The community also distributed metaphysical booklets through its correspondence schools, at one time claiming over a thousand followers. In the 1990s, with the rise of extremist antigovernment communes, local officials descended upon Shamballa Ashrama, only to find it a peaceful community of seven hundred members, only half of whom belonged to the movement. The Brotherhood, however, ranked among the first of what would become a widespread postwar growth of similar quasi-religious utopian organizations in the Mountain West.[48]

The Latter-day Saints shared fully in the western church expansion of the era. About 25,000 attended the dedication of the modernistic Idaho Falls temple, overlooking the Snake River, in 1945. At the closing session, President J. Reuben Clark, Jr., urged the faithful of the church "to be charitable and reasonable in their attitudes toward others of the world recognizing their rights to act and believe as they wish but that tolerance must never lead to acceptance."[49]

The pace of LDS temple building increased in the postwar years. Ground was broken in Los Angeles in 1951 for what was described as "the largest temple ever built in this dispensation."[50] Situated on a thirteen-acre site at Santa Monica and Overland Boulevards in West Los Angeles, the ninety-room temple became the second tallest building in the Los Angeles area, subordinate only to city hall. In the weeks prior to the formal dedication, 662,361 Gentiles viewed the interior. Many were impressed at the beauty, harmony, and design of the building, and city officials predicted that the eleventh LDS temple would become a major tourist attraction for the area.[51] LDS symbols were muted in this structure, but one could still see images of the sego lily (which had saved the Saints on their move west) in grill work over window openings and a fifteen-foot statue of the Angel Moroni sounding his trumpet.

Other western temples soon followed. Oakland's was dedicated in 1964. With its five gleaming gold towers, it became a well-known landmark in the San Francisco Bay area. The dedications of the Ogden temple (1972) and the Provo temple (1972), both situated in the heart of Mormon country, drew large crowds, as did the Seattle temple, dedicated in 1980. For the public viewing of the Seattle structure, LDS missionaries knocked on all doors in the South Bellevue area to invite families to the open house. Thousands accepted. "It's a great missionary tool," said the president of the Seattle North Stake.[52] Dallas (1954), Boise (1984), Denver (1986), Portland (1989), Las Vegas (1989), San

An architectural model of the Mormon Temple in Los Angeles. This striking structure reflects the increasing importance of the Latter-day Saints all through the West.

Diego (1993), and Bountiful (1995) rounded out the western LDS temple dedications. Albuquerque's opened in spring 2000.

There is little question that these LDS temples formed the most impressive religious structures of the entire western postwar building boom. In a very real sense, these temples reflected both the growth and at least partial mainstreaming of the LDS faith. By 1999 the Saints had grown to become the nation's seventh largest denomination; there are more Mormons than Episcopalians.

While sociologist Armand L. Mauss sees considerable ambiguity in the Mormon struggle with assimilation, historian Jan Shipps believes that the Saints are steadily entering the American mainstream. Not only are the Mormons solidly middle class, since around 1980 *The Book of Mormon* has carried the designation "Another Testament of Jesus Christ" on its cover. Some have even begun to use Mormon in adjective form, as in "Mormon Christianity." A fall 1997 poll discovered that 26 percent of the Mormons could be considered born-again Christians. "Being born Mormon 50 years ago was analogous to being born Jewish," Shipps observed. "No more."[53] Although one-third of the Saints still live in Utah (75 percent of the state's population), they now have homes not only in all western states but across the globe. Of all the changes in western religious history, this one may have the most significant long-term consequences.

If the rise and spread of LDS temples signified a major shift in western religious history, so too did a 1952 decision by the Southern Baptist Convention (SBC). In the immediate postwar era, the Southern Baptists remained what they had always been: a theologically conservative, somewhat disputatious regional denomination. Unlike other major Protestant denominations that had found ways to combine religious education and evangelism, the Southern Baptists traditionally focused primarily on the latter. In fact, the terms "Southern Baptist" and "conservative evangelical" often overlapped.

By the early 1950s the denomination had established a radio commission with a full-time director who argued that radio provided the best opportunity to spread the Gospel message since the invention of the printing press. It also began serious exploration of the possibility of religious films. During the postwar decades, the various state Baptist conventions kept up a fairly steady denunciation of what they perceived as the evils of the day: crime, the degeneration of home life, obscene literature, especially in comic books, and internal moral decay. They laid these evils at the feet of the "secular society."[54]

Only two years after the war, the SBC invited New Mexico Baptists to sponsor evangelistic work in the far western states. The New Mexico Baptist Convention rejected the offer, concentrating instead on evangelizing the Native Americans and Hispanic peoples of the region.[55] Five years later, the SBC decided it would have to undertake the task itself. In the fall of 1952 SBC officials voted to expand into eight western states where it had hitherto never been: California, Arizona, Colorado, Wyoming, Montana, Oregon, Washington, and Nevada. In spite of the fact that many Southern Baptists had traveled west to work in the wartime industries and then remained there after the war, the SBC still termed this region "pagan land."

At a September 1952 gathering in Dallas, fifteen hundred Southern Baptist ministers met to promote this expansion. Dr. W. A. Criswell, powerful pastor of the First Baptist Church of Dallas, led the crusade. On a recent visit to Oregon, Criswell declared that he had driven an entire day without spotting a single (Baptist?) church. Another pastor claimed that millions of westerners had never heard a genuine Gospel sermon. The SBC blamed this situation on the far-less-evangelical American (Northern) Baptist Convention. Ever since the nineteenth century, the SBC had established a comity agreement that had allotted the far West to its northern brethren. This comity plan came to an abrupt end in 1952. That year the SBC resolved that it could no longer sacrifice its distinct message on the "altar of ecumenicity."[56] Within two years the SBC had created the motto "a million more in '54" and had begun its penetration of the Far West in earnest. Seattle's 1965 celebration of itself as "the most western city in America" only spurred the SBC's efforts.[57]

It was not long before the Southern Baptists became a significant force in far western life. In 1973, for example, the Riverside (Southern) Baptist Church in Denver, with approximately 3,000 members, claimed to be the largest denominational church outside the Deep South. Five years later, First Baptist of Phoenix also claimed this honor, declaring itself the largest Baptist church in twenty-nine states.[58] By 1990 the New Mexico Southern Baptists had become larger than all the other New Mexico Protestants put together. Their Conference Center in Glorieta, New Mexico, built in the 1950s, has achieved a national reputation. In 1996 the First Baptist Church of Las Vegas, Nevada, completed a quarter-of-a-million-dollar building complex, one of the largest modern church plants in the state. Although the Saddleback Valley Community Church in Orange County, California, has dropped the "Southern Baptist" name, it too grew from those origins and still retains the denomination's traditional evangelical emphasis. With over 10,000 members, it is one of the largest churches in the nation. This "southernization" of the American West in terms of religion—led by southern Baptist immigrants—would also have considerable consequences in the future.

During the 1940s and 1950s, religious life in the American West echoed many of the national trends. The church building boom affected most western cities, especially Denver, which doubled its population from 1936 to 1952 (300,000 to over 600,000).[59] Simultaneously, the Mormons began their systematic construction of impressive temples in the major western cities. Religious leaders of the day, such as Archbishop James Byrne of New Mexico and Cardinal James Francis McIntyre of Los Angeles, were accorded greater respect than elected officials.[60] For many in the 1950s, church or synagogue attendance denoted respectability. As the next decades would show, however, that situation was not to last.

Chapter 6

Western Religious Personalities

On the national scene, there was a number of preeminent religious figures during this era: Reinhold and Richard Niebuhr, Fulton J. Sheen, and Paul Tillich, just to name a few. No western figure ever achieved these heights, but a number of clerics carved out considerable local reputations. This chapter discusses three of these men and women: Aimee Semple McPherson; Brother Mathias Barrett, founder of the Little Brothers of the Good Shepherd; and Rabbi Isadore Budick and the "crypto Jews" of the Southwest.

Of all the western religious figures mentioned so far, Aimee Semple McPherson (1890–1944) would probably rate the highest name recognition. During the mid-1920s, it would have been no exaggeration to say that Sister Aimee was the most famous American woman of her day, a position she held until the appearance of Eleanor Roosevelt.[1] Visitors to Los Angeles during this era ranked a trip to her five-thousand-seat Angelus Four-Square Temple as equal to strolling on the beach or hunting for movie stars along the boulevards of Hollywood. When Sister Aimee died of an accidental overdose of sleeping powders in 1944, the city of Los Angeles mourned. Moreover, unlike many western clerical figures, her fame has persisted. To date she has been the subject of five biographies. Contemporaries termed her a "national institution," and later historians have labeled her an "American phenomenon."[2]

All such phenomena are easier described than explained, but perhaps Aimee Semple McPherson's career may best be understood as a juxtaposition of three items: the Pentecostal/Fundamentalist movement, the emerging mass media, and the city of Los Angeles. Drawing upon these themes, Aimee emerged as the first "superstar" of Ameri-

Aimee Semple McPherson playing with her son, Rolf. Founder of the Four-Square Gospel Church in Los Angeles, Sister Aimee probably ranked as the best-known American woman before Eleanor Roosevelt. For many, she virtually embodied American popular religion during the 1920s.

can popular religion, surpassing her equally controversial predecessor, Billy Sunday, with whom she was often compared. Later popular religious figures would borrow the techniques she pioneered, but they seldom had her flair or sincerity.

Born into a Salvation Army/Methodist family in Ontario, Canada, Aimee was converted at a Pentecostal revival and later married the man who led the services, Robert J. Semple. In 1890 the Full Gospel Assembly ordained her a preacher, and together the Semples left for missionary work in China. Unfortunately, Robert died only three months after their arrival, and Aimee, with their infant daughter, Roberta, soon returned to North America. In 1912 she married Harold S. McPherson, with whom she had a son, Rolf. In 1915 she and her mother (and, for a brief while, McPherson) toured the nation in a "Gospel auto," holding Pentecostal healing revival services; these, unlike most services of the day, were usually racially integrated. It was hard work, and Harold McPherson soon left the enterprise. The couple eventually divorced in 1921.

In 1918 Aimee arrived in Los Angeles seeking both personal solace and renewed health. Five years later she dedicated her Angelus Temple as the Church of the Four-Square Gospel (salvation, the presence of the Holy Spirit, healing, and millennialism). The tenets of the new denomination differed little from other Pentecostal/holiness groups save in the acknowledged charisma of the leader.

Sister Aimee merged her techniques as an evangelist with vaudeville routines (an early Angelus Temple convert had once worked as a vaudeville stage manager) as well as with the acting styles of the first generation of Hollywood film icons such as Mary Pickford and Clara Bow. Her services pioneered elaborate staging and colorful costumes, many of which she purchased while traveling the globe, as well as simple, dramatic sermons. Her most familiar outfit, a white dress and a flowing blue cape, virtually anticipated the superheroes of the later comic book industry. A *New Republic* reporter termed this combination of vaudeville, Hollywood, Broadway, outdoor revival preaching, and sex appeal as "supernatural whoopee."[3]

Sister Aimee well realized the value of publicity and lost no opportunity to garner newspaper coverage. She preached from a boxing ring and at a fire station when the firemen sought a pay raise from the city. She met with infamous speakeasy proprietor Tex Guinan and once rode a motorcycle across her platform for a sermon entitled "Stop, in the Name of the Lord." There was even an attempt to sell burial plots using the slogan "Go up with Aimee."[4]

Given this bent, she quite naturally gravitated toward radio to help spread her message. She always claimed to have delivered the nation's first radio sermon, and she was indeed the first American woman to hold a radio license with her station KFSG (Kall Four-Square Gospel). Other Los Angeles pastors such as Robert ("Fighting Bob") Shuler followed suit, and soon the airwaves of southern California were filled with religious radio stations.[5] Freethinker Mike Schindler complained vigorously in 1926 that local ministers held radio services every night. "I am told that there is scarcely an evening here in Los Angeles that one cannot tune in at least one of these heaven peddlers."[6] A number of Aimee's recordings survive, revealing her voice as pleasantly husky and melodious.

This combination of gospel drama, a positive sermonic message (she said little about sin or evil), and a charismatic personality filled Angelus Temple pews with (usually) transplanted midwesterners from a middle- to lower-class background. "I bring spiritual consolation to the middle classes," she once remarked, "leaving those above to themselves and those below to the Salvation Army."[7]

The middle classes responded. Aimee regularly asked her congregation to donate canned food to her church, and they always obliged. They supported her other efforts through "special gifts" for KFSG and through regular contributions. Whenever the ushers took up a collection, they passed Bibles, rather than plates, through the congregation. Aimee would then remind her audience that while coins might fall out of Bibles, paper would stick just fine.[8]

Then came the kidnapping. In May 1926 Aimee went swimming, disappeared, and was presumed drowned. In late June, however, she reappeared near the little Mexican town of Agua Prieta, across the border from Douglas, Arizona, looking quite haggard but otherwise unharmed. To everyone's astonishment, she spoke of being kidnapped by three crooks, Steve, Jake, and Mexicali Rose, and being held captive in a Mexican desert shack until she cut herself loose and escaped. Few believed this tale, and rumors quickly circulated that she had spent the time in a lovers' tryst with her married radio operator, Kenneth G. Ormiston. The city of Los Angeles threatened to bring her up for trial (although she had committed no crime), and the national press covered the event in a manner reminiscent of the 1995–96 trial of former football star O. J. Simpson.[9] Los Angeles bars advertised "Aimee cocktails," and virtually every nightclub comedian developed an off-color "Sister Aimee" routine. Freethinker Louis Adamic recalled over a hundred ribald Aimee stories.[10] Eventually the city district attorney declared that there was insufficient evidence for an indictment, and the case faded from the public eye. As the *Los Angeles Record* put it in a front-page editorial: "It is about time that all of us—the newspapers included—find something more worthwhile to discuss than whether or not a well-known Los Angeles woman, 34 or 35 years of age, of previously unblemished reputation, committed a quite human indiscretion in Carmel, Salinas or Timbuctoo."[11] It is not clear whether such adverse publicity helped or hurt her movement. It did, however, forever cement Sister Aimee in the popular mind.

But other aspects of her career proved far more significant in the long run than the kidnapping. First of these was the establishment of her Lighthouse of International Four-Square Evangelism Bible School. Over the years, this institution graduated thousands of young men and women to spread the Pentecostal message. In 1993 the denomination boasted about 27,000 churches worldwide, with over 200,000 adherents.[12] Most major western cities today house a Four-Square Church.

Second, from the late 1920s forward, Angelus Temple gave away free meals to the poor. During the Depression, the church utilized a donated building (staffed by volunteers) to distribute over 1.5 million free dinners without distinction of race, color, or creed. The food was also distributed without forcing the hungry to listen to an evangelical sermon (termed "ear banging"). No person had to profess belief of any kind to be served.[13] During World War II Aimee preached to thousands of soldiers in uniform. She also led a number of rallies to sell government Victory Bonds.

Complex popular religious personalities such as Aimee Semple McPherson are difficult to explain. A number of people, however, have been eager to try. During her lifetime, Aimee had more than her share of critics. Liberal journalists, Freethinkers, and several regional clerics lambasted her with regularity. Fellow Los Angeles pastor Bob Shuler made her his bête noire. But never did she return this opprobrium. Skeptical journalist Carey McWilliams, who listened to her speak numerous times, once commented that he never heard her attack any individual or group.[14] Even her widely publicized disaffection with her mother, her estrangement from her daughter, and her failed third marriage did not seem to dampen her popular reputation. Sister Aimee also had many contemporary supporters. William Jennings Bryan thought highly of her and spoke at the Angelus Temple at least twice. Actor Charlie Chaplin said that Aimee was essentially an actor, whether she knew it or not.[15]

Historians have had equal difficulty in assessing her place in American religious history. In general, modern feminist scholars have kept her at arm's length, probably because of her field of work. Most biographies are laced with cynicism, although journalist Mark Epstein's recent study treats her healing crusades sympathetically.[16] Historian Edith Blumhofer's recent account is probably the most balanced assessment.

Perhaps the most telling observation regarding Sister Aimee came from actor Anthony Quinn, who had actually assisted her at the Angelus Temple in his youth. Although Quinn had met Ingrid Bergman, Greta Garbo, Ethel Barrymore, and Katharine Hepburn, he described Aimee Semple McPherson as "the most magnetic personality" he had ever encountered.[17] In spite of, or perhaps because of, these contradictions, she has become the most well known figure of early-twentieth-century western religious history.

The impact of the Irish on the story of modern American Catholicism has been incalculable. The Irish and Irish-Americans have filled the pews, dominated Catholic universities, and formed the mainstay of the American clergy. There were so many Irish-born priests in the Diocese of Sacramento in 1950 that they established their own Sacramento Gaelic football (i.e., soccer) team.[18] Popular priest John J. Ryan, who led Las Vegas, Nevada's Saint Anne's Catholic community during the 1950s, boasted that he once danced the finest jig in all of Ireland. The archbishop of Los Angeles, John J. Cantwell (1936–47), earned similar fame as the "Irish-born Apostle to the Mexicans." From the logo of Notre Dame's athletic teams to the contemporary sociological findings of Rev. Andrew Greeley, the legacy continues. The story of one man, Brother Mathias Barrett, will have to represent this aspect of western Catholic Church history for the 1920–60 era.

Maurice Barrett was born on March 15, 1900, in Waterford, Ireland, and from his earliest youth expressed a desire to serve the Church. Ordained in 1921, Brother Mathias joined the Hospitaller Order of Saint John of God, which devoted itself to caring for members of the lower strata of the social order. Sent to Dublin, Paris, and finally in 1927 to Montreal, Brother Mathias and his colleagues found considerable need for their services. By 1930 they had established five Montreal institutions, including a hospital, a home for epileptics, a convalescent home, and a soup kitchen. Mathias also became head of the Brothers of Saint John of God for all Canada.[19]

Mathias hoped to expand his Canadian operations still further, but the authorities balked. Consequently, in 1941 he moved to Los Angeles. Since his archbishop, John J. Cantwell, had been born in Tipperary, he realized the role that the Order of Saint John of God could play in wartime Los Angeles. Cantwell later provided partial funding to allow the brothers to purchase a house to use as a sanitarium; by then they had established a convalescent home and a home for delinquent boys. Within three years, they had added a night shelter, a social center for soldiers and sailors, a novitiate, and a hospital. When interviewed by a California reporter, Mathias said, "Our vow of hospitality commands us to see in the poor, the sick, the homeless and the needy, the suffering Christ."[20]

After a brief stint in Boston and again in Ireland, in 1950 Mathias moved to New Mexico, where he promised to work at Via Coeli, established in Jemez Springs, New Mexico, by the Servants of the Paraclete as a home for aged, infirm, and mentally disturbed priests. New Mexico archbishop Edwin V. Byrne, who also shared an Irish heritage, proved supportive, but Mathias found he could not get along with his immediate superior at Via Coeli, Father Gerald. Consequently, in 1951 Mathias left Jemez Springs to move to Albuquerque to establish a settlement house similar to those he had helped develop in Los Angeles. His brotherhood would "do the work nobody wants." Within a short time, this program had evolved into a new religious order: The Little Brothers of the Good Shepherd.

As biographer Carol Lovato has shown, Mathias drew on the techniques that had served him well in Montreal, Los Angeles, and Boston. Largely through the force of his personality, he forged an alliance among the Catholic hierarchy, the labor unions, the various ladies' auxiliaries, and members of the wealthy business community to enact his goals. When he first arrived in Montreal, for example, Mathias combed the telephone book for Irish surnames and then called on them for donations. Shortly after landing in Los Angeles and down to his last five dollars, he wired Rome: "Foundation established. Send Brothers." Two brothers from Canada arrived shortly thereafter, and together they opened their first shelter in Watts.

Mathias's Albuquerque tactics drew from the same well. He convinced a local parish priest to lend him two vacant houses that lay at the back of his church. He borrowed three old beds, chairs, and bedding from the Sisters of Charity at Saint Joseph Hospital. He cajoled day-old bread from Chiordi's Bakery and vegetables from local wholesalers. He borrowed used coffee grounds from Saint Joseph and "biled" them again. He convinced Catholic craft union members to donate countless hours to help remodel his shelters. When the *Albuquerque Tribune* printed a list of the city's best-dressed men, he approached each of them to ask for their old clothes.[21] As a reporter observed in 1961, "He knows exactly what he wants and uses only good humor, shrewd insight, native charm and stubbornness to get it."[22]

Single-minded in his devotion to the poor, Mathias soon became a local institution. A governing board of Protestants, Catholics, and Jews helped oversee his projects. In the late 1950s the board institutionalized the fund raising by staging an annual, citywide gala Saint Patrick's Day dinner of corned beef and cabbage that was also billed as "Brother Mathias's birthday." The proceeds all went to his organizations.

Brother Mathias was featured in *Time* magazine, and a number of men joined his order, although the turnover remained high. Still, the Little Brothers of the Good Shepherd with their motto "Charity Unlimited" spread steadily across the land. In 1973, the order had twenty houses in six states, Canada, and Great Britain. Mathias became one of the most respected clerics in the American Southwest. In 1965 the archbishop of Santa Fe celebrated a special Mass in honor of his fifty years of religious life. "Thank God for Brother Mathias," the Most Rev. James Peter Davis said.[23] The former archbishop of Los Angeles also praised his work, and the archbishop of New Mexico, Robert F. Sanchez, compared him with Mother Teresa of Calcutta.[24] Mathias himself remained far more modest, summing up his life as "fifty years of dishwashing."[25] "You know," Mathias mused in 1967, "sometimes I can hardly believe all this has happened." Once he compared his success to that of the Peace Corps, where everybody did a little bit, and to the mood of the American nation, where people had such confidence.[26]

In 1928 the National Conference of Christians and Jews was organized at the University of Illinois. Viewing the post–World War I religio-cultural clash with alarm, the founders hoped to "strike a deadly blow at bigotry and intolerance." The founders felt that such hatred, which they blamed for all wars, lay primarily in ignorance of other groups. During the Depression decade, the National Conference was sobered by the news that the FBI had compiled lists of hundreds of hate organizations. In 1944 there were predictions that these groups were ready to revitalize immediately after World War II.[27]

During the 1930s, western Jews occasionally were the targets of discrimination. Harry Rosenberg, a medieval historian at Colorado State University who grew to maturity in Vernal, Utah, met this sentiment first hand. He recalled childhood taunts of "dirty Jew" and "Christ killer" from his mostly LDS classmates. After one gathering of the local Mormon Stake, a shower of rocks landed on the roof of the Rosenberg family store. Harry's father fired his gun in the air to warn off intruders. The next day, the LDS bishop drove by, and Harry's father walked over to talk with him. With one foot on the running board of the car, Rosenberg Sr. held a long discussion with the bishop. The incident was never repeated. Harry's mother similarly recalled a group of women who stopped by to visit because they "wanted to see the Jew lady." His mother remained friendly but confessed that she really wanted to say, "See, I have horns." It was his skill at baseball that allowed Harry to integrate into the community, an aspect of life that completely eluded his father, for at that age his father had been hard at work.[28]

How representative Rosenberg's experiences were of Jews in the rural West is difficult to say. The western childhood memories collected by Myrna Katz Frommer and Harry Frommer in *Growing up Jewish* reflect more Gentile ignorance or curiosity than overt prejudice. In Wyoming, Angie Sokoloff's father always included Gentiles in his seders and enjoyed explaining the various rituals.[29] Gentiles occasionally visited the Fargo, North Dakota, temple simply to see how Jews worshiped. Yale Weinstein arrived in Cuba, New Mexico, in 1938 to begin his career as a forester and later declared that he encountered no anti-Semitism whatever.

Still, western rabbis in the smaller towns from the 1920s forward often assumed dual roles. Not only did they attend to the needs of their various congregations, they also served as ambassadors of their faith to the local community. The cultural broker mantle—interpreting one group to another—that Rabbi Joseph Magnin wore in Los Angeles was shared by many of his counterparts in rural western areas.

In 1943 the University of Oklahoma (OU) established a Hillel Foundation and selected Rabbi Isadore Budick as its director. With degrees from New York University and the Jewish Institute of Religion plus work toward a doctorate in history, Budick fit well into the university community. He taught credit classes in Jewish history as well as noncredit classes in Arabic and Yiddish.

Rabbi Budick turned Hillel into a showcase for Jewish culture. He arranged OU's first Hanukkah celebration at the Y Lounge and began a series of lectures on friendship for the local university community.

Budick also participated in the short-lived Oklahoma School of Religion, a separate, incorporated body that worked in tandem with the university. The brainchild of OU Dean E. Nicholas Comfort, the Oklahoma School of Religion was created in 1944 to introduce religious understanding and toleration in a largely conservative evangelical environment. Not only did it hold various conferences, it also published a journal, the *Oklahoma Journal of Religion*.

Comfort tried to make the *Journal* genuinely interdenominational. He included not only Catholics and mainline Protestant groups but also black Methodists, Pentecostals, Church of Christ leaders, and Mennonites on its board of editors. Comfort had dreamed of such an operation for forty years. Its purpose, he said, was to disseminate "information, good will, cooperation and determinism among Oklahomans to the end that an ever deepening sense of the fatherhood of God may be the inspiration and power of our lives and the practice of the brotherhood of man may be the procedure in our efforts to solve the problems that confront us."[30] The School of Religion also produced regular radio programs.

Rabbi Budick did his best to aid this ecumenical enterprise. Virtually all his actions were directed either at reinforcing the faith of OU Jewish students or acquainting Oklahoma Gentiles with the ancient heritage of Israel. He introduced regular Friday night services and the first High Holy Day services ever held in Norman. He also held regular social hours and staged both a Hanukkah party and a Purim party. About one-fifth of the people at these gatherings were Gentiles. His noncredit classes drew several faculty members as well. All eight students in his Arabic class were Gentiles, as were several in his Hebrew class. He headed a local interfaith council that held forums on minority relations and cochaired the Religious Forum of the Air. Budick also spent a number of hours speaking across the state at Kiwanis, Rotary, and Lions Clubs "for the cause of better relationships between Jew and non-Jew."[31]

In the Intermountain West, Reform rabbis continued to play the role of cultural broker throughout much of the twentieth century. For example, soon after Rabbi David Shor arrived in Albuquerque in 1948 to begin his thirty years at Temple Albert, he started building bridges between the Christian and Jewish communities. He invited Sunday school classes from various denominations to attend temple services and later served on numerous state boards and committees. "He was totally committed to helping all faiths understand Judaism," a friend said, "and know that we're all truly one world." His successor, Rabbi Paul Citrin, who arrived in 1982, continued this emphasis. Although Citrin acknowledged in 1996 that ignorance about Jewish culture remained, still, "whenever there is some kind of issue or project now, members of the Jewish community are almost always invited to participate, and we're seen as a respected and necessary participant."[32] Rabbis in smaller western communities have long considered this one of their functions.

For rabbis in the American Southwest, however, the position of cultural broker usually did not prove difficult. From territorial days forward, Jewish immigrants had played significant roles in the economic and political life of the region. Mostly Ashkenazim, those nineteenth-century Jewish migrants gained notoriety as itinerant peddlers, but they also worked as ranchers, merchants, and clothiers, both in the towns and in isolated rural communities. Historians William Parish and Henry Tobias have argued that these German immigrants, several of whom learned Spanish before they did English, led an economic transformation that shifted the Southwest from a barter system into the national capitalistic economy. In Parish's words, the Jewish merchants were the "catalytic influence in the linking of our several cultures." Tobias noted that from the Hispanic perspective, "it was not the Jew who was dangerous. It was the Anglo."[33] Thus the Jews were well integrated into the multi-ethnic society of the Southwest from the onset. Jews founded towns (Nogales began as "Isaacson") and served as mayors of Tucson, Phoenix, Prescott, Bisbee, Tombstone, and Yuma. Jewish settlers of Arizona helped found the University of Arizona in 1885 and also established the first bookstore in the territory.

Because of a shortage of women, a significant number of Jewish merchants married Gentiles. Historians have disputed the actual extent of this intermarriage, but a number of Arizona and New Mexico Christian families have Ashkenazic heritage.[34] When Yale Weinstein worked in northwestern New Mexico, a young Hispanic man once asked him if he were Jewish. "My father was Jewish," the young man said, "and I'd someday like to talk to you about it."[35] The Drachmans and Goldwaters of Arizona are probably the most famous of these mixed-heritage families.

Perhaps one reason for the acceptance of southwestern Jews lay with the possible Sephardic heritage of many Hispanic settlers in New Mexico. Santa Fe independent historian Stanley M. Hordes has vigorously argued that many New Mexican Hispanic families are Jewish in origin. He has presented his conclusions in scores of local talks and several articles, basing his argument on evidence found in the churches of Spain and Mexico and from interviews. His findings have provoked nationwide interest and the creation of a New Mexico Jewish Historical Society.[36] They have also produced a vigorous attack from critics.[37]

Hordes argues as follows. The year 1492 in Jewish history marks less Columbus's encounter with America than the expulsion of approximately 600,000 Jews from Spain. Estimates suggest that one-third fled, one-third perished, and one-third converted to become "New Christians." Some of these *conversos,* however, continued to practice Jewish rituals in secret. The Spanish Inquisition was established in 1498 to prevent such activities, and many conversos fled to the New World. Eventually, however, the Inquisition established itself in America and twice instituted periods of persecution: the 1580s–90s and the 1640s. Both of these periods, Hordes notes, coincided with times of extensive settlement into New Mexico. Sometimes the groups had priests with them, sometimes not. According to Dennis Duran, a Hispanic convert to Judaism and president of the New Mexico Jewish Historical Society, many New Mexico family surnames indicate possible Jewish ancestry. These include Carbajal, Chavez, Coca, Flores, Gomez, Leyba, Medina, Mendez, Nuñez, Rael (Israel?), Rivera, Rodriguez, Salas, and Sena. In addition, many New Mexican children traditionally bore popular Old Testament forenames. Perhaps as many as fifteen hundred New Mexico families have some cognizance of their Jewish heritage.[38]

Through interviews, Hordes has discovered a number of local Hispanic family traditions that seem to suggest crypto-Jewish ancestry: lighting candles on Friday evening; avoiding pork; observing the Sabbath on both Sunday and Saturday; covering mirrors during periods of mourning; circumcising males; leaving pebbles on cemetery headstones; playing with a gambling top that has letters on four sides (the *pon y sera*), a toy that resembles the Hanukkah dreidel; giving Old Testament names to their children; bathing and changing the linen on Fridays; distorting the traditional Jewish/Christian symbol of the fish so that only other Jews would recognize it; butchering livestock in a certain way; and baking unleavened bread at certain seasons.[39]

This early-twentieth-century tombstone, located in a Roman Catholic cemetery in northern New Mexico, combines the symbol of the cross with the first five commandments in Hebrew, suggesting an ancient Sephardic crypto-Jewish presence in the Southwest.

A number of oral history tales lend credence to this argument. Presbyterians in the Taos area were successful in converting Hispanic Catholics during the late nineteenth century, the argument goes, because they allowed converts to "get back to the book," that is, the Bible. According to another legend from Mora, when two German-Jewish peddlers came to visit for the first time, an elderly Catholic grandmother proudly brought forth her teenaged granddaughters and urged the girls to "get back to their roots." In a 1920s wedding photo Benino Garcia seems to be wearing a Jewish prayer shawl. Daniel Yocum recalled that his grandmother called his grandfather "Judio." When his sister died in 1961, the mother of Carlos Vélez-Ibáñez whispered to him a long-held family secret: "Somos Judios" [We're Jews].[40] Photographs of Hispanic houses often include mezuzahs, while Hebrew letters are found carved on tombstones in Catholic cemeteries.[41] Several families recalled celebrating Saint Esther's holiday, dedicated primarily to women. (It's really Purim; there is no Saint Esther in the Catholic hagiology.) Some have even suggested that the altar of San Felipe de Neri Church in Old Town, Albuquerque, actually contains a slightly modified version of the Star of David.[42]

Interest in the cryptic Jews of the West has grown steadily. It has led to the formation of the New Mexico Jewish Historical Society, the Society for Crypto-Judaic Studies in California, an organization in Denver, and historians' discoveries of similar communities in Colorado, Arizona, and Texas.

A contemporary Albuquerque rabbi has had several *reconversios* attend his services, perhaps out of curiosity. Several New Mexican Catholic Hispanics have converted and occasionally still call the rabbi "Father." Others attend both Catholic and Jewish services. But the end result is to accentuate the long-term mainstreaming of the southwestern Jewish community.

Scholars in the 1950s discovered that Jews in Santa Fe and Albuquerque had not only intermarried with Gentiles, they had completely integrated into the social life of the cities. In Albuquerque the chief cultural tension lay less between Jews and Gentiles than between Reform and Conservative congregations.[43] From the beginning Jews sat on the board of the Albuquerque Country Club. In the scientific community of postwar Los Alamos, they were always present in large numbers. This heritage may account in part for the relatively peaceful integration of Jews into southwestern life.

———

Except for Aimee Semple McPherson, none of the dominant western religious personalities of this era achieved national reputations. But in their various ways, each ministered to his or her congregation, aided the less fortunate, and—especially the western Reform rabbis—tried to build bridges between the various faiths. In the American Southwest, this undertaking was aided by the crypto-Jewish heritage of many citizens as well as the historic tolerance of the dominant Roman Catholic faith. In the next decades, however, various western religious personalities would acquire far more dramatic reputations.

PART III
The 1960s to the Present

Chapter 7

Western Religion Confronts the Modern World

The course of American life during this era bears a strange resemblance to national events of a century earlier. In each case, a cataclysm that occurred in the sixties set the stage for the drastically altered society that would follow.

For the twentieth century, the decade of the sixties (roughly 1963–1975) represents as much mood or attitude as it does an actual ten-year period. In many parts of the interior West, the sixties arrived a decade later. In terms of political history, the sixties abounded in cataclysms: the assassination of John F. Kennedy, Robert Kennedy, and Martin Luther King, Jr.; the Vietnam War; the unfulfilled promises of the Great Society; the civil rights crusade; the feminist revolution; the gay rights crusade; the rise of Native American and Chicano advocacy groups; the Pill and the sexual revolution; and widespread disillusionment with hierarchy of any type, symbolized by the ubiquitous bumper sticker "Question Authority." Many of these political/social events—Vietnam, civil rights, and issues involving sexuality—intersected with the world of organized religion at numerous points. Religious studies scholar Robert S. Ellwood has argued that the religious and political sides of the sixties formed parallel bands of a single spectrum that he considers spiritual at its core.[1]

Even if one takes a more restricted definition, the impact of the sixties on western religion proved tumultuous. Consider how it affected American Judaism. The 1967 Six-Day War both ensured Israel's independence and galvanized American Jewish support all through the West. Moreover, the near defeat of Israel spurred increased interest in study of the Holocaust. The pessimistic works of Rabbi Richard L. Rubenstein, especially his *After Auschwitz* (1966), were widely read.

The impact of the sixties on Roman Catholicism was equally earth-shattering. When Pope John XXIII called the Second Vatican Council, he set in motion a movement that not only revolutionized four hundred years of interfaith tension, it also virtually institutionalized dissent in the hitherto tightly structured American Catholic community. Afterward, public quarrels among western nuns, priests, and bishops—especially in Los Angeles—became almost commonplace. The issues of sexuality, birth control, abortion, divorce, and homosexuality increased the divisions within the Church community. The result, some complained, was to produce a "cafeteria Catholicism," where believers simply selected the aspects of Church teaching they wished to follow. (Still, as other observers note, one can get a full meal from a cafeteria.)

Although the mainline Protestant churches lacked a single dramatic event such as the Six-Day War or Vatican II, they too underwent profound transformation. Fresh from the building boom of the previous decade, the mainline denominations watched helplessly as parishioners left by the thousands from about 1975 forward. The increased success of a more moderate conservative evangelical movement seemed to portend the arrival of a "new Protestant establishment."

Historians of American religion concur on the long-term significance of these radical changes. As early as 1970, Sydney E. Ahlstrom noted that "the 1960s *did* experience a fundamental shift in the aesthetic, moral, and religious attitudes of Americans. It will probably be seen as a decisive turning point in American history."[2] Historian Ronald B. Flowers has entitled his study of this era *Religion in Strange Times* (1984). Robert Ellwood has marked this decade as the time when American religion moved from modern to postmodern, because since then no single narrative, including both the Hebrew/Christian mythos as well as the Enlightenment faith in science, has been able to encompass the whole of American life.[3]

In truth, the most insightful analyses of religion in the modern era have seldom come from historians. Rather, religious studies scholars and sociologists of religion have usually led the way. Although many of the founders of sociology, such as Emile Durkheim and Max Weber, focused on religion, the field of the sociology of religion achieved its great popularity after the Second World War by creating a variety of theoretical models.[4] These constructs have brought forth vigorous debate, and the most provocative have entered the common realm.

The first of these models is secularization. This idea suggests that as the Western world modernized, the realm of religion slowly shrank, rather like the escape of air from a balloon. Secularization could be easily seen in contemporary Europe, where the great cathedrals today serve more as artistic marvels than as thriving centers of worship. Religious attendance in all the European nations (Ireland excepted) is very low. Aberdeen sociologist Steve Bruce is the foremost contemporary advocate of this position.[5] Although secularization theory fits Europe more precisely than America, the United States has experienced it as well.[6] In this world, Luck has replaced Providence as the chief arbiter of human destiny.

Persuasive though this theory might seem, other sociologists are much less convinced. Thomas Luckmann has argued that the idea of transcendence is a universal human concept that will never disappear from society. Rather, it simply changes form. Since around 1970, he noted, American religion has emerged primarily in alternative modes, chiefly in private, individualized faiths.[7] Thus religion has not disappeared; instead, it has cut itself loose from its historic institutional bases to produce a "third disestablishment" of religion in America.[8]

The second model treats the collapse of faith communities and the growth of religious individualism. This theme has often been noted and has been especially well analyzed by Robert Bellah and others in *Habits of the Heart*. First published in 1985, *Habits* sold almost half a million copies, sales figures that ranked it with the Lynds' *Middletown* and David Riesman's *The Lonely Crowd* as the three sociological books to reach the largest popular audience. In *Habits* and in the follow-up volume, *The Good Society* (1991), the authors discuss the consequences of radical individualism on national life. They found what they termed a "crisis of social capital," a loss of civic identity with the whole.[9] Their term "Sheilaism," named for a woman who left her traditional church home and cobbled together a synergetic, totally individualized faith, has become generic. The standard "Sheila" response—"I'm not religious but I'm very spiritual"—has evolved into a modern cliché.

Finally, and perhaps the most provocative of all, sociologists Robert Wuthnow and James Davison Hunter have defined modern American life in terms of a bipolar religio-cultural war. Drawing on the earlier work of Dean M. Kelley, they argue that American religion has begun to reposition itself regarding a historic Judeo-Christian "conventional morality."[10] This split has divided virtually every major group. On one side, defending traditional revealed mores and religion, are *conservative* Protestants, Catholics, Jews, and Mormons. On the other, one finds groups that have tried to adapt traditional biblical teachings to the modern day—*liberal* Protestants, Catholics, Jews, and Mormons. The well-publicized quarrels between the two, aided by the prominence of such secular organizations as the American Civil Liberties Union, has often made the religion section of local papers as acrimonious as the front page.

An unexpected consequence of this, as has been observed by Lutheran-cleric-turned-Catholic-priest Richard John Neuhaus, is to create a "naked Public Square." In Neuhaus's analysis, the resulting attempts to exclude faith or religiously grounded values from the conduct of public life have been harmful. The public square cannot remain "naked." If it is not clothed with "meaning" that is based on a religious tradition, the modern state will impose a meaning all its own. Neuhaus argues that God's promise to the world is a *public* promise. To argue for a completely secular public square, devoid of religious meaning, both demeans the transcendent authority and promises future social chaos.[11] This situation has emerged, in the words of Wuthnow, as "the struggle for America's soul."[12]

One does not have to look far for evidence of this cultural war in the American West.[13] Because of the unique nature of post–World War II western religious life (no real mainstream faith; a widespread nonreligious contingent; a growing evangelical movement; rumors of geographical-spiritual "vortices"; increased appreciation of the Native American concept of "sacred space"; and a relative lack of population density), the West has proven home to some of the most intense cultural battles.

Although the religio-political conflicts have received wide publicity, the question of the actual numbers involved on each side still remains uncertain. In 1957 the Bureau of the Census conducted a preliminary survey on religious affiliation but ultimately issued only a partial report. Jewish groups, Christian Scientists, and various civil liberties organizations protested the questions as a violation of the separation of church and state. Later demographers had to resort to the Freedom of Information Act to examine the data.[14] The Census Bureau has been somewhat skittish about religious questions ever since.

But the post–World War II era does not lack for religious statistics. Since 1937, Gallup Polls, in conjunction with the Religion Research Center in New Jersey, have regularly asked Americans questions pertaining to religion. The surveys conducted during the 1950s showed a very high enrollment in churches or synagogues, around 63 percent. During that decade, 96 percent of Americans identified themselves as Protestants, Catholics, or Jews.[15] However, a 1980 Gallup study classified 61 million people—41 percent of the nation's adults—as "unchurched." The pollsters also professed to discover a "hunger of the soul" and a "spiritual void" that created both a judgment on and an opportunity for the nation's religious forces.[16] In 1984 George Gallup, Jr., declared that "religion is growing in importance but morality is losing ground."[17] A 1988 similar poll found that 96 percent said they believed in God and 17 percent considered the Bible as a book to be read literally. From this, the pollsters concluded that "religion permeates American life."[18]

Putting the religious survey results in the proper perspective, however, has always been a challenge. In 1990 a respected East Coast polling firm worked with Columbia University sociologist Barry Kosmin to meet this dilemma. Over a period of several months, they conducted the largest-ever national survey on religion in American life. Chartered to fill an information void, this elaborate survey provided statistical confirmation for a number of widely held opinions. It was later published under the title *One Nation under God*.

Pollsters discovered that most Americans were quite willing to discuss their faith. They also discovered that 86.5 percent of the nation identified with one of the Christian denominations and 2 percent with one of the branches of Judaism. Only 7.5 percent identified themselves as having no religion. This meant that religion played a larger role in America than in any other similarly industrialized country.[19] "What's interesting," observed Kosmin, "is that our religion cuts across class, ethnic and regional differences. You look at race or ethnic origins and we've become very diverse, but you look at religion, there is much more commonality."[20] The figures showed that the majority of Asian Americans were Protestant, that over a third of the Hispanics fell into the same category, and that in spite of considerable publicity, New Age adherents formed a statistically insignificant number.

This elaborate survey once again accented the unique history of religion in the American West. Western respondents were twice as likely to state "no religion" as any other sector of the nation. Seventeen percent of Oregon residents made this claim. Of the ten highest "no religion" states, nine were western.[21] "Is Oregon Atheist?" commentators later asked. The *Seattle Post-Intelligencer* reported that the Pacific Northwest might be God's country, but no region in the nation was less formally religious.[22] Western Catholicism also fell behind eastern cities as the most active sector of church life. Citizens of historically Catholic New Mexico were surprised to find that one tenth of the state identified themselves as nonbelievers.[23]

Most historical sociologists agree that having a dominant religious group in a region functions as a mechanism of social control. West Texas/Oklahoma and Utah both contain such groups. But in the religiously pluralistic society of the rest of the West, such social controls have been considerably weakened. Perhaps this situation best explains the persistent lack of religious affiliation in the West, or perhaps the spectacular natural environment detracts from regular attendance at worship. In addition, the fact that western states have historically functioned as homes for migrants from elsewhere might play a role as well. During their move, the immigrants, in sociologist Peter Berger's words, may have snapped "the thin thread of conversation" that linked them to previous religious organizations. Whatever the reason, in 1990 the Pacific states boasted the highest percentage of religious switchers—16.5 percent.

The absence of any western religious mainstream would surely enhance the appeal of various new religions, for joining such a group would result in far less social disapproval.[24] Perhaps this is one reason why the various New Faiths and New Age movements have flourished in western environments. These, of course, are questions that statistics alone cannot answer. There has, however, been much speculation. A number of people have emphasized that region goes a long way toward determining religious affiliation. "Geography is Destiny," proclaimed one commentator, or, as religious writer Bruce Bauer once phrased it, "Denominations no longer matter. Geography does."[25]

These polls seem to suggest three conclusions. Except for Utah and parts of Oklahoma, most areas of the West show a weakened religious cultural influence. Many regions, especially the Pacific Northwest and California, contain large bodies of nonbelievers. Simultaneously, however, all areas of the West have become home to significant neo-evangelical movements, claiming perhaps 26 percent of the population, who are turning to the political system, usually via the Republican Party, to voice their opinions. One observer described the 1996 conservatism of white evangelicals as "the most powerful political force in the country."[26] Thus it should not be surprising that the 1960s–90s West became the focal point of a variety of religio-cultural clashes (to be discussed in chapter 8). In many regions, culture and theology met head on.

To a large extent, many western mainline groups simply continued doing what they had always done for their local communities. They responded to the entry of women into the work force by establishing day care centers and after-school programs and by opening their meeting rooms to a variety of support groups. In addition, the better-funded denominations borrowed a leaf from the traditional Jewish Homes for the Elderly to introduce their own retirement home programs. In 1979, for example, Utah Episcopalians dedicated a one-hundred-unit apartment building in Salt Lake City for the elderly and handicapped, the first of its kind in the state. Evangelical Lutherans and Congregationalists have opened numerous similar facilities throughout the western region.[27]

The mainline groups proved quite creative in their responses to the social upheavals of the era. The Society of Friends (Quakers) led the crusade to allow the Puget Sound Native Americans to fish wherever they chose. The Quakers' lengthy report, *An Uncommon Controversy* (1970), provided the first comprehensive study of this decades-old conflict. In addition, the Friends played a prominent role in the West Coast opposition to the war in Vietnam. In 1960s Denver several downtown churches established shelters for homeless youth. One basement housed upward of 150 a night. The Saint John's African Methodist Episcopal Church in Pueblo inaugurated a free store.[28] In 1965 a United Church of Christ minister in Las Vegas, Nevada, became a specialist in pastoral counseling, divorce rehabilitation, and suicide prevention for workers on the Las Vegas Strip. His clientele consisted largely of gamblers, casino pit bosses, professional entertainers, and showgirls. The "Strip chaplain" program lasted about two years until denominational protests cut off funds.[29] A decade later, an Episcopal rector in Salt Lake City assumed the role of "motel chaplain" for the city's downtown Holiday Inn. After several years on call, he summarized his new ministry. He concluded that his male clients were largely middle-class men facing severe crises of self-esteem, job loss, or family problems. Although his female clients were equally middle class, they were most often fleeing bad marriages or were young women grappling with unwanted pregnancies. Before Utah legalized abortions, he occasionally sent people on to various clinics in Los Angeles.[30]

In the early 1990s the Presbyterian Church (U.S.A.) established a unique urban ministry to Native Americans in Los Angeles. By 1980 about 100,000 Indians lived in the Los Angeles area, the largest urban Indian population in the United States. Ordained pastor Buddy Monahan of the Cree Nation organized this social gospel effort, meeting in four different Presbyterian churches on a once-a-month basis. The Presbyterian program included Natives from a variety of faith traditions, including a large number of non-Christians.[31]

The Unitarian-Universalists (UU) have similarly engaged in numerous progressive social programs, often involving racial, feminist, or sexual-orientation issues. They have long been active on the Pacific Coast and, since the Second World War, have flourished in many western university towns such as Albuquerque, Laramie, and Tucson. Although never large in numbers (approximately 215,000 in 1999), the UU churches have had great appeal for those in transition from one denomination to another. They have also been attractive to families of mixed marriages, since most UU churches celebrate Jewish as well as Christian holidays. Thus, from the mid-1980s to the present, UU membership has increased about 25 percent. By combining social liberalism with a broad theism, the Unitarian-Universalists have provided a place under the tent for many westerners who might otherwise have left organized faith entirely.[32]

During this era, the mainline denominations all strengthened their university chaplain programs. By the 1960s most western students attended large, often impersonal state universities. The denominational chaplains, whose buildings frequently ring the region's various campuses, found that they were much in demand. They discovered that modern young people tended to have similar problems, regardless of denominational background.

Likewise, many western hospitals began ecumenical hospital chaplain programs. Dominican priest Al Lopez, who moonlighted as a hospital chaplain while completing a Ph.D., dealt with the entire range of society, from prostitutes to businessmen, and all ranges of faith perspectives. In the end, he concluded, everything boiled down to prayer.[33]

In addition to such direct action, western church buildings continue to house an incredible variety of support groups. Alcoholics Anonymous, Overeaters Anonymous, Parents at Risk, Sexaholics Anonymous, Mothers of Twins Club, Mothers Against Drunk Driving, Adult Children of Alcoholics, and numerous other organizations have found homes in various church basements. These proliferating support groups help provide a form of community, if only on a temporary basis.

As the nation's inner cities steadily sank into decay, the western downtown churches were forced to become especially creative. Trinity Methodist Church in the heart of Denver was virtually dead by 1980 but turned itself around through a variety of measures. It became the permanent home of the Denver Chamber Orchestra and also opened its rooms for square dance classes as well as courses in accounting, aerobics, and race walking. On the other end of the social scale, Trinity Methodist established a twenty-four-hour ministry for the street people who walked by its doors daily. By the mid-1980s the church also housed AA meetings and instituted a job placement center.[34] In Denver, at least, these were not new social roles. The pastors of the 1890s would have found them very familiar.

━━━━━

One of the most creative approaches to western social concerns came from organized church efforts to deal with migrant agricultural workers, the "Migrant Ministry." The political dimensions of the crusade to better the life of migrant agricultural workers received little national publicity until Arizona-born labor leader Cesar Chavez led a nationwide boycott of California grapes in the late 1960s. Although virtually all of the migrant workers were Catholic by tradition, Chavez became the first leader to draw upon Mexican religious symbolism, especially the Virgin of Guadalupe, to bolster their cause. The public support given by such figures as Catholic radical activist Dorothy Day also aided the publicity. As the following case study of the Idaho Council of Churches shows, however, the western Catholic and Protestant churches had inaugurated a social gospel program for these migrant workers long before Chavez brought the issue to national attention.

In 1960 the National Council of Churches, which had been concerned about migrants for some years, evaluated the state programs and established ten goals for local groups. National and local organizations officially deplored the current state of seasonal farm worker life. They argued that the responsibility for improving conditions should be shared by growers, workers, consumers, labor unions, government agencies, and community residents. But the National Council placed the most responsibility on the local churches, declaring that the situation was one to which Christians needed to respond. Although the Migrant Ministry program was nationwide, fourteen western states participated. The smooth cooperation between Protestants and Catholics, both through the National Migrant Advisory Commission and at the local level, led the Migrant Ministry to be termed "the most extensive ecumenical field program in the United States." In fact, the Migrant Ministry contributed to the establishment of the Idaho Ecumenical Council. At one time, the Migrant Ministry program had a staff of 600 and about 15,000 volunteers in various levels. Overall, they supplied various social services to about 200,000 members of the migrant community.

Working closely with Title 3B of the Federal Economic Opportunity Act, the ministry crossed denominational lines. Catholics, Mennonites, Evangelicals, and liberal Protestants all participated in programs to provide pastoral care, Christian education, community development, health and welfare services, recreation, citizenship classes, libraries, job placement, teenage centers, vocational retraining, vacation church schools, classes in English and Spanish, and adult literacy classes.

Southern Idaho established one of the more extensive Migrant Ministry programs. The fertile Boise Valley had long had historical links with the Hispanic world. Mexican packers had been an integral part of the nineteenth-century mining era, and Boise had boasted a Spanish neighborhood for over a century. During World War II, Mexican women worked in the region via the bracero program. The postwar agricultural expansion continued the demand for largely Hispanic agricultural workers.

By the early 1950s mainline Protestants and Roman Catholics had each instituted separate social and educational programs to try to improve housing conditions in the camps. They also tried to mitigate, although with minimal success, the migrants' social and cultural rejection by the local community. The conservative political climate of southern Idaho, bolstered by a strong anti-union emphasis, made it difficult for organized labor to make much headway. In fact, given local suspicion of both the federal government and national unions, the Idaho Council of Churches was probably the only organization that could have implemented such social programs. In Idaho, as elsewhere, organized religion has long been the safest avenue by which a minority could present its case. Thus the churches spoke out for collective bargaining rights for migrants and also urged that the migrants be included in Idaho state workmen's compensation coverage.

After about a decade of parallel services, in 1964 local Protestant churches, via their Southern Idaho Migrant Ministry organization, began to create a cooperative body that included significant participation by the Catholic Diocese of Idaho, headed by Bishop Sylvester Treinen. Because the majority of migrants came from Hispanic Catholic culture, Protestants took care not to proselytize in any of their programs. Instead, they agreed to concentrate exclusively on social services.

President Lyndon Johnson's 1964 War on Poverty and the ensuing federal Office of Economic Opportunity (OEO) programs aided this effort, for the region needed a single Idaho agency to apply for federal funds to begin community action programs. In February 1965 an Idaho Farm Workers Services organization appeared. It worked with long-term Valley Hispanic residents, such as Jesse S. Berain of Twin Falls, to set up a variety of community action initiatives.

Over the years, as mechanized field equipment replaced hand operations, hundreds of Hispanic farm workers settled in Idaho. Their children soon became a prominent minority in what had hitherto been a largely homogeneous school system. Much of the local council's emphasis lay with promoting the dignity of Hispanic culture and the Christian responsibility of Idaho churches to acknowledge the human worth of the newcomers. The following incident highlights the need for the council's actions. When Cesar Chavez visited the Boise Valley in the late 1960s to see what could be done to improve conditions, the organizers had to keep his visit secret from the mainstream community because of their fear of harassment.[35]

At their height, church-government programs touched on many areas. They included a Mennonite Voluntary Service Unit in the Caldwell Labor Camp, a Nampa group that took books to migrants, and the Idaho

Farm Workers Service, Inc., a nonprofit agency that made OEO educational and child care programs available to Idaho migrants. As the Idaho Council Assembly noted in 1967, "The ordinary layman can best help the migrant problem by being aware of the problem and of its possible solutions, and by extending some sort of Christian welcome to migrants in the community where contact is possible."[36]

At its height (1965–67), the Migrant Ministry in Idaho set up an impressive set of social programs, including a migrant day center, which supplied bathing facilities, daily vitamins, regular cereal, fruit and vegetables and a play area for small children. Supervisor Eloise Ward praised the love that Hispanic families showed to their little ones, noting, "We discovered the physical needs are greater than the emotional needs." One mother told Ward that she could double her daily wage because of the program. The day care center meant that she did not have to make constant trips to the car to take care of her children.

But other, more complex programs ran into difficulty. Max Vargas, a Migrant Ministry official, discovered that Jesse Berain, whom he labeled the "self-appointed leader" of the Twin Falls Mexican community, wanted to control all federal patronage himself. Berain also discouraged attempts to alter the migrants' lifestyle. Adult classes for migrant workers proved far less successful than the popular day care centers. "Don't hold classes whenever there is a Mexican movie on," one man told Vargas, "for the workers wouldn't miss a Mexican movie to go to any classes." Several migrants suggested that they be paid for attending such classes. Vargas actually toyed with the idea, arguing that when one worked in the field all day, two to three hours of class would seem like overtime. The fact that the adults' command of English varied considerably frustrated the English teachers. Unlike the children, who were virtually all at the same language level, the adults needed almost individualized instruction. Thus, it is not surprising that a 1967 report showed 581 children involved in child development centers but only 87 adults enrolled in classes. Still, Vargas pushed adult education programs. He helped administer a migrant higher education project in which twenty-one young people would live for a year on a college campus, pass their high school equivalency test, and prepare to enter either the University of Oregon or Washington State University.[37] Unfortunately, these dreams collapsed in 1967 when Congress disestablished educational and other grants to nongovernmental community action programs, causing nonprofit corporations such as

the Idaho Farm Workers Service to become obsolete. During its hey-
day, however, over half a million dollars in federal grants had funded
a variety of programs, with the churches serving as the chief conduit
for the funds.[38]

It is impossible to catalog the modern social gospel efforts of western churches and synagogues. Seldom do their programs reach a national audience, but at a local level they have clearly been extensive.
Perhaps the best way to illustrate this is to imagine different scenarios.
What would Los Angeles have been like without the Catholic parochial school system? Or Denver without the National Jewish Hospital?
Or Albuquerque without the Baptist Noon Day Free Food program,
which fed over 10,000 people? Or Boise without its Migrant Ministries? Although these contributions cannot be measured, seldom do
they go unnoticed. As historian Edwin S. Gaustad once observed, "Thomas (Tip) O'Neal once remarked that all politics is local. Perhaps all
church history is as well."[39]

————————

As sociologist Wade Clark Roof noted, by 1978 the mainline Protestant churches were experiencing "severe problems of plausibility."[40]
By that time the traditional biblical doctrines of divine revelation, the
uniqueness of Christ, the authority of Scripture, and church attendance
as a mark of respectability suddenly found themselves called into question by the public.[41]

The decline of the liberal churches and the collapse of liberal theology opened the door to a conservative evangelical subculture that
still found its belief system largely intact. All religions are not equal,
this group said. Scripture reveals God's message to humanity. Christ is
the only way. Over time, these evangelical groups received rather unexpected support from the Missouri Synod Lutherans and from conservative Catholics. As one controversial nun remarked, "Enough. I'm
tired of you, liberal church in America. You're sick."[42]

The 1952 decision of the Southern Baptists to expand their ministry, followed by other evangelical groups, resulted in a heightened
evangelicalism in the American West. The move was aided by the 1947
founding of the Fuller Theological Seminary in Pasadena, California.
Historian George M. Marsden credits Fuller with playing a central role
in evangelizing the West as well as in creating a new, more open evangelical theology. Prior to the founding of Fuller, a harsh, antimodern

Fundamentalism seemed to characterize much of conservative evangelical Protestantism. Since around 1960, however, Fundamentalism and conservative evangelism have developed clearly distinct identities.[43] Fundamentalists faded into rather bitter enclaves, where they denounced the evil nature of the world, but a revived neo-evangelism grew steadily into a major western sociocultural phenomenon. Biblically based, it was open to metaphor and symbol, and it proved remarkably flexible when confronting the diversity of western life. Fuller Seminary also drew support from evangelist Billy Graham, who gained prominence in Los Angeles in 1948, and from Dwight Eisenhower's widely publicized opinion that America was, at heart, a religious nation. Outside of the Dallas area, Fuller had virtually no competition on the western evangelical front. It enrolled over a thousand students in its School of Theology and had extension ministries in seven other cities. It also established active black and Hispanic programs.[44] Within a short time, conservative evangelism had established itself in the heart of Southern California and in many other coastal regions.

With the founding of Fuller in 1947 and the Southern Baptist decision to move west five years later paving the way, the West continued to attract other important evangelical churches. Campus Crusade for Christ found a home on most western university campuses. From the 1980s forward, Calvary Chapels, with their evangelical, upbeat message, spread across the region as well. In the 1990s the Promise Keepers, a Colorado-based evangelical movement that met in football stadiums for massive rallies, achieved a great deal of publicity.

This western evangelical upswing was firmly linked with the religious interests (or lack thereof) of the much-studied members of the baby boom generation born between 1945 and 1964. As Wade Clark Roof's superb recent study shows, the boomers have become a "generation of seekers."[45] The defection of this age group from its birthright churches seems to be behind most of the widely reported national decline of the mainstream denominations.[46] But while this group has deserted the mainstream, it has not deserted all organized faiths. As Roger Finke and Rodney Stark have noted in their more controversial study, conservative groups have risen at steady rates to assume the mainstream's former role. In 1990, for example, the black Baptists, with their dynamic worship services and strong social outreach programs, had grown to become the nation's fourth largest denomination. Similarly, the Latter-day Saints are currently the eighth largest denomination, ahead of both Episcopalians and the United Church of Christ.[47] Of the ten largest individual churches in America in 1990, five were located in large western cities. Calvary Chapel of Costa Mesa, California, claimed 12,000 members, and First Assembly of God in Phoenix, 9,500. The West Los Angeles Church of God in Christ had about 8,000.[48] These western "megachurches" and their smaller counterparts (serving 2,000–3,000 each) in the Intermountain West are currently thriving. Their evangelical services combine informal dress with Pentecostal-derived (often rock-and-roll) "praise" songs. The buildings are new and expensive and filled with the latest multimedia technology. The pastors are dramatic personalities who stress practical situations in their sermons, and the well-trained staffers can provide services for just about every imaginable need. Perhaps most of all, these churches are tolerant of human frailties, especially divorce, depression, relationship problems, and various forms of addictions. As one pastor confessed, "I deal with the walking wounded."[49]

The chief critique of these energetic, thriving churches is that they lack both historical and theological rigor. Historian Dan Carnett has discovered that recent converts to New Mexico's growing Southern Baptist churches know nothing of the denomination's historic insistence on the separation of church and state or its central concept of "soul competency" (the idea that all people have the capacity to read and interpret the Bible for themselves).[50] Similarly, a *Rocky Mountain News* reporter observed of the 3,500-member Heritage Christian Center: "This is one of Denver's largest community churches, where the most complex theology is boiled down to sound bites, and salvation is reduced to a few simple steps."[51]

The growth of these churches reflects a new western openness to various forms of evangelical religion. Sociologist Mark A. Shibley has noted that although the steady rise of the historically southern evangelical groups has seemingly plateaued, other evangelical churches that exhibit more flexibility, such as Calvary Chapel, have continued to expand exponentially. These groups have been able to compromise with the openness of western culture more easily than some of the more rigid southern groups.[52] They continue to exhibit high profiles in many western communities.

Given the presence of such strong secular and religious forces, it was virtually inevitable that the West would witness socioreligious clashes of the first order. Because of the advent of the birth control pill, the renewed emphasis on personal autonomy, and "liberation," the most hotly contested issues have often involved lifestyle issues, especially those of abortion and homosexuality. The chief gay/lesbian organization of Montana, Pride Montana, has argued that sexual questions have become the most volatile issue of the 1990s.[53] The Conservative Campus Crusade periodical *Critical Issues* agreed. It suggested that the last decade of this century would probably share the sobriquet of the previous one: "The gay nineties."[54] These concerns were nationwide, of course, and they split the denominations along a distinct conservative to liberal axis, with Missouri Synod Lutherans, Southern Baptists, and Catholics bunching at the conservative end and Unitarian-Universalists, the United Church of Christ, and the Protestant Episcopal Church at the liberal end.

The western states were home to some of the fiercest public debates. In Washington state, Republican delegates in 1988 favored televangelist Pat Robertson as their presidential choice. In the fall of 1992 Oregon conservatives placed a measure on the ballot that would have denied public funds to any effort to portray homosexuality in a positive light. (It failed.) In Colorado, however, voters passed Amendment 2 to the state constitution. This amendment sought to overturn any local law that gave "minority status, quota preferences or protected status or claims of discrimination" to homosexuals. The measure was specifically directed at local ordinances from the liberal communities of Boulder, Aspen, and Denver, which had passed antidiscriminatory laws to protect local gays and lesbians. This measure also failed, overturned by a 6–3 Supreme Court decision. In Utah the Salt Lake City local school board voted 4–3 to ban *all* extracurricular clubs rather than sanction a homosexual student organization.[55] In addition, Utah became the first state to pass a law against gay and lesbian marriage, a measure also under consideration by South Dakota, Washington, and California. When a gay Catholic priest officiated at a New Mexico gay "marriage," the archdiocese deplored the ceremony as noncanonical.[56] Similarly, a Colorado rabbi who had been active in civil rights issues refused to sanction homosexual marriage.

The rhetoric proved fierce in every one of these encounters. A Montana gay spokesperson declared, "We're a minority that does not have equal rights under the law and it's time to claim those rights."[57] Activists blamed Fundamentalist Christianity for most of the evils in the world. In turn, an Albuquerque pastor said gays were no more a minority than rapists, murderers, or burglars. He declared that homosexuality was a sin. "And that's not what we say: it's what the Word of God says."[58]

In such an atmosphere, moderate voices could scarcely be heard. Many liberal-to-moderate churchgoers complained that once they declared their faith, they were instantly labeled antigay. In many circles, "Christo-centric" became almost an insult. The press helped fuel this controversy by seeking out the most extreme statements. The charismatic lesbian pastor who argued that Christian spirituality was compatible with intimate gay/lesbian relationships received far less press than the gay Episcopal priest who termed both celibacy and monogamy "unnatural" and declared that Mother Teresa would have been better off if she had had sex. (He later apologized.)[59] When the New Mexico legislature debated a gay rights bill in Santa Fe in November 1990, 5,000 Pentecostals, charismatics, and conservative evangelicals confronted 1,000 prohomosexual advocates on the grounds of the capitol. In the ultimate battle of symbols, the gays erected a twelve-foot-high paper penis in the form of a cross. The shouting between the two sides reached such intensity that police officers manning the barricades had to hold their hands over their ears.[60]

In many areas of the West, the forces of organized religion found themselves at the very center of this controversy.[61] For example, in 1972 in Lincoln, Nebraska, the Universalist-Unitarians inaugurated a bold program of sex education, "About Your Sexuality," that included film strips and recordings of adults talking about their first sexual experiences.[62] Four years later, Grace Community Evangelical Church of Lincoln hosted a "God, Country and Decency" rally on the campus of Lincoln's Nebraska Wesleyan University. There Jack Wyrtzen, head of Word of Life International, denounced pornography, alcohol, the ERA, homosexuality, abortion, astrology, horoscopes, violence on television, and Ouija boards. The same night, First Plymouth Congregational Church in Lincoln hosted a speech by gay rights advocate Barb Gittings.[63]

In the Colorado fight over homosexual legislation, Episcopalians, Presbyterians, Quakers, and several Jewish groups decried Amendment 2 as subjecting gays to second-class citizenship. On the other side, the Southern Baptist Convention, Missouri Synod Lutherans, Roman Catholic Legal Society, and National Association of Evangelicals argued that the amendment protected the civil rights of those who viewed homosexuality as a sin. There seemed no end to the controversy.

Thus the 1990s West proved far different from the 1890s West in terms of the use of religious symbols. In 1896 presidential candidate William Jennings Bryan rallied the region by denouncing those who would "crucify mankind upon a Cross of Gold." No modern candidate would make such Christian allusions. If the 1890s shared a common biblical rhetoric—the Kingdom of God—that allowed various religious groups to work together for eventual reform, the 1990s religious rhetoric was invariably couched in exclusivist terms.

Nowhere was this standoff more loudly announced than on the region's rear bumpers. During the 1920s and 1930s, public debates over religion retained at least a modest popularity in certain southern Plains circles. In a strange way, the "bumper sticker war" of the modern West replicates this exchange but without the question-and-answer period or the "vote" that followed. There is not much dialogue involved with such messages as "America is not a theocracy"; "The last time religion became involved with politics, people were burned at the stake"; "My goddess gave birth to your god"; "Honk if you love Darwin"; "I'm doing the best I can to annoy the Religious Right"; "The moral majority is neither"; the Christian fish symbol upside down and dead; the split red circle (i.e., "forbidden") superimposed over the cross. The latter two, prominent in Colorado in the 1980s, were perhaps the most blatant antireligious public statements since Germany of the 1930s. A California company produced most of these bumper stickers. On the other side, one sees various forms of the fish symbol; "Pray the Rosary"; "When the Rapture comes, this car will be empty"; and a fish swallowing Darwin with the message "survival of the fittest."

This is a theological "symbolic war" if ever one existed. Biblical metaphors and symbols that once united the West now form instant lines of cleavage. The multiplicity of metaphors has proven unsettling. As sociologist Peter Berger has noted, the key question is not whether modern life will be "religious" or "secular" but which set of transcendent symbols will provide the "sacred canopy" under which westerners, and all Americans, must make their way.[64]

The religious writings of Kathleen Norris provide a welcome relief from this noisy cultural clash. In the 1970s Norris and her writer husband moved back to her family home in Lemmon, South Dakota. This vast Plains region that lies west of the Missouri ("West River" to locals) is one of the most sparsely settled areas of the nation and also one of the poorest. They have lived there ever since.

As Norris reveals in *Dakota* (1993), her grandparents represented both sides of the cultural wars (the Fundamentalist-modernist controversy) of their day. Her paternal grandmother was a rigid Fundamentalist who often asked people if they had been saved; her maternal grandmother reflected a more liberal Protestant stance. A somewhat bohemian skeptic who initially rejected her inherited religious tradition for literature, Norris found herself gradually drawn back into spiritual and (later) church life.[65] She was led to this position in part by the daily challenges of survival in West River country, in part by a gradual re-acquaintance with Scripture, and in part by her term as an oblate at a North Dakota Benedictine monastery. The latter theme she details in *The Cloister Walk* (1996).[66]

Both works, *Dakota* especially, became surprise national best sellers. Critics praised Norris both for her felicity of language as well as her insights into human nature. Within a year, Kathleen Norris had moved from relatively unknown western regional writer to literary celebrity.

Her books firmly reject the religious dualism sketched out in the previous section. Rather, she focuses on both geographical and biblical insights to try to comprehend the sacred, the cosmos, the nation, her neighbors, and herself. For example, she suggests that gossip—a staple of small town life—is at its heart theological. "When we gossip we are also praying," she notes, "not only for them [the people about whom we are gossiping] but for ourselves."[67]

Her months as an oblate in the Benedictine seminary attuned her to the virtue of silence, causing her to despair over the noisy media quarrels concerning intimate matters. Some aspects of life such as sex, she says, are both private and, ultimately, mysterious. As such, they deserve to have "the glow of silence" draped around them.[68]

In a consumer-oriented world that attempts to elevate every whim into an urgent need, she writes of the contentment that Benedictines and West River people have found by surrendering themselves to reduced circumstances. When one is surrounded with little, especially within monastery walls, one often can discover a radically new way of understanding who one really is.

Norris is similarly enchanted with the concept of place, in her case, the vastness of the northern Great Plains. A land of extremes, the Plains serve locals as an ever-present "school for humility." While urbanites often find the Plains either barren or boring, Norris sees Dakota life as infused with mystery. "Maybe the desert wisdom of the Dakotas can teach us to love anyway," she observes, "to love what is dying, in the face of death, and not pretend that things are other than they are."[69]

From contemplating the mystery of life amidst this overwhelming geography, Norris moved gradually to contemplating the mystery of Scripture, especially as expressed through Benedictine liturgy ("the poetry of theology"). From listening both to the daily recitation of the monks and to the argot of locals, she has realized the crucial role that language and stories play in human life. One's stories determine who one is. More generally, she celebrates the concept of metaphor in all such renditions. The liberal attempts to reduce religious language to politically correct verbiage will invariably fail. So, too, will conservative efforts to extol biblical literalism and reduce faith to media evangelism. Both impoverish an ancient tradition.[70] With *Dakota* and *The Cloister Walk,* Kathleen Norris has emerged as the foremost western religious writer of the 1990s.

Chapter 8

Western Religion as Public Controversy

For the last quarter of the twentieth century, western religion found itself much in the news but seldom for reasons that would please the theologians. The incidents were legion: a variety of extreme political groups with millennial views and tangential religious affiliations; the February 1993 shoot-out of the Branch Davidian offshoot of the Seventh-Day Adventists in Waco, Texas; the March 1997 mass suicide of the "Heaven's Gate" UFO followers in California; and the seemingly endless sex scandals that rocked the powerful Roman Catholic Church to its foundations. All this proved genuinely unsettling to western religious life.

Prior to the 1960s, the words "sect" and "cult" were hardly recognized by most Americans. Eccentric polygamous LDS groups in Arizona or isolated communities in the Colorado back country might occasionally attract reporters, but this interest quickly faded. Yet from the 1960s forward, these "new religions" commanded the evening news on a regular basis. Some observers have estimated the number of cults and sects at over a thousand. Both federal officials and sociologists have devoted considerable effort to watching them. Sociologist J. Gordon Melton has compiled a superb *Encyclopedic Handbook of Cults in America* (1989). According to Melton, these alternative and nonconventional religious movements "have settled into the American religious landscape and show every sign of staying in place for the foreseeable future."[1] The cult phenomenon has proved worldwide in scope, but the largest American groups were all based either in the San Francisco area, other Pacific coastal cities, or isolated regions of the Intermountain West. Beginning in the late 1960s, each decade produced vast media concern over at least one of these western new religions.

This chapter illustrates the variety of western religious controversies by discussing the Jesus Freaks (1960s); the Divine Light Mission (1970s); Jonestown (1970s); and Rajneeshpuram (1980s). In addition, it examines the furor in Utah over the sudden appearance of forged LDS historical documents and the advent of renewed clashes, all through the West, over the theory of evolution. For over a quarter of a century, these incidents turned much of the world of western religion into a gigantic public controversy.

———

The media coverage of these new faiths probably began in the middle 1960s in the Sunset Strip section of Hollywood, then the microcosm of California popular culture. The area teemed with militant street evangelists who termed themselves "Jesus Freaks" or "Jesus People." Led by Arthur Blessitt, a Baptist seminary dropout, this militant band of evangelists passed out evangelical literature in the Tenderloin area and operated rescue missions for refugees from the ever-present drug culture.[2] Even more extreme were the Children of God, founded by David Berg, who went by the name "Moses." Moses denounced the "watered-down Gospel" of contemporary Christianity and preached "on-demand" revolution.[3] These militant evangelistic sects made some inroads into the California motorcycle gangs—"Bikers for Jesus"—and gradually merged under the vast umbrella of California conservative evangelical Protestantism. Extreme though they might have been, the initial militant evangelical groups retained at least a tenuous link with historic Protestantism.

———

The Divine Light Mission (DLM) became the first popular western new religion to emerge from a non-Christian (Hindu) background. The father of Guru Maharaj Ji (born Prem Pal Singh Rawaf in Hardwar, India, in 1957) founded the DLM. Maharaj Ji allegedly began delivering sermons at age two and a half and when his father died in 1965 inherited his spiritual authority. He made his initial "world peace tour" in 1971. His second trip to America the next year drew a rally of 5,000 in Montrose, Colorado.[4] Organizers gained great publicity from millions of leaflets that asked, "Who is Maharaj Ji?"

In 1972 the DLM moved its headquarters to Denver, "spiritually the darkest place in the world."[5] There the young guru lived in comfortable surroundings filled with electronic gadgetry that he often had difficulty operating. From there he also proclaimed his plans for the United States. His goal was to build a "Divine City" in America that would demonstrate that human beings can live together in peace. To promote this goal, he staged a much-publicized three-day festival at the Astrodome in Houston entitled "Millennium '73." Although the "Soul Rush" brought 25,000 followers to Houston, including converted political radical Rennie Davis, critics judged the event a major disappointment. Houston Baptists put forth considerable opposition. "Beware false prophets," warned the marquee of the First Baptist Church. Another Baptist cleric termed the Maharaj Ji one of "a long list of anti-Christs."[6]

Reporters covered the Maharaj Ji's activities with zeal. The majority were critical, but more than a few were deeply puzzled over the adoration that American young people expressed for the chubby teenager from India.[7] His followers, who derived from Protestant, Catholic, and Jewish backgrounds, viewed him as an "enlightened master." They believed that he transmitted the ancient knowledge, given to humankind by Moses, Jesus, Buddha, and Krishna, to the contemporary world. They credited his five commandments to spiritual wholeness for leading them to a high energy bliss that for many seemed to be a last resort from severe personal problems.[8] He really loves people, said one woman convert. "I really understand from him what it means to love someone."[9]

Many followers did, indeed, change their lives. The guru's message seemed to have special appeal to former antiwar activists and ex-political radicals. The DLM ashrams forbade all drug use, alcohol, tobacco, and sexual activity. They stressed meditation and vegetarianism as the paths to truth. In addition, they also engaged in modest social work. By his own account, Maharaj Ji reformed thousands of drug users, murderers, and thieves. When asked his opinion as to the percentage of his American devotees who had formerly used drugs, he replied, "How many of us were formerly children? About that percentage."[10]

By 1976 DLM income from gifts and tithes was estimated at $3.78 million. The young guru owned a private airplane, fifteen houses, and four automobiles, including a Rolls Royce. Although the Denver Hare Krishnas denounced him for posing as God and for exploiting his followers, he claimed 300 local supporters and 50,000 worldwide. As adverse publicity mounted, however, the DLM ordered its followers to discard the trappings of a mission and to deny they were a "religion." The Maharaj Ji even considered changing DLM church status to that of a nonprofit corporation.[11] Shortly after, the young man married an American follower and moved to California, whereupon publicity rapidly declined. Critics might denounce Maharaj Ji as a naive philosopher who relished American technology, but at least he did no overt harm. The same could not be said for many of the others.

———

The saga of Rev. Jim Jones, the San Francisco People's Temple, and the over 900 murder/suicide victims in Jonestown, Guyana, reveals a far more sinister side of the new religions. It is no exaggeration to say that the story of Jonestown became the most dramatic religious happening of the entire 1970s. The memory of Jonestown still elicits both horror and bewilderment.[12]

James W. Jones was born in 1931 in Indiana. He grew to maturity in that southernmost section of the Midwest, surrounded by Pentecostalism, socialism, and racial segregation. As a young man he attended Butler University and entered the clerical profession, and during the 1950s he became fascinated by Father Divine's Peace Mission. Borrowing from this idea, he founded in Indiana a racially integrated People's Temple that in 1960 became affiliated with the Disciples of Christ. After receiving a vision of imminent nuclear destruction, Jones took his family to Brazil for almost two years. In 1964 he and 140 followers moved to Ukiah, California, just north of San Francisco. Within five years, he had erected a People's Temple complex there, complete with swimming pool, senior citizens center, and child care center; the next year he established a branch People's Temple in the black Fillmore district of San Francisco. His sermons reflected great concern for contemporary racial prejudice and for the problem of poverty. They reflected his belief (also borrowed from Father Divine) that he was a human god. During this time he sired a child by the wife of his legal advisor with the permission of all involved.[13]

It was not long before Jones became prominent in San Francisco. The local press termed him "a charismatic figure," and his sermons drew crowds that approached a thousand each Sunday. When he threw his political weight behind successful Mayor George Moscone, he found himself appointed to the City Housing Commission. Famed San Francisco columnist Herb Caen spoke well of him.[14] He also had brief meetings with First Lady Rosalyn Carter, California Governor Jerry Brown, vice-presidential candidate Walter Mondale, and other national political figures.

As Jones's reputation grew, his enemies also began to surface. Temple defectors termed him a liar, cheat, and cruel taskmaster. They challenged his "healing ceremonies" as mere "sleight of hand" magic performances. When the story of his illegitimate child reached the press, it proved especially scandalous.

Jones refused to answer his critics on any charge. Instead, he began to devote more attention to his multiracial Agricultural Mission (begun in 1975) in Jonestown, Guyana. Sociologist David Chidester has termed this experiment "a utopian heaven on earth, a socialist paradise in the jungle where racism, sexism, ageism, and classism would be eliminated."[15]

In 1977 *New West* magazine ran an especially damning article on Jones and Temple policies. This led Jones and several of his closest followers to permanently depart San Francisco and join the group in the still-uncompleted Jonestown. Acting on the *New West* and other complaints, California congressman Leo Ryan made an official visit to Guyana on November 17, 1978, where he was ambushed and killed along with three companions. Immediately afterward 914 men, women, and children either killed each other or killed themselves by drinking cyanide mixed in Kool-aid. Five more suicides followed at various other locations. Although the tragedy occurred in Guyana, it was largely an American phenomenon. Never had the nation witnessed anything like this before.

National media reaction proved extensive. Both *Time* and *Newsweek* devoted much attention to the story.[16] Investigative reporters soon discovered that the community had actually planned for this probable outcome via ritual suicide drills and paranoid atrocity tales against American authorities all told to them by Jones. Reporters who searched for historical precedents found them principally in the story of the Jews at Masada and the Japanese kamikaze pilots of the Second World War. But as Herb Caen argued, the Masada warriors and kamikaze pilots at least died for a higher purpose. Since the cause of the Jonestown tragedy remained largely unexplained, the people there were considered to have died in vain.[17]

In the past thirty years, scholars have penned over twenty books on the Jonestown experience. Valuable though they have been, few have placed the movement in the context of western religious history. Although the People's Temple began in Indiana, it did not flourish until Jones moved to northern California, as far as one could get without falling into the Pacific, he once stated.[18] San Francisco in the sixties and seventies reflected the ferment of the countercultural attacks on the war in Vietnam, denunciations of racism, distinctive music, a mixed racial atmosphere, and a plethora of drugs. Sociologist James T. Richardson has argued that Jones's organization drew far less from alienated white middle-class youth than from the impoverished local black community and the charismatic heritage of Father Divine.[19] This point is well taken, for Jonestown followers were about 75 percent black, 20 percent white, and 5 percent Hispanic and Asian.

Still, the atmosphere of San Francisco provided an environment that allowed his message to flourish. (What if he had moved to Hartford, Connecticut?) The world of Black Power, Jesus Freaks, and Hare Krishna followers formed a backdrop to his quasi-socialist community's demand for a shared intense experience. In that turbulent, unstable social world, people's expectations turned utopian. The most utopian move of all, of course, was Jones's claim of divinity.

Similarly, Jones's initial dedication to social welfare programs in the Tenderloin allied him with the prominent Black Brothers and other radical groups. Jones's Native American ancestry also gave him social cachet.[20] Sociologist David Chidester is correct in arguing that Jones and the People's Temple can best be understood as a religious movement. But it is one that could only have succeeded in 1970s San Francisco.

━━━━━━

The dominant western religious story of the 1980s involved not urban San Francisco but rural Antelope, Oregon. From 1981 to 1985, reporters penned an estimated 4,000 articles on the Bhagwan Shree Rajneesh and his community, Rajneeshpuram, in eastern Oregon. Since then there have been at least six book-length studies (two by ex-members), one fictionalized account (John Updike's novel *S*), and countless articles by sociologists.[21] It is fair to say that the rise and fall of Rajneeshpuram ranks as the most thoroughly covered tale of western religious history for this generation.

Born into an Indian family of cloth merchants following the Jain faith, Chandra Mohan Jain (his family called him Rajneesh) graduated from college in 1955 and later earned a master's degree in philosophy in India. He then began a career teaching at the university level. During the early 1960s, a series of public lectures brought him great notoriety (and followers) as he attacked Gandhi, denounced socialism and Hinduism, and praised capitalism, technology, science, and birth control. In addition, he declared that sexual energy was divine and that human sexuality should be freely expressed. The goal of true religion, he said, was to show people how to enjoy life.

Aided by funds from a wealthy Jain convert, the Bhagwan founded a meditation center outside Poona, India, that attracted a number of Western followers. Given its location and the cost, the Poona clientele was highly self-selected. It attracted Western intellectuals, a few European aristocrats, and numerous members from the loosely organized human potential movement, largely based in California. By 1981 the Bhagwan greeted over 30,000 visitors annually.

Unfortunately, many of these visitors had had previous difficulties with drugs and/or psychological problems, and a number ended up either in jail or in Indian hospitals. Reacting to this local wave of hostile publicity, an American follower, Mo Anand Sheela (née Silverman) oversaw the community's move to the United States. In August 1981 Sheela purchased for the Bhagwan the 64,000-acre Big Muddy Ranch in the high desert John Day country of eastern Oregon. The price was $5,350,000.

Oregon east of the Cascade Mountains is both spectacular and sparsely settled. There are no large towns, and most residents are familiar with weapons and hunting. In general, citizens of the region are independent and politically conservative. Prior to 1980 one heard numerous complaints about "government regulations." Into this isolated region came one of the most educated, articulate communes since Scottish reformer Robert Owen brought his "boatload of knowledge" to New Harmony, Indiana, in the late 1820s. Mostly white, middle-class professionals, many adherents initially worked in the health care professions. The community boasted a variety of Ph.D.s and a staff of highly trained lawyers. They were incredibly well funded, over $30 million by some estimates, and situated in one of the poorer sections of Oregon.[22]

Through leases from the Bureau of Land Management, the community of "Rancho Rajneesh" acquired a land base approaching 85,000 acres. The new arrivals worked hard. By 1985 they had built first-rate roads, schools, banks, office buildings, and an airport.

The ranch had several goals, but residents' primary aim lay in their plans to transform the community into a city of perhaps 10,000 adherents saved from the three Armageddons predicted by the Bhagwan: earthquakes, AIDS, and nuclear holocaust. Massive "celebrations" from 1982 to 1984 also brought in between 7,000 and 15,000 annual visitors to the region, many of whom remained.

The widely publicized tales of sexual freedom in the compound gave the Bhagwan considerable publicity.[23] The fact that the Bhagwan owned a large number of Rolls Royce automobiles—ostensibly to show that material wealth "didn't matter"—became a similar source of notoriety. Articulate spokespeople for the community vigorously denied that they were a "cult"; rather, they were only expressing a "philosophy." Later the Bhagwan himself denied that he had founded a "religion."

Historian Carl Abbott has described Rajneeshpuram as a "New Age theme park," while journalist Frances FitzGerald has termed it "a year-around summer camp for young urban professionals."[24] By the mid-1980s, everything was in place for a profound western religio-cultural clash.

The opposition was not long in forming. It began in a local conservative Baptist congregation in nearby Madras, Oregon. Led by the pastor, Baptists denounced the "immoral" display of wealth and the nonconventional sexual practices. But the protest soon extended to the religiously neutral. Other Oregonians argued that the issue was not religion but water. Long-time ranchers feared that introducing a community of several thousand people into the area would forever lower the water table.[25] The commune's widely known contempt for the local "rednecks" and "bigots" did little to smooth over feelings.

Frances FitzGerald drew on terms like "range war" and "Belfast" to describe this situation. Local bumper stickers such as "Bag a Bhagwan" reflected a more direct approach. Several commune windows were shot out, and someone allegedly planted a bomb on ranch property.[26]

Soon the commune guards began to arm themselves with M-14s. Security became a central issue, and Sheela herself donned a sidearm to greet newcomers. Some worried that the Bhagwan might be assassinated. From an open community expressing free sexuality, Rajneeshpuram had turned into a closed society, literally, an armed camp.

In other circumstances, this situation might have evolved into a twentieth-century version of the shoot-out at the OK Corral. But opponents of Rajneeshpuram chose another route: Oregon's extensive bureaucratic local and state regulations. Ever since the 1920s quarrel over Catholic schools, Oregon had been very sensitive to issues involving church-state matters. Since the early part of the century, regional conservationists had enacted a dense mass of land-use regulations. Any proposed city such as the Rajneesh had in mind would inevitably run into a tangle of bureaucratic county and state planning laws.[27]

Eventually, in true western fashion, the citizens of Oregon ran the Rajneesh and his followers out of town. But the victory bore little resemblance to Gary Cooper's famous showdown in *High Noon*. Instead, the local victory emerged through the efforts of ordinary bureaucrats in blue jeans and bifocals. Wasco County land-use planners and federal judges became local heroes as they stymied various development plans via obscure regulations and/or injunctions. The climax came on December 10, 1985, when a federal judge declared that the incorporation of Rajneeshpuram was illegal because it violated the constitutional clauses separating church from state.[28]

Locals also won the battle of public opinion as the new community members committed a series of quasi-legal and illegal actions in their efforts to win control of local government. These included

—the 1984 busing to Oregon of 3,500 "street people" from California and the East Coast;

—sham marriages to give foreign members of the community U.S. citizenship, which eventually brought in the U.S. Immigration Service;

—attempts to sabotage the computer system utilized by *Portland Oregonian* reporters who were writing an exposé on the community;

—illegal wiretaps;

—rumors (later proven true) that the Bhagwan desired to purchase a 1.4-million-dollar watch;

—the complete takeover of Antelope, Oregon, driving out the locals and renaming it "Rajneeshpuram";

—salmonella poisoning in several restaurants in The Dalles in an alleged effort to influence a local election;

—an attempt by Sheela and others to poison the Bhagwan's personal physician with an injection of adrenaline;

—the October 1985 guilty plea by the Bhagwan on federal immigration charges, for which he paid $400,000 in fines and court costs and was expelled from the country.

The Rajneesh finally admitted that the move to America had been a "mistake" and urged all his followers to leave Oregon. In 1986 Sheela and two other female leaders were sentenced to prison terms on a variety of charges.

The Bhagwan died in 1990, and the future of his movement remains uncertain.[29] Tourists continue to visit the city (now renamed Antelope), but there is little to actually see. However, citizens have erected a plaque in downtown Antelope that bears a quotation from Edmund Burke: "The only thing necessary for the triumph of evil is for good men to do nothing."[30]

———

In 1953 Arizona governor Howard Pyle sent a small cadre of law officials into Short Creek, an isolated community in the Arizona Strip (the region between the north rim of the Grand Canyon and the Arizona/Utah border), and arrested scores of male polygamous Latter-day Saints. This raid, which turned into a public relations disaster, proved to be the last official state assault on the outlawed but still extensive Fundamentalist Mormon branches. (Estimates vary from 6,000 to 30,000 regionwide; there are a variety of such groups.)

Although the Utah, Idaho, and Arizona governments still keep a wary eye on the various polygamous communities, especially that of Short Creek (now renamed Colorado City), Arizona, they generally leave these tight-knit bands of millennialists to themselves. Indeed, in the wake of the sexual revolution of the 1960s, the polygamists' insistence on plural marriage has almost a Victorian ring to it.[31] Consequently, the most disruptive incident in LDS life during the last quarter of the twentieth century did not involve polygamy, which had been outlawed in 1890. Rather, it revolved around the tragic consequences of forged Mormon historical documents.

By the 1980s, only the most extreme evangelicals still termed the Mormons a "cult." In the eyes of most of the nation, the Saints had become simply another denomination, wrestling among themselves as to the proper degree of assimilation with mainstream American life.[32]

But the powerful LDS Church experienced a severe public setback during the early 1980s when former LDS missionary Mark W. Hofmann was exposed not only as a forger of LDS historical documents but as a murderer as well.

Mark W. Hofmann was born into a strict LDS family, served his mission in southwestern England, and entered Utah State University in 1976. Along the way, Hofmann somewhere lost his faith in church teachings but simultaneously became obsessed with church history.[33] A promising student, Hofmann soon became friends with Jeff Simmonds, curator of Special Collections and Archives at Utah State. He often did research in their excellent collection of LDS documents.

After graduation, Hofmann began dealing in historical documents himself and by the early 1980s had achieved a considerable local reputation. He discovered autographed first editions by Mark Twain and other American writers, which he sold at considerable profit. He also found a rare copy of "The Oath of a Freeman," the first document ever printed in North America. The Library of Congress hoped to purchase the oath but was unable to raise his asking price of $1 million.

Hofmann's discoveries regarding early LDS history proved equally startling. He found a document by Martin Harris (who had known Prophet Joseph Smith but had left the early church) that confirmed the story of Smith's first vision. Even more amazing, he found another letter that suggested that Smith had been led to discover the buried golden plates not by an angel, as Smith had always claimed, but by a "white salamander." This letter implied that Smith was deeply steeped in the prevailing folk magic of his upstate New York home.

Church officials were shocked at this "salamander" letter and the ensuing negative publicity it engendered. When Hofmann spoke of a "McLellin Collection" that contained even more potentially embarrassing information on early church life, he had the instant ear of the highest LDS officials. It seems that Hofmann planned to undermine the beliefs of the entire Mormon Church through these "discoveries."

In the early 1980s the Mormon Church found itself under grave national scrutiny. LDS authorities had recently excommunicated feminist Sonia Johnson for publicly supporting the Equal Rights Amendment. A proposed series of books on LDS history overseen by respected historian Leonard J. Arrington was quietly terminated as not being sufficiently "faith promoting." Potentially damaging historical documents were rumored to be locked in the church's "secret vault."[34] The 1978 revelation admitting black men to the priesthood only partially softened this criticism.

As was eventually proven, Hofmann had forged the majority of his discoveries. His considerable income—estimated at $2 million—derived from his facile pen. So clever was he that the extent of his forgeries will probably never be known. Noted documents expert Charles Hamilton (who had himself authenticated several of Hofmann's discoveries) declared him "the world's greatest forger."[35]

Mark Hofmann might never have been uncovered except for the fact that in October 1985 he deposited two pipe bombs that killed Steven Christensen and Kathleen Webb Sheets (probably intended for her husband, Gary), who had both been associated with him in trading documents. The next day, Hofmann was himself injured when a third bomb, prepared for another, unidentified person, accidentally detonated in his car. The subsequent investigation of this case became the largest in all of Utah history. The publicity surrounding the trial dominated local media for months. The foremost non-Mormon expert on the Saints, historian Jan Shipps, found herself besieged by reporters who, in many cases, had never heard of the golden plates.[36]

The case and trial took over a year and a half to complete. The surrounding publicity not only drew many LDS skeletons from the closet, it also re-emphasized the LDS doctrine of "blood atonement," which states that some crimes (including murder and adultery) are so heinous that Jesus' crucifixion cannot redeem them. The perpetrator of any of these actions has to pay for the crime with his life. For months, Hofmann's father took this position and only reluctantly gave it up.[37] After a guilty plea, Hofmann apologized to his victims and began a prison sentence that some critics felt was far too light for the crimes.[38]

———

The previous incidents garnered incredible regional controversy for Colorado (Divine Light Mission), northern California (Jonestown), Oregon (Rajneeshpuram), and Utah (Hofmann). But one religio-social issue touched almost every hamlet or city throughout the entire West. This was the postwar incarnation of a familiar question: should evolution be taught in the nation's public schools?

As discussed in chapter 4, the clash over evolution in the mid-twenties was largely an eastern one, affecting few western states.

Only Oklahoma and, to a lesser extent, Arizona and California witnessed any serious public controversy. When the quarrel revived, however, this was completely reversed. From the 1960s forward, the locus for anti-evolution sentiment lay in the West, primarily in southern California. From bases in Los Angeles and San Diego, the anti-Darwinian groups have spread their messages to the entire nation.

As historians Ronald L. Numbers, George E. Webb, and Edward Larson have shown, dispute over the theory of evolution remained quiescent from the late 1920s throughout the 1950s.[39] In 1957, however, the Russian success with *Sputnik* sent American educators scurrying to improve the nation's science teaching. Aided by a National Science Foundation grant, biologists established a center at the University of Colorado in Boulder to improve the teaching of biology in the high schools. Their Biological Sciences Curriculum Study (BSCS) placed evolution at the core of their program, and by the mid-1960s about half the nation's high schools used the BSCS books.[40]

Simultaneously, in 1963 a group of scientists and engineers, led by Henry M. Morris, founded the Creation Research Society, which soon moved its headquarters to San Diego. Originally linked with evangelical Christian Heritage College, by 1972 the group had established an independent organization: the Institute for Creation Research. The founders included Baptists, Missouri Synod Lutherans, and other denominations and drew heavily on the anti-evolution writings of various Seventh-Day Adventist spokesmen.

The institute received much support from the Bible Institute of Los Angeles (BIOLA) and from Herbert W. Armstrong's Worldwide Church of God (WCG) headquartered in Pasadena. The WCG published a slick, glossy magazine, the *Plain Truth,* nearly every issue of which contained an attack on evolution. Distributed gratis, the *Plain Truth* reached an untold audience, estimated in the millions.[41] The creationist/anti-evolution crusade probably also drew from the increased western disenchantment with science in the Vietnam era.

During the 1920s opponents of evolution had concentrated on convincing state legislatures to outlaw the teaching of the theory in tax-supported schools, arguing that teaching evolution denied the truth of Scripture and undermined the civic morality of the students. Pro-evolution forces of that decade all declared that evolution lay at the core of human and natural world development. A significant number denied that the theory of evolution clashed with Scripture. Kirtley F.

Mather, chairman of the Geology Department at Harvard, for example, served as an expert witness at the Scopes Trial in Dayton, Tennessee. Afterward, he spent much effort in arguing for the essential harmony of science and religion. Evolution is a process, Mather insisted; God is a power, a force. Until his death, Mather argued that many people of science believed in theistic evolution as the process God used in effecting his will on earth.[42]

The new creationists did not necessarily dismiss this position, but they took a very different tack. Led by Berkeley-trained biochemist Duane T. Gish, who earned his Ph.D. in 1953, many were credentialed scientists, although not always in biology or geology. Indeed, a significant number were trained as engineers deeply committed to an "empiricist folk epistemology." Consequently, they argued that the theory of evolution was scientifically false and could be refuted on a *scientific* basis and that to teach that biological evolution occurred via completely naturalistic means was really to teach another "religious faith," one held by "secular humanists." Thus, they maintained that teaching naturalistic evolution in state-supported schools violated the civil rights of religious children (mostly, but not exclusively, conservative evangelicals), not unlike forcing Jewish children to write essays on Jesus or sing "Silent Night" at a Christmas assembly. The creationists would not forbid the teaching of evolution but only asked for "equal time" to present their "equally scientific" point of view. The students could then decide for themselves.

The majority of scientists leaped to this bait. Evolution formed the basis for all twentieth-century science, they said. To ignore evolution was to deprive California children of the best of science education. Moreover, creationism was not science but "religion" and thus should be excluded from public schools along the lines of the First Amendment.

From the 1970s forward, the creationists staged numerous public debates, often on college campuses, to spread their position. These public spectacles usually generated considerable controversy but probably convinced few onlookers to shift their points of view. The public usually viewed these clashes as another round of the science versus religion quarrel. But historian David Wilson is correct in asserting that it should more accurately be described as one "cluster" of science *and* religion versus another.[43]

In truth, the issues were incredibly complex. The creationists were not of a single mind, as they argued amongst themselves about the disappearance of the dinosaurs, the exact timing for creation, the precise overlapping of science with Scripture, the nature of the Noachian flood, and so on. Similarly, the theory of evolution came in a number of varieties: Darwinian naturalism, punctuated equilibrium, theistic evolution, and so on. Indeed, by the early 1970s the theory of evolution had become the prime cosmic origin myth for the late twentieth century. The complexity of comprehending all aspects of the process seemed daunting. Since no one could be an expert in all the fields involved (paleontology, biology, neurophysiology, zoology, etc.), each person had to rely on the conclusion of experts. But which "experts"? There lay the rub.

Most western towns did not harbor extreme cults or sects, but all had public schools. Thus, in one form or another the evolution issue affected every western school board or state legislature, albeit at different times and in slightly different ways. Prior to the 1982 Arkansas Federal Court decision that creationism was "religion," three western states had placed "equal time" bills in their hoppers. Much of the controversy—virtually impossible to track down—occurred on a local level as local school boards, from Denver to Seattle to Los Alamos, wrestled with some version of this issue. Since the State of California educated 4 million students in its public school systems, it was frequently in the news in the 1970s and 1980s in this regard.[44] Although the case of *Edwards vs. Aguillard* officially quashed the legal aspect of the equal time argument, creationists continue to advocate it on a local, cultural level. During the early 1990s the Atomic City of Los Alamos, New Mexico, almost elected a creationist majority to the school board.

Why the West? When *New Yorker* writer Calvin Trillin covered the 1973 California hearings on the matter, he offered an answer: internal migration from the South. Whenever he heard an Oklahoma or Arkansas twang, Trillin knew that this person would oppose evolution.[45] The fact that California rates number one and Texas number two in textbook sales might be another reason for western involvement.

But there may be yet another reason for the western dimension of the fight. In the late twentieth century the theory of evolution emerged as the ultimate "origin myth" for the modern world. Given the symbolic importance involved in teaching the "myth of creation," the emotional stakes run high. A standard part of the western myth has always involved belief in democracy and fair play. "Let the people decide"—the creationist motto—has long been a western populist watchword. Berkeley law professor Phillip Johnson has written several volumes along these lines to denounce an elite scientific establishment's naturalistic interpretation as the sole possible source of creation.

Recently the scientists have borrowed back that slogan with their own compromise. Teach creationism in high school if we must, they say, but in comparative religion classes rather than in biology. Catholic liberals have similarly sought a way to accommodate the anti-evolution forces.[46] What the outcome will be is anyone's guess. All that can be said at the moment is that this is the most widespread religio-cultural conflict in western life.

———

Because of these various incidents, religion in the West received a great deal of adverse publicity from around 1965 to the end of the century. Unlike the equally mean-spirited cultural wars of the 1920s, which seldom extended beyond words, a number of the post-1960s incidents ended in tragedy. In 1999 organized anti-Semitism again raised its ugly head. Fortunately, the most widespread manifestation of the cultural clash, the quarrel over teaching evolution in the public school system, has remained nonviolent. But the issues involved are deep-rooted and unlikely to soon disappear.

Chapter 9

Religious Personalities of the Modern West

The dominant western religious personalities from the 1960s forward have been legion. Thanks to extensive media coverage, a number of regional figures have achieved national reputations. Each decade produced at least one prominent person in this regard.

For the 1960s, the person probably would be James A. Pike, Episcopal bishop of California from 1958 to 1966. Pike then resigned to work for the Center for the Study of Democratic Institutions in Santa Barbara. He died the next year in the Judean wilderness on a quest to find the Dead Sea Scrolls.

Pike formed as much a part of 1960s California as the antiwar movement, the Beach Boys, and campus unrest. He took radical positions on church doctrinal items such as the Virgin Birth, the authority of Scripture, and the role of Jesus, for which he received official church censure and barely avoided a heresy trial. An advocate of the "new morality," his personal life was filled with tragedy. His son and mistress both committed suicide, and his daughter also attempted to kill herself. With his third wife he wrote a book that describes his claim to have successfully contacted his dead son through a medium. As his biographers have noted, the term "controversial" became as much a prefix to James A. Pike's name as his title "bishop."[1]

For the decade of the 1970s, one might highlight Peace Pilgrim, a silver-haired woman who since 1953 had been walking across the nation to proclaim her message that God resides within each person, that good can overcome evil, and that the goal of life is internal as well as national peace. Beginning in the McCarthy era, Peace Pilgrim vowed to remain a wanderer across the land until "mankind learned the way of peace, walking until I am given shelter and fasting until I am given food." She walked over 25,000 miles and spoke to whoever would listen, often high school and civic groups. Her arrival in a western town usually produced considerable newspaper coverage for her message. Only her death in 1981 ended her crusade. Shortly thereafter, friends in Santa Fe published a book based on transcripts of her many talks. Her writings and speeches have been donated to the Peace Center at Swarthmore College.[2]

During the 1980s, New Age spokesperson J. Z. Knight emerged as a prominent figure. A native of West Texas/eastern New Mexico, Knight survived a childhood of poverty to rise steadily in the world of business. She achieved national notoriety, however, for her claims of divine healing, UFO contact, and, especially, her statement that a former inhabitant of Atlantis, "Ramtha," was channeling his message to the world through her. During the 1980s, Knight provided spiritual advice from Ramtha to thousands of followers, including actors Shirley MacLaine and Richard Chamberlain, and amassed a considerable fortune along the way. She built a three-million-dollar compound south of Seattle as her headquarters. Cartoonist Gary Trudeau burlesqued this phenomenon when he portrayed his character "Boopsie" as receiving similar messages. Knight's personal life proved equally turbulent. Her third husband claimed at their 1992 divorce proceedings that Ramtha had told him that he could not die from his HIV positive diagnosis.[3]

One does not have to look far to find problematic western religious personalities in the modern era. The same is true for religious movements and institutions. The controversial role played by Theosophy in the early years of the century was assumed by Scientology and the Unification Church two generations later. Scientology traces its origins to the World War II years when science fiction writer L. Ron Hubbard met John Parsons, wealthy Los Angeles pioneer of Cal Tech rocketry and later founder of the Jet Propulsion Laboratory. Parsons also dabbled in the occult arts, and it is likely that Hubbard borrowed in part from this when he founded his technological faith of Scientology. Official publications also credit his interest in British Columbian Native American mythology as a source for his philosophy of survival. Hubbard's publication *Dianetics: The Modern Science of Mental Health* has become perhaps the world's best-selling self-help book. Scientology promised adherents that all followers could become "clear" of all harmful events in their past.[4] Attaining such a position, however, was often expensive.

The Rev. Sun Myung Moon's Unification Church has been only slightly less controversial. The faith was born in Korea in 1954 from a combination of anti-Communism, Presbyterianism, and personal insight, and the "Moonies" first arrived in the United States in 1959. Their essential message was that Jesus had failed in his mission because he had fathered no children, but that another person had been chosen to fulfill that purpose in modern times. Reverend Moon, who arrived in the United States in 1971, waited until 1990 to proclaim officially in San Francisco that he was that person.[5]

In the 1960s and later, opponents accused the church of brainwashing and kidnapping its followers. Later, federal officials sentenced Moon to over a year in jail for tax evasion. But the political conservatism of the 1980s allowed the Unification Church to assume a more moderate role.[6] Church emphasis on family values and multicultural marriages also placed it more in the cultural mainstream. Today Unification Church pastors are often members of local western ministerial alliances.

There are scores of other groups that could be mentioned. Consequently, when one is dealing with the modern period, one simply has to be arbitrary. This chapter focuses on three prominent movements: the rise of Native American faiths; Seventh-Day Adventist founder Ellen Gould White and her Loma Linda University; and the rise of Asian faiths. It also treats four dominant personalities: black activist Rev. Cecil Williams; the two foremost antinuclear western Catholic bishops, Raymond G. Hunthausen and Leroy T. Mathiesen; and the country's most well known television evangelist, Robert Schuller. Admittedly fragmentary, these selections will have to represent the panorama of the whole.

———

The most hallowed of all phrases in American religious history is "separation of church and state," whatever that may mean in light of various specific Supreme Court decisions. During the two-hundred-plus-year relationship between the federal government and Native Americans, however, that position was most often honored in the breech as the government openly drew upon the nation's churches to help "civilize and Christianize" the various Indian tribes. Not until the Meriam Report (1928) and the appointment of radical reformer

John Collier as commissioner of Indian Affairs five years later did the government begin to acknowledge the centrality and integrity of Indian spirituality.[7]

In 1978 President Jimmy Carter signed the American Indian Religious Freedom Act (AIRFA) to officially recognize this change. Although not without its limitations, AIRFA legislation had considerable impact on western America, for most reservations lay west of the Mississippi. The 1978 act also emphasized the importance of communal Native identity (tribalism) and correctly placed Native spirituality, or traditional religion, at the heart of this corporate identity. AIRFA also acknowledged the importance of traditional Native sacred sites, scattered all through Indian country, and the need to protect them from degradation.[8] Additional amendments passed in 1994.

These concepts of Native spirituality and Native sacred space often proved bewildering to non-Indians who hailed from a Judeo-Christian framework. As anthropologists were quick to point out, there is no single Native American religion. Instead, Native America contained a vast variety of spiritual traditions.[9] Most Native faiths emphasized a spiritual relationship to the various animals in their region: deer, elk, salmon, or buffalo. This close human-animal connection, dating back perhaps 20,000 years, produced a connection that is almost completely lacking in Judeo-Christian Scripture.[10] The Ogalala Sioux, for example, celebrate the birth of a rare white buffalo calf as an omen of impending social good. Athabaskan hunting rituals involve prayers of thanks to the hunted (deer or bear) for donating its life so that others may live. The skinning of the animal must similarly follow prescribed rituals, not unlike Hebrew regulations for the slaughter of animals.

Indeed, exact performance of ritual is crucial to sustaining all Native spirituality. From the sacred pipe of the northern Plains to the seasonal dances of the southwestern Pueblos to the healing ceremonies of the Navajo, proper ceremony is essential to insure good crops, restore health, and integrate the individual into the harmony of the universe. Generally speaking, tribal groups do not mind if non-Indians observe these ceremonies. As writer Peggy Pond Church once noted, when the Pueblo Indians dance, they dance for us all.[11]

Most non-Indians can appreciate the Native American reliance on properly performed ritual to sustain their faith. Non-Indians who share strict divisions between the secular and the sacred (Saturday night/ Sunday morning, earthy blues/gospel hymns, etc.) have had more dif-

A dance at Santa Clara Pueblo, New Mexico, c. 1930. Ever since the 1970s, outsiders have become more aware of the ancient Native American spiritual traditions. Historic Native concern for the natural environment may well provide a basis for ecumenicism in the twenty-first century.

ficulty in comprehending the Native position that nothing in life stands outside the realm of religion. Yet this too lies at the heart of Native faith. From this perspective the concept of "church" can never be separated from that of "state," for both are subsumed under a larger, sacred umbrella. Everything in life is thus linked to everything else through a "sacred reciprocity."[12] "The whole universe is one perfect being, and we fit in there somewhere," a Navajo leader remarked in 1991. "We spend our lives trying to find a way of fitting in perfectly, and in the process we gain knowledge."[13] If everything is sacred, however, Judeo-Christian terms like "theology," "religion," and "church" have much reduced significance.

This umbrella concept of the sacred stands in sharp contrast to Judeo-Christian understanding. In the western world, the sacred is often limited. It encompasses items such as a church, the Bible, the consecrated host, an altar, the Ark of the Covenant, or burial grounds. The sacred is best expressed in symbols: Scripture, a Star of David, a crucifix, a cross, the golden plates, sometimes an altar. To desecrate any of these symbols is to engage in symbolic warfare. But if the sacred encompasses all aspects of life, where does one draw the line between ordinary activity and "desecration"?

The presence of Native sacred sites on federal or state land has produced a variety of compromises in this regard. In several cases, such as Blue Lake (sacred to Taos Pueblo) and Mount Adams (sacred to the Yakama), the government has returned the sites to Native control. Local federal and state officials also try to insure regular access to other sacred sites for seasonal rituals. Yet this is fraught with controversy. Cave Rock near Lake Tahoe, Nevada, for example, has attracted rock climbers from around the world, and the climbers have drilled several hundred bolts into the rock's surface. The Washoe, however, consider this the desecration of a sacred site used for spiritual renewal, not unlike rappelling over the Western Wall in Jerusalem or up the sides of the National Cathedral. The Forest Service, which manages the site, has had to mediate between these groups, so far with minimal success.

Equally troublesome for federal managers are the various New Age borrowings of Native American ceremonials and sites. Perhaps the most prominent Native American religious symbol is the medicine wheel. These stone circles have been found in several areas of the northern Plains. The most well known is probably the Big Horn Medicine Wheel, which lies at 10,000 feet in the Big Horn Mountains in Wyoming. Numerous New Age adherents have re-created similar medicine wheels in various western areas to perform eclectic ceremonial rites. In Sedona, Arizona, federal land officials have spent much effort dismantling these crude circles. Finally, they decided to leave the largest intact, hoping it would suffice for all ceremonies. Every New Age holiday—May Day, the spring and fall equinoxes, Midsummer Night's Eve, Halloween, the winter solstice—inspires a rash of ceremonies at various locations that are deemed to have "harmonic convergences." Park rangers in Chaco Canyon National Park have had to close Casa Rinconada to the public because of these activities. Federal officials at Bandelier National Park have been similarly forced to delete the site of the ancient stone lions (sacred to the Cochiti) from park maps to discourage such observances.[14] Once when two northern Plains medicine men approached the Big Horn Medicine Wheel, they discovered a nude white woman stretched out, she said, in prayer. (This is not a traditional Native ceremony.)[15]

Native spiritual leaders have been perplexed by this situation. Although Native ceremonies are intended for all people, they complain that New Age groups have "stolen" their concepts for their own purposes, sometimes for financial profit. So far this protest has had little deterrent effect. As the western New Thought groups could not control the spread of metaphysical ideas during the fin de siècle years, so too have modern Native leaders had difficulty restricting the borrowing from Indian spirituality.

As the ceremonies surrounding the quincentenary of Columbus showed, the five hundred years of Native-European-African interaction have had many ramifications. In the wake of these observances, angry Natives often blamed the arrival of Christianity in America as the cause of all their woes. The anti-Christian response has taken on a number of forms. One southwestern pueblo publicly desecrated the cross, while another interrupted a 1996 Christmas Eve Mass by holding a Native dance in the church sanctuary. On the northern Plains the Sioux have reinstituted the once forbidden Sun Dance. Everywhere long-neglected ceremonies have suddenly taken on new life for a younger generation of Native people. A Christian/traditionalist tension exists on many reservations.

Spokespeople for several churches have recognized the legitimacy of many of these Native claims. There have been two prominent attempts at reconciliation. In November 1987 a task force that included Roman Catholics, Episcopalians, Presbyterians, the Lutheran Church of America, the United Church of Christ, and others issued a formal apology to the Natives in the Pacific Northwest for the actions of their ancestors. Known as the "Bishops' Apology," this document asked forgiveness and concluded: "May the God of Abraham and Sarah, and the Spirit who lives in both the Cedar and Salmon People, be honored and celebrated."[16]

In August 1993, on his way to a mass rally in Denver, Colorado, Pope John Paul II gave a speech in Izamal, Mexico. There he admitted that the early Christians from Spain had treated the Native peoples badly. But the pontiff assured his audience that the contemporary Catholic Church fully supported their crusades for human dignity.[17]

During the 1980s this historical tension between Catholicism and the Native faith tradition was brought into the headlines again by the California Catholic community's efforts to beatify Franciscan Junipero Serra, founder of the California mission system. California's active Catholic lobby had long been engaged in this quest, and Father Serra had passed the first of three hurdles necessary for sainthood. But in the late twentieth century, California Natives began to protest. What the Church did was its own business, they said, but since Serra had whipped and punished their ancestors, they argued that he should not be officially recognized as a California state hero.

Serra defenders, usually Franciscan historians, suggested that eighteenth-century figures should be judged by eighteenth-century standards. Although Serra may have been harsh toward the Indians, they noted, he was equally harsh toward himself. The Indian missions were but an extended patriarchal great family, argues Francis J. Weber, the archivist for the Archdiocese of Los Angeles. "To call it slavery as unscrupulous writers do is evidence of a warped mind."[18] At this time, the canonization of Father Serra has stalled. This incident shows the limits of *any* religious tradition encompassing the entirety of the western social order.

In spite of these tensions, the dominant religious aspect of this five-hundred-year-old encounter between Christianity and Native faiths has been one of syncretization, which has occurred along numerous lines. An old Native joke states that when the Cherokee are asked to sing a traditional song, they often choose "Onward Christian Soldiers." Many of the prominent Native revival movements reflect a Christian component. Lakota Sioux holy man Black Elk's writings reveal this syncretization to perfection. When John G. Neihardt published *Black Elk Speaks* (1932), Neihardt portrayed the old Sioux as thoroughly Native. As recent studies by ethnohistorian Ray deMallie have shown, however, Black Elk was simultaneously an active Catholic apostle to the Sioux. Throughout his life, Black Elk was a typical example of walking multiculturalism.[19] Contemporary Native worship services reflect this syncretization on a number of levels. Perhaps the ultimate example may be seen in the 1995 passing of a middle-aged Navajo woman. The funeral was held at the Presbyterian church in Piñon. Burial was in the traditional family burial ground in Smoke Signal on the reservation. Rosary was recited in Cope Memorial Chapel in Gallup.[20]

━━━━━━━

In 1909 black scholar W. E. B. DuBois termed the church "the social centre of Negro life in the United States, and the most characteristic expression of African character."[21] In 1939 historian Carter G. Woodson observed that a definitive history of the African-American Church would touch on virtually all aspects of African-American history.[22]

These statements have assumed canonical status. Scholars might dispute the persistence or absence of African features in contemporary American religious life or debate whether the black church has been primarily liberal or conservative, but they concur that, as an institution, the church has lain at the heart of the African-American experience in the United States. As Constance Thomas of Seattle recently recalled, "If you were a young black person [new] to the city, the first place you would always go would be the church. . . . That's how you met black people. Social events and musicals—all that was part of the church; the biggest barbecue of the year was held at Mount Zion. We knew everybody through the church."[23]

African Americans' sense of themselves as a people has historically included a religious dimension. Consequently, the churches found themselves playing many roles. First, they interpreted and reinterpreted what modern scholars have termed the "black sacred cosmos."[24] This worldview, which reflected the continuous presence of the divine, derived in part from indigenous African themes and in part from appropriation and internalization of borrowed aspects from (primarily Protestant) Christianity.[25] African-American Islam and African-American Judaism show similar convergence. In addition, the black church has echoed the ideas of "freedom," "deliverance," and, especially, "love and forgiveness." Outsiders have usually been welcome at black services, and rarely has black Christianity held grudges.[26] On a social level, church involvement in the community remains strong. As Rev. Wyatt Tee Walker recently commented, "The most important ministry of the African-American Church is that it heals the brokenness so rampant in Black life."[27]

Since slavery days produced primarily an oral culture, the African-American community has long recognized the person who displayed the "gift of words." Frequently this person became a preacher. A 1944 observer described the black minister in Oklahoma as "lawyer, preacher, doctor, and business manager for his church. He is the Moses of his people."[28] From the days of Nat Turner forward, black clerics have been prominent beyond their numbers. Martin Luther King, Jr., was probably the most important minister of the entire postwar American world, regardless of color.

Because the black church reflects a corporate as much as an individual identity, it has persisted at the same time white mainline churches have seen their numbers tumble. In the 1990s nine of the fifteen fastest growing American churches were primarily black. Black Pentecostals have been the leaders in this regard. Perhaps one reason for this sustained growth may concern local involvement. A national survey discovered that while white churches expressed much interest in national or international affairs, black churches were primarily concerned with filling local needs.[29]

In the American West, black churches assumed all these roles. Seattle's First African Methodist Episcopal Church dates from 1886 and Mount Zion Baptist from 1890. Members often met newcomers at the railway station to invite them to supper. Similarly, the "Baptist Prayer Band" of 1890s Salt Lake City formed the core of the first African-American church in the heart of Zion. The 1906 Azusa Street revival in Los Angeles had one foot in the black experience, and during the Great Depression the black churches in the rural West survived—sometimes on two cents per person—when black businesses often did not.

The greatest growth, however, came with World War II. From the 1940s onward, observers considered the West as the place to pioneer new race relations. While North and South had their racial customs firmly in place, the rapidly developing West Coast cities were viewed as a new frontier for cultural interaction. (Black migration largely bypassed the Intermountain West.) San Francisco served as home to many of these experiments. Rev. E. E. Hamilton (Church of God), Rev. H. B. Gantt (First African Methodist Episcopal), Rev. Hamilton T. Boswell (Jones Methodist), Rev. F. D. Haynes (Third Baptist), and Rev. Howard Thurman (Fellowship Church) all pastored important World War II–era black churches in the Bay Area. They led the black ministerial alliance that continually argued for equal employment, housing, and public services.[30]

Rev. Howard Thurman assumed an even more challenging role. Enticed to San Francisco by liberal Presbyterian cleric and San Francisco State University philosophy professor Alfred G. Fiske, Thurman arrived to head an interracial church in wartime San Francisco. The Church for the Fellowship of All Peoples had a racially mixed board, Sunday school, staff, and choir. Thurman always claimed it as the first fully integrated church in the United States.[31] Thurman also interacted with the white ministerial world as well.

In Los Angeles the black church assumed a similar role. The oldest L.A. black denomination, founded by former slave Biddy Mason in her living room in 1872, became the powerful First African Methodist Episcopal Church. Rev. H. H. Brookins served as long-time pastor (1959–72) and as L.A. bishop (1976–84). During this time he oversaw church growth to five thousand members and molded the political career of later mayor Tom Bradley. First AME also played a major role in the California civil rights movement.

First AME continues its prominence up to the present day. The church runs twenty-five task forces, maintains a program for reclaiming street people, and oversees numerous housing units. It also has a strong focus on programs for boys and young men, perhaps as a rival to the message broadcast from Louis Farrakhan's Nation of Islam. Even so, First AME has long maintained a relationship with the Black Muslims and has held Muslim funerals in its sanctuary. With pulpit exchanges with the local Jewish Temple Isaiah and community meetings with local Asians and Latinos, it has remained vital for over a century. Said Rev. Cecil L. Murry, current pastor, "A useless Black church is demonic."[32]

Other contemporary West Coast black churches have had similar regional impact. At the Crenshaw Christian Center of Los Angeles, an independent charismatic church, Rev. Frederick Pierce preaches the controversial Word of Faith message. This position claims that God will supply anything if followers will only believe sufficiently. More traditional are Rev. J. Alfred Smithing, Sr., who pastors Oakland's popular Allen Temple Baptist Church, and Rev. Samuel McKinney, pastor of Seattle's Mt. Zion Baptist Church. The Seattle area today claims over a hundred black churches.[33]

Rev. Cecil Williams has emerged as perhaps the most important of the West Coast African-American clerics. In 1963 he moved to the Glide Memorial Methodist Church in San Francisco (the gift of Lizzie H. Glide, wife of a Sacramento oil millionaire) as director of community involvement. Three years later he took over as minister. Since that time Glide Memorial and Cecil Williams have become well known throughout the West and the nation.

Born September 22, 1929, in San Angelo, Texas, Albert Cecil Williams suffered a mental and physical breakdown at age twelve because of racial discrimination in his hometown. He became healed through the ministrations of his family and the local black community. Williams attended Huston-Tillotson College in Austin for his B.A. and Perkins School of Theology in Dallas for his B.D. (1955). He soon became involved in the emerging civil rights movement and also worked as chaplain and taught at his undergraduate alma mater. In addition, he served a year in a segregated Methodist church in Hobbs, New Mexico.

When he arrived at Glide Memorial, Williams quickly realized that the small (roughly thirty-five people), mostly white church on the edge of San Francisco's Tenderloin district could never be a traditional church. After experimenting with a variety of techniques, he brought in John Handy and his jazz group for a Christmas Eve service. This filled the church pews, and they have remained filled for thirty years.

Williams has played a visible role in virtually every social issue for three decades. Named local "Man of the Year" in 1967, the next year he became embroiled in controversy with San Francisco State University President S. I. Hayakawa over campus racial matters.[34] In 1974 his name was found on the "death list" of the young black man who shot and killed Mrs. Martin Luther King, Sr.[35] When heiress Patty Hearst was abducted by the Symbionese Liberation Army that same year, Williams served as a liaison between the organization and the Hearst family.[36] By this time he had emerged as one of the most prominent black clergymen in the West. In the 1980 presidential election, candidate John Anderson sought and received his endorsement.

Williams's reputation largely derived from two trends: his unique spiritual message and his thorough grounding in the black Methodist social gospel tradition. Williams once termed himself a "folk minister" who drew on the folk tradition of "honesty"—the message from the heart—that he perceived in the historic black community and in the Hebrew community that wrote the original Scriptures.[37] The church exists as an extended human family, he said; it is not simply an organization for believers. Jesus Christ "came to bring us life, to bring us freedom, to empower us, and to bring us together."[38] Thus, Glide Memorial services tended to be largely celebratory, filled with powerful music and personal testimony. Herb Caen called them "theatrical in the extreme," but Oprah Winfrey's comment proved more charitable. "I haven't seen a church like this," she said. "I haven't seen a church that is really racially mixed and where the White folks can sing!"[39]

The second part of his message rested in an extensive social gospel program. Williams's church not only provided the same sort of services that one found in San Francisco at the turn of the century, it also added newer, appropriate social services for the modern day. These included computer instruction and classes to aid people with drug and alcohol addiction and anger management.

Williams proved very creative in these areas. Given the location of his church, he tried to develop a "theology of recovery" that relied on the presence of the Holy Spirit to liberate people from a variety of addictions. Every person has power, he notes, but no individual has ultimate power. This alone is reserved for God. True empowerment is measured by the good that is offered to the extended family of humanity.

Williams was one of the first clerics to recognize the dangers of crack cocaine to the local black community, and in 1969 he organized a national conference on this theme. He also tried to evolve a specifically black version of the twelve-step recovery programs that relied on traditional African-American community support as well as individual actions. All along he stressed the power of narrative and story as a means of healing. When the AIDS epidemic broke out, he established the Glide/Goodlett AIDS Project, which gave out "safe sex" kits and provided AIDS testing after Sunday services. In all these endeavors he has been aided by his wife and chief assistant, Janice Mirikitani.

The services at Glide Memorial have not only regularly filled the pews, they have drawn visits from a wide variety of public figures, including comedian Bill Cosby, San Francisco mayor Willie Brown, athlete Willie Mays, poet Maya Angelou, activist Angela Davis, musician Leonard Bernstein, John F. Kennedy, Jr., and President Bill Clinton. Once President Clinton personally called Reverend Williams to thank him for organizing a free Thanksgiving Day meal for 6,500 people. Williams has promoted tolerance for divergent lifestyles (Glide has many gay members) and religious diversity and argues that the nation must do the same if it is to survive. As he once phrased it, "We've got black and white, gay and straight, upper class, lower class, and no class here at Glide."[40] The church is just completing a million-dollar homeless shelter next door. Under the guidance of Rev. Cecil Williams, Glide Memorial Methodist Church has become the most comprehensive provider of human services for the entire city of San Francisco.

Cecil Williams also drew heavily on the power of music for his success. His services have assumed a "performance" quality. He has included many aspects of the black musical tradition, especially the gospel songs pioneered by Thomas Andrew Dorsey. Dorsey began his career by composing double entendre (Saturday night) blues songs, but in 1928 he underwent a conversion and devoted the rest of his career to writing Sunday morning Gospel music. As critic Arthur Kempton noted, Dorsey's gift was to "transmute blues into sacred song." He did so through such classics as "Take My Hand, Precious Lord," "If You See My Savior (Tell Him That You Saw Me)," and "Peace in the Valley." So popular was he that during the 1930s gospel songs were actually termed "Dorseys." Singers Mahalia Jackson, Sam Cooke, and Aretha Franklin took this Gospel genre into the public and popular realm.[41] Glide Memorial services insure that it remains prominent.

In the early 1960s the son of a seminary-trained minister moved to the West Coast. There he exchanged his European name for an African one, Maulana Karenga, and currently serves as chairman of the Black Studies Department at Cal State University, Long Beach. In 1966 Karenga created a new holiday he termed Kwanzaa to celebrate African-American heritage. Lasting seven days and straddling the New Year, Kwanzaa devotes each day to a major concept. They are:

1. Umoja, December 26, devoted to unity and peaceful togetherness.
2. Kujichagulia, self-determination.
3. Ujina, community and collective responsibility.
4. Ujamaa, cooperative economics, that is, patronizing black businesses.
5. Nia, purpose.
6. Kuumba, creativity.
7. Faith.

In numerous speeches Karenga has argued that the appeal of Kwanzaa is a universal one, open to blacks and whites alike, for it is based in "spiritual grounding and moral achievement."[42] From this base, Kwanzaa has grown to national status. It now shares the winter holiday season with Christmas and Hanukkah.

One of the most striking aspects of the post-1960 western religious scene lay with the emergence of Asian faiths. In *Turning East* (1977)

Harvard theologian Harvey Cox charted his personal experience with this phenomenon, voicing his concern in his subtitle: "the promise and peril of the new Orientalism."[43] By the time Cox wrote, however, Asian faiths had become a very visible part of West Coast life.

The Asian faiths had a long history on the West Coast, especially in California. By 1900 Chinese immigrants had established perhaps four hundred temples in the region. Located in the hearts of the various Chinatowns, these modest organizations often provided a unique mixture of Taoism, Confucianism, and Buddhism.[44] In 1899 the Japanese Buddhists established a mission that later evolved into the Buddhist Churches of America. These groups provided the same social support as the ethnic churches of the Great Plains.

Asian philosophy initially reached non—Asian Americans through Transcendentalism, Theosophy, and the spokesmen who attended the World's Parliament of Religions, held in conjunction with the Chicago World's Fair of 1893.[45] The American lectures of D. T. Suzuki (1950–58) influenced a wide number of literary figures, such as Allen Ginsberg, Jack Kerouac, and Gary Snyder, as well as composer John Cage. The 1959 flight from Tibet by the Dalai Lama and over 100,000 Tibetans also popularized such thinking.

The most successful popularizer of Buddhism during this era, however, was probably English-born former Episcopal priest Alan Watts. Moving to California in the 1950s, Watts formed the American Academy of Asian Studies in San Francisco, the first center strictly devoted to Asian philosophy. Through hundreds of public lectures and over twenty books, Watts argued for the necessity of mysticism in religious life.[46] His message merged with the California-based human potential movement, the consciousness explosion, the popularity of drugs, and the general hunger for meaning that pervaded the 1960s.[47] Through his lifestyle and his connections with the West Coast literary scene, Alan Watts became a central religious popularizer of the 1960s, the "Norman Vincent Peale" of Zen. From fad of the 1950s, Buddhism by the 1970s appeared to offer a viable alternative to Christianity and Judaism in West Coast America.

Scholars puzzled over the appeal of Buddhism, particularly Zen. Zen's emphasis on the goal of Enlightenment through overcoming self-will, the Four Noble Traits and Eightfold Faith, and an emphasis on quietism seemed very foreign to the American character of pushing to get ahead. One observer felt that the growth of Buddhism could be traced to "widespread disillusionment with Christianity and Judaism in having failed to respond adequately to the ills of society."[48]

Although statistically few non—Asian Americans actually joined Buddhist churches, many Christians and Jews embraced their idea of meditation. While the Judeo-Christian tradition contains a meditational heritage of its own, meditation in Western life had historically been restricted to monks, nuns, and mystics. Thanks to Suzuki, Watts, and the Buddhist centers in Berkeley and Boulder, however, meditation has become "democratized." Both Roman Catholic and Episcopal writers soon began to merge Zen ideas with historic Christianity.[49] As the religious editor of *Publishers Weekly* has noted, during the last fifteen years many major book reviews have been sympathetic to Buddhist writings.[50]

Moreover, from another perspective, many Buddhist ideas seem to be congruent with western concepts: individualism (one can achieve Enlightenment on one's own), secularism (Buddhism is nontheistic, and some deny that it is truly a religion), democracy (Buddhism transcends race, class, and gender), and ecology (most Buddhists are vegetarians, and all adherents respect Nature).

Whatever the reason, since the 1970s Buddhism has spread throughout the West. A Wasatch Zen group emerged in Salt Lake City by 1984, and several hundred more appeared along the Pacific Coast a decade later. California alone had perhaps a dozen Tibetan retreat centers. The culmination came on June 1996 when Buddhists erected a twelve-million-dollar temple and monument complex near Sonoma, California. Located on a 1,000-acre plateau overlooking the Pacific, this complex has been compared favorably with any Asian monument. One observer termed it a "tour de force" of Buddhist architecture.[51] Since the new complex houses a massive library that includes many priceless documents from Tibet, the structure will serve scholars and researchers as well. It also firmly announces the Buddhist coming of age in the American West.

Although there were individual exceptions, most Protestant, Catholic, Jewish, and Mormon communities made little protest to the onset of the Cold War and national nuclear defense policy. The polemics of theologian Reinhold Niebuhr, especially his argument for the need to oppose force with force, the traditional Catholic doctrine of a "just war," and Jewish concern over the survival of Israel, made for few religious protests from 1945 to the early 1960s.[52]

The multifaceted American peace movement proved the major exception. Formed by a loose alliance among the historic peace churches (Mennonites, Quakers, Church of the Brethren) plus Catholic radicals and the *Christian Century,* American pacifism remained an elitist, marginal crusade until the mid-1960s. As late as 1960, scientist J. Robert Oppenheimer remarked, "I find myself profoundly anguished over the fact that no ethical discourse of any nobility or weight has been addressed to the problem of atomic weapons."[53]

Vatican II, the Vietnam War, the nuclear build-up of the 1970s, and the election of Ronald Reagan in 1980 led to a variety of changes. Afterward, churches and synagogues returned to biblical admonitions and to prophetic condemnation of America's nuclear weapons program. The pope played a major role here as well. Ever since he assumed the pontificate in 1978, Pope John Paul II has called for the elimination of nuclear arms.

Although early-twentieth-century pacifism had largely been a Protestant position, radical Catholics such as Dorothy Day, Robert Ludlow, and Ammon Hennacy helped extend the pacifist view into the Catholic Church. The formation of Pax Christi, a Catholic peacemaking organization, plus the popular voice of Trappist monk Thomas Merton (the first "nuclear pacifist"), helped to forge what critics have termed the "great Catholic peace conspiracy."

The strongest statement in this regard came from the National Conference of Catholic Bishops in May 1983. After months of discussion they issued a 44,000-word pastoral letter, *The Challenge of Peace: God's Promise and Our Response,* which Cardinal Joseph Bernardin of Chicago termed "perhaps the most important and timely Pastoral Letter ever to come from the American hierarchy in its nearly two centuries of existence." This document reflected a clear break from the government's positions on nuclear arms and nuclear deterrence. In it the bishops set forth a Catholic theology of peace that dismissed both first use of such weapons and retaliation against any nuclear attack. Their opposition to nuclear war was unequivocal: no Christian could carry out orders that were aimed at destroying noncombatants, they said. They accepted the overall umbrella of nuclear deterrence, but only as a framework by which to negotiate nuclear arms control, the reduction of the arms race, and eventual disarmament.[54]

A number of clerics were involved in the movement. Radical Josephite priests Daniel and Philip Berrigan, founders of the Catholic Peace Fellowship, were early pacifists. Omaha priest Jack McCoslin was arrested so many times for protesting America's nuclear policy that the conservative bishop of Lincoln threatened to excommunicate him. But the two most noted figures in this crusade were western bishops: Bishop Leroy T. Matthiesen of Amarillo and Archbishop Raymond G. Hunthausen of Seattle. Their positions extended well beyond mere theory, for each had a major nuclear installation within his diocese.

Born into a German-American family in central West Texas, Leroy T. Matthiesen grew up familiar with both hunting and guns. He served in Amarillo as a parish priest from 1948 forward. He was appointed bishop in 1980. One of the largest industries located in the Panhandle region is Pantex, the final assembly plant for the nation's vast nuclear weapons industry. (With the end of the Cold War, it serves as a *dis*assembly plant for nuclear weapons.) In the early 1980s it employed over two thousand people, many of them members of the Catholic Church. Matthiesen confessed that he had thought little about the situation until 1981, when a Catholic employee of Pantex and his wife sought his counsel regarding the morality of weapons work. The issue was complicated by public hearings over possibly locating the elaborate MX missile defense system west of Amarillo, plans to store nuclear waste in the Panhandle, and the announcement by President Ronald Reagan in August 1981 of plans to proceed with the production of the neutron bomb, which killed people by radiation but left equipment largely intact. After rereading the works of Martin Luther King, Jr., Matthiesen concluded that the national choice lay between "nonviolence and nonexistence."[55] A member of Pax Christi, Matthiesen had lobbied to strengthen the pacifist passages in the bishops' 1983 statement. He received the most notoriety, however, from a brief statement in the Amarillo diocese newsletter. There he called on all individual Catholics involved either in the manufacture or stockpiling of nuclear weapons at Pantex to quit work and find employment elsewhere. He argued that continual preparation for nuclear warfare was a sin and that reasoned objection to such work formed an act of responsible Christian witness.[56]

Local newspapers instantly seized on this appeal, and soon the shy bishop found himself featured in numerous periodicals. He even appeared on television talk shows. His position also provoked intense local discussion. The opposition proved strenuous, with many Methodists and Baptists holding contrary views. Although some of his attackers implied that Matthiesen might be a Communist or even a traitor, they never descended to the rhetoric of traditional anti-Catholicism.[57] Although Catholicism has never been the predominant faith in this region of the Panhandle, for several years in the early 1980s Bishop Leroy T. Matthiesen was the area's most celebrated cleric.

The archbishop of Seattle, Raymond G. Hunthausen, became even more controversial than Matthiesen. Like his fellow bishop, Hunthausen was born into a German-American family but in Anaconda, Montana. He attended Carroll College and Saint Edwards Seminary in Seattle, taught at his alma mater, and was made bishop of Helena in 1962. In 1975 he was installed as archbishop of Seattle. An ascetic who lived modestly and often traveled by foot, he developed his pacifist views shortly after taking office. Although he later confessed that he had been against nuclear weapons from the moment he learned of Hiroshima, he had not spoken out on this issue until 1976. That year he read an article by Richard McSorley, S.J., called "It's a Sin to Build a Nuclear Weapon" and gradually became convinced that this issue overwhelmed all other moral concerns of his day. His diocese included Bangor Navy Base, across Puget Sound from Seattle, which housed nuclear submarines. Many of his parishioners were involved in this aspect of the defense industry.

By the early 1980s Hunthausen had become perhaps the most prominent western spokesman against nuclear weapons. He broadcast the fact that one nuclear submarine could strike 408 separate target areas. He also often pointed to the social waste that the nuclear industry entailed. All such weapons, he said, had been built at the expense of the nation's poor: "Jesus must weep at such a world."[58] He also maintained that a person should be responsible for his or her own backyard and once termed the Trident base the "Auschwitz of Puget Sound."[59]

Deciding that the Church must speak out, he called for fasting and prayer on each Monday. He publicly supported local Catholic pacifist writer Jim Douglass and appeared at antinuclear rallies at Bangor Navy Base. In addition, he called for unilateral nuclear disarmament. This caused considerable local dissension, but it was his public refusal to pay his federal income taxes that made his name a national one. In June 1982 Hunthausen declared that he would withhold half of his federal tax payment and give it to charity. After this he received endless invitations to speak and became a local celebrity. This position, plus his liberal stance on homosexuality, also led to a two-year apostolic investigation by representatives from the Vatican. When the Holy See tried to reduce his diocesan power in 1986, public outcry was enormous. Over three thousand Catholics, including two hundred Seattle priests plus sixty fellow bishops, wrote to support his stance. Eventually the Vatican backed down.[60]

Such views, naturally, brought forth rebuttal. Conservatives declared that the antinuclear bishops were out of their depth when they ventured to discuss the intricate world of defense systems. One Catholic writer described Hunthausen's position as "noisy pacifism."[61] The Catholic Church of Los Alamos compiled a hefty pamphlet that argued in favor of the nation's elaborate nuclear defense systems.

As the Cold War has officially ended, it is difficult to evaluate the momentarily high public profiles given to Matthiesen and Hunthausen. But the widespread publicity surely elevated a local issue involving a nuclear installation into a national one. It also transcended traditional Catholic Church boundaries to encompass people from all religious persuasions. In Utah, for example, a combination of Catholic, Shoshoni, and LDS sentiment halted the potential placement of the MX system along the Utah/Nevada border. The Native Americans, Catholics, and Mormons utilized essentially religious arguments to halt this program.[62] During the 1980s the question of defense systems, nuclear arms buildup, and deterrence moved from religious circles to the public realm, from where it has not yet retreated.

———

This section profiles a unique western religious institution: Loma Linda Sanitarium/College of Medical Evangelists, renamed Loma Linda University in 1961. Located near Redlands, California, the school was founded by the Seventh-Day Adventists (SDA) in 1905. Although the church is, of course, worldwide, a significant SDA minority live in southern California, and Loma Linda has emerged as the most prominent sectarian medical school of the region.[63]

The Seventh-Day Adventists trace their origin to the millennial expectations fostered by Baptist preacher William Miller in upstate New

York during the 1840s. After Miller's predictions of End Time failed to materialize, a small band of Adventists looked to the teachings of Ellen Gould Harmon White (1827–1915), who helped organize the denomination in 1863. White experienced "visions" or trances from age seventeen on, and her followers considered her able to foretell the future. They credited her with predicting the American Civil War and the San Francisco earthquake of 1906, among other events. They also viewed her writings on health as special gifts from the Holy Spirit.[64]

It is in the realm of health care that the SDA movement has had the biggest impact on American life. White considered Christianity and health as interrelated. She wrote and spoke prodigiously on health improvements of all kinds. She advocated vegetarianism, especially supplemented by dried fruits and nuts, and denounced salt, sugar, tobacco, alcohol, coffee, tea, stimulants, and drugs. Her writings on these and other matters were extensive. She published over thirty books in her lifetime, and her followers have gathered her materials together to produce about thirty more. Although not well known outside SDA circles, Ellen G. White was perhaps the nation's most prolific woman writer of her day.

In 1866 one of her long-held dreams, the Western Health Reform Institute in Battle Creek, Michigan (later Battle Creek Sanitarium, with a related American Medical Missionary College), opened its doors to treat an epidemic of Gilded Age health care problems. Dr. John Harvey Kellogg soon took over the leadership of the institution and in his quest for "biologic living" invented flaked wheat, corn flakes, granola, a sorghum coffee substitute, peanut butter, and a number of other health foods. One patient, C. W. Post, allegedly "borrowed" the recipes to create his own Post Toasties and Postum. By 1900 thousands had sought improved health at Battle Creek, and John Harvey Kellogg had become the most famous Seventh-Day Adventist in the world.[65]

Eventually, White and Kellogg quarreled, and in 1907 the church officially "disfellowshipped" Kellogg. One point of disagreement lay with Kellogg's wish to make the Battle Creek Medical Missionary College nondenominational. One result of this clash, however, was to send White (who had moved to northern California) in search of a new medical college that would remain under SDA denominational auspices.

After her husband's death in 1881, Ellen White had traveled the world to follow the spread of Adventism. During her time in Australia she realized that church medical work proved the best way to dispel prejudice against the movement's view of End Time. In 1899 she concluded that nothing converted "the people like the medical missionary work." Consequently, in 1900 she wrote a pamphlet that urged the denomination to use medicine as the "entering wedge" for the faith.[66] For this she needed a denominational medical school. In 1905 she instructed follower John Burden to place a down payment on a twice-failed sanitarium complex near Redlands, California, called Loma Linda.

Establishing a sectarian medical school during the Progressive Era was fraught with difficulties. The SDA church had only 11,000 members, few of them wealthy.[67] In addition, the 1910 report by Abraham Flexner animated the powerful American Medical Association to either weed out or improve the various "one-horse" medical schools of the day. The SDA's fledgling College of Medical Evangelists barely survived AMA inspections until 1922, when it finally earned its first "Class A" rating. As the denomination's only medical school, Loma Linda introduced new themes of SDA dietetics and steadily graduated both nurses and physicians (many female) during the interwar years. During the Second World War, Loma Linda boosted its physical therapy and radiology programs and in 1948 organized the School of Tropical and Preventive Medicine (later the School of Public Health). The Loma Linda School of Dentistry graduated its first class in 1957. In 1963 a traveling medical missionary team pioneered open heart surgery in a number of Third World countries. Missionary work, either overseas or on the Navajo Reservation, has long been part of Loma Linda medical training.

Although southern Californians were well acquainted with Loma Linda University, the world first learned of it on October 26, 1984. That day a surgical team from the medical school transplanted a baboon's heart into a twelve-day-old girl named Baby Fae who had been born with a fatal heart defect. Although Baby Fae lived only twenty days, she became the forerunner of Loma Linda's more successful surgeries: infant human-to-human heart transplants. Because an infant's body has an underdeveloped immune system, such organ transplants often have better chances of success than those involving adults. As of 1991 Loma Linda has performed ninety of these operations on infants, of which seventy-one have been successful.[68]

Naturally, a great deal of controversy surrounded these ventures.

Since most donor baby hearts came from anencephalic infants (babies born with most or all of the brain missing), the medical community had to develop an elaborate protocol regarding such actions. The ethics of such ventures became grist for many a television talk show. The enormous publicity surrounding this event—1,500 media contacts every day for a brief period—introduced many Americans to both Loma Linda Medical Center and the tenets of the SDA denomination.

Self-described as conservative evangelical Christians, the approximately eight-million-member denomination emphasizes biblical literalism (including a strong suspicion of evolution); keeping the Sabbath (a foretaste of heaven) from Friday night to Saturday night; anticipation of an imminent Second Advent (the door to Heaven); and, especially, an emphasis on vegetarianism and healthy lifestyles (the cafeteria at Loma Linda University has long been famous for its "health burgers").

The medical missionary work of Loma Linda University forms an integral part of the SDA faith perspective. From modest beginnings at the turn of the century, Loma Linda has grown into one of the foremost sectarian medical schools of the West.

During his 1997 State of the Union speech, President Bill Clinton singled out Rev. Robert H. Schuller, who sat at the side of First Lady Hillary Rodham Clinton, for special recognition. Investigative reporters soon discovered that the head pastor of California's Crystal Cathedral had quietly been advising Clinton since the midterm election of 1994. He had even shared a private prayer with the president in the Lincoln Bedroom of the White House. After the Democratic election victory in November 1996, Schuller congratulated Clinton and included his favorite Bible verse, Isaiah 58:12: "You shall be called the repairer of the breach, the restorer of paths to dwell in." Clinton asked his speechwriters to work that passage into his inaugural address.[69]

In 1997 Robert H. Schuller needed little introduction to most Americans. At that time he was, perhaps, the most widely recognized cleric of the late twentieth century. Schuller is the author of thirty-one books, and his "Hour of Power" Sunday morning television program has been reaching an estimated 20 million viewers in 184 nations for more than twenty-five years. During his worldwide travels, Schuller has conversed with the great figures of the day: India's Mother Teresa, members of

Dr. Robert H. Schuller, pastor of the Crystal Cathedral in Garden Grove, California. With his widely televised "Hour of Power" church service and his over thirty books, Schuller is probably the most famous cleric in the contemporary West.

the Israeli cabinet, Palestinian leader Yasir Arafat, and key Russian officials. His Crystal Cathedral had become world famous not only for its architectural beauty and multicultural staff but also for its full line of programs. The cathedral offers worship services, support group classes, counseling centers, telephone crisis counseling, singles and divorce recovery programs, a senior ministry, and a youth ministry. In addition, it boasts a gymnasium and workout facility. In his forty-year career, Schuller built it all from scratch.[70]

Although generally slighted by students of American religion, Schuller has become a major postwar religious figure, both theologically and culturally. A native of Iowa, he made a career move in 1955 that made him the right person in the right place. The place was Orange County in southern California.

Born on September 16, 1926, Robert Schuller grew to maturity in a family of five amidst a Dutch-American community in northwestern Iowa. His parents were staunch members of the First Reformed Church in Orange City, Iowa, and they struggled constantly to make their small farm succeed. Schuller later confessed that his philosophy of life was largely shaped by watching his family and neighbors battle the drought and storms of the Depression years.

After high school, Schuller attended the Dutch Reformed Hope College in Holland, Michigan, and after graduation in 1947 enrolled in the nearby Western Theological Seminary. His B.D. thesis consisted of a scriptural and topical index for John Calvin's *Institutes of the Christian Religion*. To prepare this work he read through Calvin's *Institutes* ten times. During this period he courted and married Arvella De Haan, who became his life-long rock of stability, chief advisor, and an author in her own right. Together they raised five children.[71]

In 1955 Rev. Schuller accepted a call to Orange County, California, where the family arrived with two small children and $500. His assignment was to start a Dutch Reformed Church in that rapidly burgeoning area. Nationwide, his church contained only 200,000 members, and after surveying the neighborhood he found only two denominational families.[72] Thus, Schuller discarded the term "Reformed" and began the "Garden Grove Community Church." He held his first services in the Orange County drive-in movie theater, preceded by an advertising campaign that suggested: "Come as you are in the family car."[73]

One of the best-selling books of the mid-1950s was Rev. Norman Vincent Peale's *Power of Positive Thinking*. A fellow Dutch Reformed cleric and pastor of the Marble Collegiate Church in New York City, Peale had great influence on young Schuller. Not only did Peale write introductions for Schuller's first books, Mrs. Peale first suggested the term "possibility thinking" that Schuller utilized in his first volume, *Move Ahead with Possibility Thinking* (1967).

Schuller always manifested a keen awareness of place. His Orange County world of the 1950s and 1960s teemed with migrants from elsewhere, most of whom had left their inherited religious affiliations behind. Schuller's environment reflected, in extreme, the westward tilt of the nation and the late-twentieth-century version of individualism. Orange County migrants were disconnected from the traditional support systems provided by social order, neighborhood, or family. Unlike the individualism of Emerson and Thoreau, which maintained strong links to the cosmos (Emerson's "Oversoul"), the new western individualism proved predominantly secular. As such, it quickly led to anomie, despair, and depression. Psychologist Martin E. P. Seligman coined the phrase the "California Self," but Schuller broadened the concept to the "modern International Secular Self."[74] As he admitted in 1982, most of his ministry had been "a mission to the unbelievers."[75] His *Believe in the God Who Believes in You* (1989) contains three prefaces: one to the agnostic/atheist/secular reader, one to the religious reader, one to the Judeo-Christian reader.[76] This "mission to unbelievers" approach led him to search for a universal theological ground, and he found it in the concept of the "Dignity of the Person." He termed this pride in being human "self-esteem." In his most trenchant book, he called this "the single greatest need facing the human race today."[77]

This quest to enhance every person's self-esteem lies at the center of Schuller's thirty-one books and countless sermons. Arguing that the will to self-respect (self-esteem) is the most fundamental of all human desires, he has concluded that the failure to achieve a healthy self-pride is disastrous. The lack of self-esteem is not humility, he argues, but rather shame. Reminding people that they are sinners simply reinforces this negative self-image. Indeed, he once redefined sin as the sense of shame and uncertainty that derives from a person's lack of trust in God.

Schuller argues that only awareness of God's love can allow a person to claim a position of healthy self-esteem. He maintains that neither money, power, fame, nor sex can produce fulfillment. Any "success," however defined, can be boiled down to its core: creating self-esteem in one's self and in other people, and this can be brought about only by service to others.[78] In later books, he interpreted both the Ten Commandments and the Beatitudes from this perspective.[79] His other books and his TV shows tell stories of people who have faced and overcome great obstacles by holding to the premise of "possibility thinking." The Schuller family has had its own share of obstacles. Their daughter Carol lost a leg in a teenage motorcycle accident, his wife suffered breast cancer, and he twice underwent serious brain surgery. He has, therefore, practiced what he preached.

But Schuller's theology also reflects his position as a child of the southern California media world. The free brochures for the Crystal Cathedral gleam like Hollywood posters. For the tenth-anniversary celebration of the cathedral in 1990, sky divers dropped from 12,000 feet to form a floating cross in the sky. The media propensity for sound bite slogans is echoed in Schuller's list of 366 responses to "faith is."[80]

The Crystal Cathedral, Garden Grove, California. Designed by architect Philip Johnson, this striking glass church was dedicated in 1980. The congregation numbers over ten thousand, ranking it as one of the West's "megachurches."

His *Power Thoughts* (1997) echoes the same theme, as does his *Success Is Never Ending/Failure Is Never Final* (1988).

Schuller also well understood the key role played by religious architecture. After the initial success of his drive-in theater church, he decided to construct a more permanent building. Impressed with George W. Truett, who had remained at Dallas's First Baptist Church for a lifetime, Schuller hoped to do the same in Orange County. Thus, he wanted a building that would reflect both permanence and elegance. He sought out Richard Neutra, one of southern California's most famous architects, and became enthralled with Neutra's ideas of "Bio-Realism." Neutra maintained that much of world tension could be traced to the fact that human beings have been forced to live outside their natural surroundings. Humankind was originally destined to live amidst flowers, trees, birds, and gardens, not freeways, high-rise buildings, and asphalt. A properly designed building could enhance the spiritual that is so often lost in the modern world. Neutra convinced

Schuller that grass, flowers, trees, and pools of water were not only beautiful, they were practical as well. A proper church environment should allow a person to be receptive to the presence of God.

When Schuller later decided to build an even more elaborate cathedral, he hired New York architect Philip Johnson, who shared Schuller's architectural ideas if not his religious philosophy. Johnson designed a glass cathedral to seat 4,000, and in 1980, after three years and $20 million, it was finally completed. *Newsweek* termed the building "one of the most spectacular religious edifices in the world." Journalist Norman Cousins called it "the kind of church God would build—if he could afford it."[81] The Crystal Cathedral of the Reformed Church in America attracts over 200,000 visitors every year. In a strange way it echoes the appeal of Aimee Semple McPherson's Los Angeles temple during the 1920s. Each incorporates the regional embodiment of "popular religion."

Given his prominent position and his theology, Schuller has had his share of criticism. From around 1975 to the late 1980s, "Schuller shooting" proved a popular form of theological discussion. It came from all sides of the political/religious spectrum. Liberals attacked his religious "Disneyland image." As *New Republic* reporter T. D. Allen noted in 1976, "His critics contend that Schuller has done for Jesus what Colonel Sanders has done for chicken, that he offers a kind of fast-food franchise salvation bearing the same relationship to the Christ of the Cross that the plastic automaton Abraham Lincoln at Disneyland does to the American Civil War."[82] *Theology Today* writer John M. Mulder termed Schuller primarily a salesman peddling his own philosophy, a "sanctified exploitation" that reflected the cultural captivity of the American churches.[83] University-based theologians dismissed his theology as "shallow." Even his friends called him a "Johnny-one-noter."[84] Others found fault with his worship and marriage fees, accused him of contributing to southern California pollution, and critiqued his absolute silence on the issues of the day: Vietnam, Watergate, abortion, race, homosexuality, drug use (especially among middle-class families in Orange County), and the ordination of women. In critiquing the manuscript of *Self Esteem,* Martin Marty asked Schuller if his perspective were not "a philosophy which makes room for God more than a theology that incorporates psychology."[85]

Religious conservatives have had their innings as well. They criticized Schuller for neglecting the Gospel tradition, for downplaying sin, and for creating a twenty-million-dollar "eyesore." In 1984 the conservative evangelical journal *Christianity Today* sent a team of scholars to grill Schuller on these and other questions. In a careful interview, Schuller discussed with them his views of sin.[86]

Although stung by these criticisms, Schuller declined to respond publicly to his detractors.[87] Sometimes his friends replied for him, but Schuller steadfastly refused to enter into public debate on any issue. He always maintained that the pulpit was not the place for controversial positions. Those seated in the pews could offer no reply. Controversial subjects should be aired in small groups, he said, where all sides could be discussed.[88]

In several cases, however, his critics ended up changing their minds. Although Berkeley Congregationalist Browne Barr found Schuller's message "pretty thin gruel," he stood in awe of Schuller's ability to reach people who stood outside the moral and religious structures of the day. By speaking to them in terms of their own experiences, Barr noted, Schuller has tried to draw these outsiders within earshot of the biblical message. In this respect—winning a hearing from the unchurched—no one could approach Schuller's success.[89]

And this, Schuller has always insisted, has been his primary goal. As he once noted, "One of my non-Christian friends said, 'I love to listen to you because you don't get to Jesus Christ until the end, and when you do, I can turn it off.' Don't you see? That's my strategy."[90] Although he has left his inherited Calvinism far behind, by grounding his self-esteem theology in "service to others," Schuller reflects much of the original Christian message.

In the modern era, the American West has provided more than its share of prominent religious personalities. The range has been prodigious: from Robert Schuller and Cardinal James McIntyre, who have international reputations, to Cecil Williams and Thomas Banyacya (the Hopi leader who spoke to the UN in 1948), who have national ones, to "prairie preacher" Gertrude Horn, whose reputation, despite a sixty-four-year ministerial career, has never extended beyond northern Weld County, Colorado.

These figures were not united by denominational theology or even a shared social vision. Rather, they shared a common sense of place: the great American West. From the 1960s forward, the West proved broad enough, in both geography and attitude, to encompass a multitude of powerful religious personalities.

Epilogue

In 1902 the Episcopal bishop of Boise argued that "the American who is being developed in the Far West is going to be quite as important a factor in our country's future for good or evil as the one who is being molded in our great [eastern urban] centers."[1] I believe the bishop to have been an able prophet, and I think his statement is even more applicable for the twenty-first century. Consequently, I would like to conclude this study with six general observations on the nature of religion in the modern American West.

First, although one need not accept the position that American society currently pits a "nihilistic hedonism and secular belief pattern" against a "spiritual system,"[2] it does seem clear that traditional forms of Judeo-Christian morality no longer hold the same cultural dominance over national life. As Catholic historian Charles R. Morris phrased it, modern American culture has become "highly latitudinarian."[3]

Deciding which purveyor of a "symbolic reality" sets the prevailing western cultural tone is a risky business, but one can hazard a guess that it somehow revolves around the media. Hollywood, television, rock music, comic books, the Internet, the press, modern novelists, and so on have combined to create a cultural atmosphere that if not exactly "secular" is not exactly "religious" either. Film and, by extension, video and television have usually been targeted as the chief agents in this cultural transformation. The *New York Times* recently noted that over six million video cassette movies are rented each day, compared to three million items checked out of public libraries, and that the average American watches fifteen hundred hours of television per year.[4] By its very nature, film cannot easily convey Judeo-Christian symbols or ethics. This is due partly to the fact that religious themes usually do not have great audience appeal. But it is also due to

the fact, as literary critic Simon Weil has noted, that film (and literature) often turn reality upside down. In real life, evil is monotonous
and boring and good is endlessly exciting. But in film, the reverse is
true. On-screen evil is often fascinating. On-screen good, on the other
hand, usually ends up as dull. The theme of goodness simply has no
story.[5]

As historians, folklorists, and psychologists have long understood,
whoever tells the stories defines the culture. At the beginning of the
twentieth century, the dominant western stories often echoed biblical
themes—the Kingdom of God, the search for Zion, the chance of personal and social redemption. In their better renditions, these stories
were laced with irony, allusion, and mystery. No longer. The modern
storytellers have had difficulty incorporating these multiple layers of
meaning into their tales. As the twenty-first century begins, it is hard
to find a common spiritual frame of reference in the dominant forms
of storytelling. Thus, it is under a largely secular cultural umbrella
that the organized forces of western religion must prepare to meet the
new century. In some sense, then, most organized religious groups
will probably assume the roles historically played by the Mennonites,
Jews, ethnic churches, and Mormons of an earlier day: they will all
become "outsiders."

Second, although the forces of organized religion may have slipped
somewhat, the activities of western churches and synagogues are still
vital to their local communities. The prominence of parochial schools,
church-run day care centers, support groups, welfare distribution, and
involvement in environmental issues means that organized religion
remains alive and well on a local, personal level. Even if the churches
have become outsiders, they are the most important outsiders that any
western community can have.

Nowhere is this better seen than in the religious responses to the
wave of social tragedies that swept through several western communities during the 1990s: brutal murders because of race or sexual ori-
entation in Texas and Wyoming; disastrous public school massacres
in Oregon and Colorado; and bombings and tornadoes in Oklahoma.
In each case, the local clergy played prominent roles, through sermons
and counseling, in the attempts to heal these broken communities.[6]
By so doing, these clerics helped create what Peter Berger has described
as the normal social ministry of the church—"to mediate, to reconcile,

to provide a neutral ground on which societal antagonists can meet as human beings."[7] This local involvement often astounds outsiders.

For example, when the Alfred R. Murrah Federal Building in Oklahoma City was bombed in April 1995, the Oklahoma churches and synagogues provided the most prominent civil response. The Oklahoma Conference of Churches coordinated the formation of the Oklahoma City Disaster Interfaith Response Office, involving leaders from the Christian, Jewish, Islamic, and Baha'i faiths. East Coast reporters marveled at the role played by the churches of the region.

Third, the powerful Mormon Church has changed considerably during the last hundred years. In 1947 Utah held 55 percent of the world's LDS population; half a century later, the figure was 17 percent. The church expects to reach about 12 million members worldwide in the early years of the twenty-first century, doubling its size since 1980. Much of the growth has been overseas.

The celebration of the 150th anniversary of the Saints' arrival in the Salt Lake Valley in 1847 brought them considerable publicity. Most of the coverage of the re-creation of the trek West was favorable. At the turn of the twentieth century, the Saints have emerged as an international force. Indeed, the LDS Church provided the model for language training now used by the Peace Corps, and Peace Corps officials know that if the church withdraws its missionaries from a region, danger is imminent.

More than any other mainstream group (for so they have largely become), the Latter-day Saints embody traditional American middle-class, Judeo-Christian virtues. As sociologist Arnold Mauss has noted, they will probably continue to walk a delicate line between their traditional role as outsiders and their new-found position of "representative of the traditional mainstream."[8]

Fourth, the Asian and Near Eastern faiths, particularly Buddhism and Islam, are here to stay. With the enactment of new immigration laws of 1965 (with even higher Asian and Middle Eastern quotas passed in 1990), these groups are certain to increase. Islam is already on the verge of becoming the nation's second largest non-Christian faith.[9]

So, too, are the various New Age religions that often merge with or borrow from various Native faiths. The traditional Asian/Native perspective on the sacredness of the environment continues to grow rapidly. In fact, since the 1980s, numerous church groups have begun to

The Buddhist temple Higashi Honganji in Los Angeles, California. Buddhism has established a firm hold in California and in other areas of the West.

focus much attention on the religious dimension of ecology, including the Latter-day Saints, Anglicans, various Orthodox Churches, and the Assemblies of God. All have argued for a biblical basis for stewardship of the environment. This may provide a basis for twenty-first-century ecumenicism.[10]

Fifth, the western states have become home to a vigorous Protestant neo-evangelism that shows no sign of declining. This neo-evangelism has proven far more flexible than anyone could have predicted. In many cases, it has modified its stance on alcohol, homosexuality, and biblical literalism. The related Pentecostal faiths—with appeals to black and, increasingly, Hispanic audiences—also show similar growth. In fact, some sociologists such as Donald E. Miller have suggested that the West Coast–based groups such as Vineyard Fellowship, Calvary Chapel, and Hope Chapel may well serve as "new paradigm" churches for the twenty-first century.[11] The spread of these evangelical groups insures that a biblically based minority will continue to challenge mainstream society on a number of fronts.

Finally, the West continues to attract migrants, both from the South and East as well as from around the globe. The great western cities of Seattle, Las Vegas, Denver, San Diego, and San Francisco contain every religious group imaginable.

A classroom in an Islamic school in Los Angeles. Islam has become the second largest non-Christian faith in the West.

Consider Los Angeles, the urban area most likely to represent the city of the twenty-first century.[12] Surveys of the Los Angeles religious scene by historian Michael Engh and geographer Barbara Wrightman have discovered the following: the "Centrifugal City" houses the nation's largest Hindu shrine, Sree Venkateshwara Temple, north of Malibu, which serves the estimated 10,000 Hindus in the region; the Buddha Hall of Hsi Lai Temple in Hacienda Heights that not only functions as the center of the International Buddhist Progressive Society but also trains monks and nuns for the growing (Anglo and Asian) Buddhist community; a new Zoroastrian worship center in Westminster, designed to resemble a similar center built in ancient Persia by King Darius; five Islamic centers and eighty-two mosques that serve the estimated quarter of a million southern California Muslims. (A number of mosques have been built in the vicinity of predominantly black areas to serve the growing number of converts to Islam from the city's African-American community.) The Catholic Diocese of Los Angeles officially lists ninety-three different ethnic groups in its parishes. Today southern California priests offer Mass in forty-two different languages, and a new Los Angeles Catholic cathedral is scheduled to be completed in 2001. The region's 800,000 Jews recently erected three new structures: the Museum of Tolerance, the Museum of the Holocaust, and the Los Angeles Holocaust Monument. In addition, Los Angeles houses the Simon Wiesenthal Center, which relentlessly tracks down ex-Nazis. Evangelical Protestant churches, such as the South Coast Community Church in Irvine, rank as among the largest in the nation. South Coast has a staff of sixty-eight and a membership of 10,000 and boasts a 2,500-seat auditorium for health-related activities, including post-football game parties.[13] The University of Southern California has recently begun a Center for Religion and Civic Culture with the motto "The Los Angeles Religious Community: Working Together, Building City Neighborhoods."

As historian Eldon G. Ernst has noted, California never produced any religious mainstream. From the beginning, the various faiths have all been "minority" faiths, juxtaposed against a dominant secular culture. California has changed our whole understanding of what it means to be religious, Ernst argues. While one might easily comprehend what it means to be religious in, say, Boise, Amarillo, or Provo, what does it mean to be religious in Los Angeles?[14]

A 1990 Lilly Foundation report concluded that the majority of Californians were spiritual but not conventional in their religious belief patterns. Without the structures provided by historic faith traditions, however, such spirituality often becomes formless, guided by individual whim. Consequently, many describe Los Angeles as a city filled with people who lack social ties. In such a world of pluralistic belief patterns, religion has emerged as yet another "consumer item."[15] Los Angeles has enormous choice in this regard. As J. Gordon Melton notes, "Los Angeles is the only place in the world that you can find all forms of Buddhism. Not even Asian countries have all forms of Buddhism."[16] It is likely that southern California will continue to lead the nation in this tremendous range of individual religious options. If western individualism is more spiritual than atheistic (and all surveys seem to suggest that this is so), then those that can best respond to this situation will be those that will thrive in the future.

The French philosopher André Malraux once proclaimed that the twenty-first century would either be a spiritual century, or it would not be. If so, then the American West offers a variety of options from which the century might choose.

Notes

Preface

1. Gary Holthaus et al., eds., *A Society to Match the Scenery* (Niwot: University Press of Colorado, 1991); Clyde A. Milner II, ed., *A New Significance: Re-envisioning the History of the American West* (New York and Oxford: Oxford University Press, 1996); David M. Wrobel and Michael C. Steiner, eds., *Many Wests: Place, Culture, and Regional Identity* (Lawrence: University Press of Kansas, 1997); and Valerie J. Matsumoto and Blake Allmendinger, eds., *Over the Edge: Remapping the American West* (Berkeley: University of California Press, 1999).

2. Quintard Taylor, *In Search of the Racial Frontier: African Americans in the American West, 1528–1990* (New York: W. W. Norton and Co., 1998).

3. Timothy Egan, *Lasso the Wind: Away to the New West* (New York: Alfred A. Knopf, 1998); Robert D. Kaplan, *An Empire Wilderness: Travels into America's Future* (New York: Random House, 1998). To be fair, one should also mention the exception. William Cronon et al., *Under an Open Sky: Rethinking America's Western Past* (New York: Norton, 1992) contains a fine essay by D. Michael Quinn, "Religion in the American West" (145–66). See also Laurie F. Maffly-Kipp, "Eastward Ho!" in *Retelling U.S. Religious History*, ed. Thomas A. Tweed (Berkeley: University of California Press, 1997), 127–48.

4. *Atlas of the New West: Portrait of a Changing Region* (New York: W. W. Norton and Co., 1997).

5. Schmemann as quoted in John Garvey, ed., *Henri Nouwen* (Springfield, Ill.: Templegate Publishers, 1988), 17.

6. On this theme, see George M. Marsden, *The Soul of the American University: From Protestant Establishment to Established Nonbelief* (New York and Oxford: Oxford University Press, 1994).

7. Statement by the Lakota, Canadian Lakota, Dakota, and Nakota Nations as quoted in *Atlas of the American West*, 115.

8. John Clive, *Not by Fact Alone: Essays on the Writing and Reading of History* (Boston: Houghton Mifflin Co., 1989), 68.

Chapter 1. The Western "Gospel in the World"

1. See the essays on the play in *The Millennium Project: The Great Divide* (Albuquerque: NMRT, 1990), 1–11.

2. U.S. Bureau of the Census, *Historical Statistics of the United States: Colonial Times to 1957* (Washington, D.C.: U.S. Government Printing Office, 1960), 226–28.

3. H. K. Carroll, *The Religious Forces of the United States,* rev. ed. (New York: Scribner's, 1912), viii, xiv, xiv–xv.

4. "Churches," pamphlet in Sharlott Hall Museum, Prescott, Ariz. Mss. box no. 3. Taos figures courtesy of Janine Dorsey.

5. U.S. Bureau of the Census, table 3, in Lawrence A. Young, "The Religious Landscape," in *Utah in the 1990s: A Demographic Perspective,* ed. Tim B. Heaton et al. (Salt Lake City: Signature Books, 1996), 157.

6. *Idaho Daily Statesman,* February 4, 1898. Figures supplied by Carol MacGregor from her "Founding Community in Boise, Idaho, 1882–1910," Ph.D. dissertation, University of New Mexico, 1999.

7. "The Classification of Church Members," *World's Work* 18 (October 1909): 1209–10.

8. Carroll, *Religious Forces of the United States,* 474–77.

9. E. H. Abbott, "Kansas," *Outlook,* April 19, 1902: 970.

10. Eldon G. Ernst, "Baptists in the Pacific Northwest: An Historiographical Frontier," *Foundations* 11 (October–December 1969): 321.

11. William W. Manross, *A History of the American Episcopal Church* (New York: Morehouse, 1935), 332, 334; Francis Key Brooke, "Ten Years of Church Life in Oklahoma and Indian Territory," in *Oklahoma and Indian Territory* (New York: Domestic and Foreign Missionary Society of the Protestant Episcopal Church in the United States of America, c. 1903), n.p.

12. *Annual Report upon Domestic Missions* (New York: Protestant Episcopal Church, 1890), 71–72.

13. Walter Rauschenbusch, *Christianity and the Social Crisis* (New York: Macmillan, 1907); Walter Rauschenbusch, *A Theology for the Social Gospel* (New York: Macmillan, 1917).

14. See Robert W. Schneider, *Novelist to a Generation: The Life and Thought of Winston Churchill* (Bowling Green: Bowling Green University Popular Press, 1976).

15. Abbott, quoted in Ferenc Morton Szasz, *The Divided Mind of Protestant America, 1880–1930* (University: University of Alabama Press, 1982), 44.

16. C. Howard Hopkins, *The Rise of the Social Gospel in American Protestantism, 1865–1915* (New Haven, Conn.: Yale University Press, 1940), 319. See also the classic accounts by Henry F. May, *Protestant Churches and Industrial America* (New York: Harper and Row, 1949, 1967); Robert T. Handy, ed.,

The Social Gospel in America (New York: Oxford University Press, 1965); and Ronald C. White, Jr., and C. Howard Hopkins, eds., *The Social Gospel: Religion and Reform in Changing America* (Philadelphia: Temple University Press, 1976).

17. Mark S. Masse, "Social Justice in an Industrial Society," in *Church and State in America: A Bibliographical Guide: The Civil War to the Present Day* (New York: Greenwood, 1987).

18. They did not always succeed. Laurie F. Maffly-Kipp judges Protestant evangelism in gold rush California to be "an abashed failure" (*Religion and Society in Frontier California* [New Haven, Conn.: Yale University Press, 1991], 92). Later, when the gender ratio had evened out, the churches had a bit more success. See also Michael J. Engh, *Frontier Faiths: Church, Temple, and Synagogue in Los Angeles, 1846–1888* (Albuquerque: University of New Mexico Press, 1992).

19. Dale E. Soden, "Mark Allison Matthews: Seattle's Southern Preacher," Ph.D. dissertation, University of Washington, 1980; Timothy J. Sarbaugh, "Father Yorke and the San Francisco Waterfront, 1901–1919," *Pacific Historian* 25 (Fall 1981): 29–33. The best study of San Francisco is Douglas Firth Anderson, "Through Fire and Fair by the Golden Gate: Progressive Era Protestantism and Regional Culture," Ph.D. dissertation, Graduate Theological Union, 1988.

20. Facts from Uzzell Vertical File, Western Room, Public Library, Denver, Colo. See especially *Denver Times,* October 26, 1901, February 17, 1901; "He Did His Level Best," *Greeley Sunday Journal,* October 26, 1955.

21. *Colorado Graphic* 3 (October 1887): 1. Facts from the Reed file, Public Library, Denver, Colo. See especially *Daily News,* March 5, 1899; *Denver Times,* January 30, 1899; *Denver Daily News,* May 7, 1897; *Denver Republican,* February 2, 1899. The only biography of Reed is by James A. Denton, *Myron W. Reed: Rocky Mountain Radical, 1884–1899* (Albuquerque: University of New Mexico Press, 1997).

22. *American* (January 1917), Dawson Scrap Books, Colorado Heritage Center, Denver.

23. *Annual Report of the Holy Trinity Italian Evangelical Institutional Church* (Denver, 1912); *Rocky Mountain News,* December 16, 1929.

24. See Denton, *Myron W. Reed,* passim.

25. The best studies are Lawrence H. Larsen, *The Urban West at the End of the Frontier* (Lawrence: Regents Press of Kansas, 1976); and Hugh Latimer Burleson, *Our Church and Our Country* (New York: Domestic and Foreign Missionary Society, 1918), 48.

26. See J. Alton Templin, Allen D. Breck, and Martin Riat, eds., *The Methodist Evangelical Protestant and United Brethren Churches in the Rockies, 1850–1920* (Denver: Rocky Mountain Conference of the United Methodist Church, 1977).

27. Ferenc Morton Szasz, *The Protestant Clergy in the Great Plains and Mountain West, 1865–1915* (Albuquerque: University of New Mexico Press, 1988), 201–8.

28. "Churches and Schools of Rock Springs," typescript, Vertical Files, Wyoming Historical Society, Cheyenne.

29. Information from displays posted at the Carson City, Nevada, School Museum (Washoe tribe) and the Nebraska Susan La Flesch House Museum (Winnebago tribe); Anne M. Butler, "Mother Katharine Drexel: Spiritual Visionary for the West," in *By Grit and Grace: Eleven Women Who Shaped the American West,* ed. Glenda Riley and Richard W. Etulain (Golden, Colo.: Fulcrum Publishing, 1997), 198–220.

30. *As a Chinaman Saw Us: Passages from His Letters to a Friend at Home* (New York: Appleton and Co., 1910), 181–82.

31. Helen Webster, "The Chinese School of the Central Presbyterian Church of Denver," *Colorado Magazine* 40 (January 1963): 57–62 (pt. 1) and (April 1964): 132–37 (pt. 2); "Two Years–The First Baptist Church of Denver, 1890–1892," ms., Colorado Heritage Center; Grant K. Anderson, "Deadwood's Chinatown," *South Dakota History* 5 (Summer 1975): 266–85; Elizabeth Lee and Kenneth A. Abbott, "Chinese Pilgrims and Presbyterians in the United States, 1851–1977," *Journal of Presbyterian History* 55 (Summer 1977): 125–44.

32. Cited in Jack Benham, *Silverton and Neighboring Ghost Towns* (Ouray, Colo.: Bear Creek Publishers, n.d.).

33. Webster, "Chinese School," 57–62, 131–37.

34. Undated clipping, Vertical Files, Sharlott Hall Museum, Prescott, Ariz.

35. Vertical Files, Public Library, Price, Utah; Dan Carnett, "New Mexico Baptists since World War II," ms.

36. Quoted in Donald C. Yelton, *Four Studies in Collective Biography* (Metuchen, N.J.: Scribner's Press, 1978), 94.

37. Karen Shane, "New Mexico: Salubrious El Dorado," *New Mexico Historical Review* 56 (1981): 387–99.

38. *Redlands Daily Facts,* November 18, 1984; Joyce Kinkead, "The Western Sermons of Harold Bell Wright," *Journal of American Culture* 7 (Fall 1983): 85–97; James D. Hart, *The Popular Book: A History of America's Literary Taste* (Berkeley: University of California Press, 1963), 218.

39. *Albuquerque–El Paso–Phoenix–Tucson* (El Paso: Texas Western Press, 1982), 43; *La Aurora,* May 15, 1908.

40. Jake W. Spidle, Jr., "An Army of Tubercular Invalids: New Mexico and the Birth of a Tuberculosis Industry," *New Mexico Historical Review* 61 (July 1986): 179–201.

41. *La Aurora,* November 15, 1914.

42. See also John E. Baur, *Health Seekers of Southern California* (San Marino, Calif.: Huntington Library, 1959).

43. *La Aurora,* December 15, 1913; Marion Woodham, *A History of Presbyterian Hospital, 1908–1976* (Albuquerque, 1976), 1–13.

44. Anderson, "Through Fire and Fair," passim; Kevin Starr, *Americans and the California Dream, 1850–1915* (New York: Oxford University Press, 1973), 83–84, 275–77; Jay P. Dolan, *The American Catholic Experience: A History from Colonial Times to the Present* (Garden City: Image Books, 1985), 256; F. Patrick Nicholson, "Non-Protestants in Southern California," in *The West and the Religious Experience,* ed. William Kramer (Los Angeles: Will Kramer, 1975), 141.

45. Benjamin M. Read, *Illustrated History of New Mexico* (Santa Fe: New Mexican Printing Co., 1912), 559.

46. See Randi Jones Walker, *Protestantism in the Sangre de Cristos, 1850–1920* (Albuquerque: University of New Mexico Press, 1991); Mark T. Banker, *Presbyterian Missions and Cultural Interaction in the Far Southwest, 1850–1950* (Urbana: University of Illinois Press, 1993).

47. *Oklahoma Journal of Religion* 2 (March 1945): 8–9.

48. *Laramie Boomerang,* September 22, 1891; see also John R. Thelin, "California and the Colleges," *California Historical Quarterly* 56 (Summer 1977): 140–53 (pt. 1) and (Fall 1977): 230–48 (pt. 2). For a fine example of a Catholic school history, see John C. Scott, O.S.B., *This Place Called Saint Martin's, 1895–1995: A Centennial History of Saint Martin's College and Abbey, Lacey, Washington* (Virginia Beach: Downing Co., 1996).

49. Gerald McKevitt, "Jesuit Higher Education," *Mid-America* 73 (October 1991): 209–26.

50. *Denver Post,* July 29, 1902.

Chapter 2. Religious Life in the Urban and Rural West

1. This chapter draws in part on my "The American Quest for Religious Certainty, 1880–1915," in *The American Self: Myth, Ideology and Popular Culture,* ed. Sam B. Girgus (Albuquerque: University of New Mexico Press, 1981), 88–104. See also Ray S. Baker, *The Spiritual Unrest* (New York: Frederick A. Stokes, 1910); George T. Bushnell, "The Place of Religion in Modern Life," *American Journal of Theology* 17 (October 1913): 530; Gaius G. Atkins, *Religion in Our Times* (New York: Round Table Press, 1932), 64.

2. Quoted in Daniel Pope, "The Development of National Advertising, 1865–1920," Ph.D. dissertation, Columbia University, 1967, 167.

3. Commander Booth Tucker, *Prairie Homes for City Poor* (c. 1899), pamphlet, Colorado Historical Society, Denver. See also Clark Spence, *The Salvation*

Army Farm Colonies (Tucson: University of Arizona Press, 1985); Ferenc M. Szasz, "Francis Schlatter," *New Mexico Historical Review* 54 (April 1979); Charles Pierce LeWarne, *Utopias on Puget Sound, 1885–1915* (Seattle: University of Washington Press, 1975); Alice Bullock, "Shalam, 'Land of the Children,'" *New Mexico Magazine* 17 (March 1929): 38 ff.

4. Robert V. Hine, *California's Utopian Colonies* (New York: Norton, 1966). Tingley's major book was *Theosophy: The Path of the Mystic* (Pasadena: Theosophical University Press, 1922).

5. *Palo Altan,* November 1, 1912. Copy provided by Joseph Weixelman.

6. See the files of *Woodrow's Monthly* in Special Collections, University of Oklahoma Library, Norman.

7. Peter Argersinger, "Pentecostal Politics in Kansas: Religion, the Farmer's Alliance and the Gospel of Populism," *Kansas Quarterly* 1 (Fall 1969): 24–35.

8. *Intermountain Catholic,* August 14, 1909.

9. Lyle Dorsett, *The Queen City: A History of Denver* (Boulder: Pruett, 1977), 88–89.

10. "Wyoming" (c. 1936), pamphlet, Wyoming Historical Society, Cheyenne, 6.

11. Henry G. Satteder to J. Mills Kendrick, November 16, 1895, J. Mills Kendrick Manuscripts, Archdiocese of the Rio Grande, file 10, Albuquerque.

12. Scott Cline, "The Jews of Portland, Oregon: A Statistical Dimension, 1886–1980," *Oregon Historical Quarterly* 88 (Spring 1987): 13.

13. Lawrence H. Larsen, *The Urban West at the End of the Frontier* (Lawrence: Regents Press of Kansas, 1976), 31.

14. Moses Rischin, "The Jewish Experience in America: A View from the West," in *Jews of the American West,* ed. Moses Rischin and John Livingston (Detroit: Wayne State University Press, 1991), 16 (quote); Ron Robin, "Jewish Architecture and Folk History in San Francisco," *Journal of the West* 26 (October 1987): 67–73, quote on 68; "First Synagogue at Albuquerque—1900," *Western States Jewish Historical Quarterly* 11 (October 1978): 46–48.

15. *Provo Daily Herald,* July 19, 1994. The order was Saint George (1877), Logan (1884), and Manti (1895). The best book on American religious architecture is Peter W. Williams, *Houses of God: Region, Religion, and Architecture in the United States* (Urbana and Chicago: University of Illinois Press, 1997).

16. *Church Week,* ending June 3, 1978: 6.

17. LDS Church statements, found in undated clippings, Utah State Historical Society, Salt Lake City.

18. Quoted in *Deseret News,* April 6, 1993.

19. *Ogden Standard Examiner,* May 20, 1993; *Provo Daily Herald,* July 19, 1994.

20. *Lincoln Journal and Star,* May 3, 1959, Public Library, Lincoln, Nebr.

21. *Denver Republican,* January 1, 1890.

22. Myrna Katz Frommer and Harvey Frommer, eds., *Growing up Jewish in America: An Oral History* (New York: Harcourt Brace and Co., 1995), 77.

23. *75th Anniversary, Temple Emanuel* (1949), pamphlet, Western Room, Public Library, Denver, Colo.

24. Rodney Steiner, *Los Angeles: The Centrifugal City* (Dubuque: Kendall/ Hunt, 1981), 69–70.

25. Frederick Luebke, ed., *European Immigrants in the American West: Community Histories* (Albuquerque: University of New Mexico Press, 1998), ix–xv.

26. James R. Shortridge, "The Great Plains," in *Encyclopedia of American Social History,* 3 vols. (New York: Charles Scribner's Sons, 1993), 2: 1006.

27. "The Hellenic Orthodox Church: The Assumption, Price, Utah, Description of the Present and Original Physical Appearance," typescript, Public Library, Price, Utah.

28. See the essays in Frederick C. Luebke, ed., *Ethnicity on the Great Plains* (Lincoln: University of Nebraska Press and the Center for Great Plains Studies, 1980).

29. Leo Schpall, "Jewish Agricultural Colonies in the United States," *Agricultural History* 24 (July 1950): 120–46; Robert A. Goldberg, "Zion in Utah: The Clarion Colony and Jewish Agrarianism," in Rischin and Livingston, eds., *Jews of the American West,* 66–91; W. Gunther Plant, "Jewish Colonies at Painted Woods and Devil's Lake," *North Dakota History* 32 (January 1965): 59–70.

30. *Rachel Calof's Story: Jewish Homesteader on the Northern Plains* (Bloomington and Indianapolis: Indiana University Press, 1995), 33.

31. Sophie Trupin, *Dakota Diaspora: Memoirs of a Jewish Homesteader* (Lincoln: University of Nebraska Press, 1984), 1, 91.

32. *Annual Report of Domestic and Foreign Missions of the Protestant Episcopal Church* (1895), 87; Frank T. Bayley, *Twentieth Anniversary Sermon* (Denver, 1911).

33. Karl A. Peter, *The Dynamics of Hutterite Society: An Analytical Approach* (Edmonton: University of Alberta Press, 1987), 38.

34. John W. Bennett, *Hutterian Brethren: The Agricultural Economy and Social Organization of a Communal People* (Stanford, Calif.: Stanford University Press, 1967), 42; Michael Holzach, *The Forgotten People: A Year among the Hutterites* (Sioux Falls: Ex Cahina Publishing Co., 1993).

35. Michael L. Olsen, "And a Child Shall Lead Them: The Legendary Introduction of Turkey Red Wheat into Kansas," in *Great Mysteries of the West,* ed. Ferenc Morton Szasz (Golden, Colo.: Fulcrum Publishing, 1993), 164–85.

36. James C. Juhnke, *Vision, Doctrine, War: Mennonite Identity and Organization in America, 1890–1910* (Scotdale, Pa.: Herald Press, 1989), 51; Diane

Zimmerman Umble, *Holding the Line: The Telephone in Old Order Mennonite and Amish Life* (Baltimore, Md.: Johns Hopkins University Press, 1996).

37. Frederick C. Luebke, *Bonds of Loyalty: German Americans and World War I* (DeKalb: Northern Illinois University Press, 1974), xv; John David Unruh, "The Mennonites in South Dakota," master's thesis, Yankton College, 1926; *South Dakota Historical Collections* 10 (1920): 470–72.

38. *Amarillo News-Globe,* January 18, 1976; "Peace Evangelical Lutheran Church," *Oklahoma Journal of Religion* (February 1944): 3–4.

39. *Amarillo Globe-Times,* November 12, 1971.

40. Harry S. Stout, "Ethnicity: The Vital Center of Religion in America," *Ethnicity* 2 (June 1975): 204–24.

41. Robert J. Lazar, "Jewish Communal Life in Fargo, North Dakota: The Formative Years," *North Dakota History* 36 (Fall 1969): 351.

42. *Amarillo Globe-Times,* May 5, 1972.

43. Fr. John B. Terbovich, O.F.M., "Religious Folklore among the German-Russians in Ellis County, Kansas," *Western Folklore* 22 (April 1963): 79–88.

44. *Amarillo Daily News,* November 11, 1968.

45. *Call* 1 (September 1914); *History of Sacred Heart Cathedral,* pamphlet, Public Library, Amarillo, Tex.; *Laramie Boomerang,* July 19, 1891.

46. *The History of the France Memorial [Rawlins, Wyoming] Presbyterian Church, 1869–1969,* pamphlet in author's possession.

47. *Amarillo Sunday News-Globe,* c. 1938, Vertical Files, Public Library, Amarillo, Tex.

48. Paula M. Nelson, *After the West Was Won: Homesteaders and Town Builders in Western South Dakota, 1900–1910* (Iowa City: University of Iowa Press, 1986), 110–11.

49. Rev. David A. Johnson with Frank Fox, *In the Beginning: A Bicentennial History of Tucson's Religious Beginnings,* pamphlet, Arizona Historical Society, Tucson, 83.

50. Joe S. Warlick, *Some Baptist Blunders* (Dallas: John B. McCraw, 1923). A good collection of these may be found in the Arthur B. Duncan Papers, Texas Tech University, Lubbock.

51. Thomas W. Woodrow sermon, "Why Organize a Universalist Church in This City" (c. 1910), Wilson Manuscripts, University of Oklahoma.

52. Farmington, Vertical File, New Mexico Palace of the Governors, Santa Fe.

53. Mrs. R. D. Winters of Tempe, "Reminiscences" (1930), Arizona Historical Society, Tempe.

54. "Journal of Franklin Spaulding," Nevada Historical Society, Reno.

55. Austin and Alta Fife, *Heaven on Horseback: Revivalist Song and Verse in the Cowboy Idiom* (Logan: Utah State University Press, 1970), 15, 23–24.

56. A. C. Stewart, "Out Arizona Way," *Sunday School Missionary* 45 (February 1919): 1; A. C. Stewart, "Out Arizona Way," *Sunday School Missionary* 47 (December 1921): 2, typescripts, Arizona Historical Society, Tempe.

57. W. H. Schureman, "Pioneer Sabbath School Missions in Colorado and Wyoming, 1898 to 1923," typescript, Public Library, Fort Collins, Colo., 24, 26.

58. *San Angelo [Texas] Standard Times,* August 23, 1964; *Fort Worth Star Telegram,* August 23, 1964, August 14, 1966; *Texas Evangel* (July 1929); Joe M. Evans, *Bloys: Cowboy Camp Meeting* (El Paso: Guynes Printing Co., 1959), 3. See also the unpublished essays by Dave Bennett, copies in author's possession.

59. Quoted in Ollie Reed, Jr., "Church on the Range," *Albuquerque Tribune,* December 23, 1998.

60. Figures from Thomas Noel, *Denver Post,* December 15, 1998, Western Room, Public Library, Denver, Colo.

Chapter 3. Varieties of Religious Leadership

1. Ferenc M. Szasz, "The Clergy and the Myth of the American West," *Church History* 59 (December 1990): 497–506.

2. A. C. Stewart, "Trying for a Better Life," *Sunday School Missionary* 14 (February 1919), typescript, Arizona Historical Society, Tucson.

3. Arthur Cushman McGiffert, "The Progress of Theological Thought during the Past Fifty Years," *American Journal of Theology* 20 (July 1916): 325.

4. Lyman Abbott, *Reminiscences* (Boston: Houghton Mifflin, 1915), 404.

5. M. A. DeWolfe Howe, *The Life and Labors of Bishop Hare: Apostle to the Sioux* (New York: Sturis and Walton, 1911), 25, 35, 201, 236–38, 281, 291.

6. Cover of *Montana* 22 (Autumn 1972).

7. Isadore Papermaster, "A History of North Dakota Jewry and Their Pioneer Rabbi," *Western States Jewish Historical Quarterly* 10 (January 1978): 174.

8. Alma White, *The Story of My Life and the Pillar of Fire,* 4 vols. (Zarephath, N.J., 1935) 2: 32, 73, 207, 328.

9. Gunther Barth, "Donaldina Cameron," in *Notable American Women,* 4 vols. (Cambridge, Mass.: Harvard University Press, 1971), 4: 130–32.

10. Peggy Pascoe, *Relations of Rescue: The Search for Female Moral Authority in the American West, 1874–1939* (New York: Oxford University Press, 1990), 110, 158.

11. Ibid., passim; Laurene Wu McClain, "Donaldina Cameron: A Reappraisal," *Pacific Historian* 27 (Fall 1983): 25–35.

12. Mildred Cowl Martin, *Chinatown's Angry Angel: The Story of Donaldina Cameron* (Palo Alto, Calif.: Pacific Books, 1977).

13. *Idaho Statesman,* October 8, 1937.

14. Boone, typescript, ms. 4, Idaho Historical Society, Boise.

15. H. H. Miller, "Death Takes Rector Boone," Boone file, Idaho Historical Society, Boise.

16. Diary of William Judson Boone, typescript, Idaho Historical Society, Boise.

17. Friedman, Biographical Data Sheet, Vertical Files, Western Room, Public Library, Denver, Colo. See also Marjorie Hornbain, "Denver's Rabbi William S. Friedman: His Ideas and Influence," *Western States Jewish Historical Quarterly* 13 (January 1981): 142–54.

18. *Denver Republican,* September 23, 1889.

19. *Denver Post,* February 9, 1930.

20. *Denver Republican,* January 24, 1890, March 18, 1890.

21. Ibid., January 1, 1891.

22. Ibid., October 19, 1891; *Denver News,* June 18, 1899.

23. *Denver Republican,* October 19, 1900.

24. *Denver News,* August 26, 1906, January 27, 1898.

25. *Denver Republican,* March 2, 1897.

26. *Denver News,* November 14, 1905.

27. *Denver Post,* April 25, 1908.

28. *Denver News,* March 17, 1903.

29. *Denver Post,* February 7, 1916, April 21, 1919, November 29, 1906; *New Orleans Picayune,* March 9, 1907; *Denver Times,* October 23, 1910.

30. Moses Rischin, "Sunny Jim Rolph, the First 'Mayor of All the People,'" *California Historical Quarterly* 53 (Summer 1974): 165–72. See also David Max Eichhorn, ed., *Joys of Jewish Folklore* (Middle Village, N.Y.: Jonathan David Publishers, 1981).

31. Kevin Starr, *Americans and the California Dream, 1850–1915* (New York: Oxford University Press, 1973), 377–78.

32. *Nation,* December 12, 1928.

33. John O. Pohlmann, "The Missions Romanticized," in John and Laree Caughey, eds., *Los Angeles: Biography of a City* (Berkeley: University of California Press, 1986), 239–43. Lummis cited in Ferenc M. Szasz and Margaret Connell Szasz, "Religion and Spirituality," in Clyde A. Milner II, Carol O'Connor, and Martha Sandweiss, eds., *The Oxford History of the American West* (New York: Oxford University Press, 1994). See also David J. Weber, *The Spanish Frontier in North America* (New Haven, Conn.: Yale University Press, 1992), 344–45; and James J. Rawls, "The California Mission as Symbol and Myth," *California History* 74 (Fall 1992): 343–60.

34. John Bernard McGloin, "Survey: California Catholicism's Neglected Gold Mine: A Report on Research and Writing, 1850–1960," *Church History* 29 (1960): 344–52.

35. Bernard Fontana, *Biography of a Desert Church: The Story of Mission San Xavier del Bac* (Tucson: Westerners, 1961).

36. Erwin M. Thompson, "Joseph M. Cataldo, S.J. and St. Joseph's Mission," *Idaho Yesterdays* 18 (Summer 1978): 19–29.

37. Catherine L. Albanese, *Nature Religion in America: From the Algonkian Indians to the New Age* (Chicago: University of Chicago Press, 1990). See also Sandra Sizer Frankiel, *California's Spiritual Frontiers: Religious Alternatives in Anglo-Protestantism, 1850–1910* (Berkeley: University of California Press, 1989).

38. The literature on this theme is extensive. See Klara Bonsack Kelley and Harris Francis, *Navajo Sacred Places* (Bloomington: Indiana University Press, 1994); Christopher Vecsey, ed., *Religion in Native North America* (Moscow: University of Idaho Press, 1990); Howard L. Harrod, *Becoming and Remembering a People: Native American Religions in the Northern Plains* (Tucson: University of Arizona Press, 1995); Murray L. Wax and Rosalie H. Wax, "Religion among American Indians," *Annals of the American Academy* 436 (March 1998): 27–39; John D. Loftin, *Religion and Hopi Life in the Twentieth Century* (Bloomington: Indiana University Press, 1991).

39. James S. Griffith, *Beliefs and Holy Places: A Spiritual Geography of the Primeria Alta* (Tucson: University of Arizona Press, 1992), 151–52.

40. John Muir, *The Story of My Boyhood and Youth* (Madison: University of Wisconsin Press, 1965), 129. This section borrows, in part, from my manuscript "Scotland and the American West."

41. John Leighly, "John Muir's Image of the West," *Annals of the Association of American Geographers* 48 (December 1958): 309–18; Roderick Nash, *The American Conservation Movement* (St. Charles, Mo.: Forum Press, 1974), 9.

42. C. Michael Hall, "John Muir's Travels in Australia, 1903," in *John Muir: Life and Work,* ed. Sally M. Miller (Albuquerque: University of New Mexico Press, 1993), 304.

43. Cited in William Cronon, "Landscape and Home: Environmental Traditions in Wisconsin," *Wisconsin Magazine of History* 74 (Winter 1990–91): 97.

44. Thurman Wilkins, *John Muir: Apostle of Nature* (Norman: University of Oklahoma Press, 1995) presents the standard view. So does Michael P. Cohen, *The Pathless Way: John Muir and American Wilderness* (Madison: University of Wisconsin Press, 1984).

45. Mark Stoll, *Protestantism, Capitalism, and Nature in America* (Albuquerque: University of New Mexico Press, 1997).

46. The best book on restorationism in general is Richard T. Hughes and C. Leonard Allen, *Illusions of Innocence: Protestant Primitivism in America, 1630–1875* (Chicago: University of Chicago Press, 1988).

47. Don Weiss, "John Muir and the Wilderness Ideal," in Miller, ed., *John Muir*, 120.

48. William Frederic Bade, ed., *The Life and Letters of John Muir*, 2 vols. (Boston: Houghton Mifflin, 1924), 1: 179.

49. John Leighly, "John Muir's Image of the West," *Annals of the Association of American Geographers* 48 (December 1956).

Chapter 4. Religion in the West of the 1920s and 1930s

1. Dale E. Soden, "Mark Allison Matthews, Seattle's Southern Preacher in Quest of a Righteous Community," typescript based on author's Ph.D. dissertation, University of Washington, 1980, 223.

2. J. B. Gambrell, *Ten Years in Texas* (Dallas: John F. Worley Printing Co., 1910), 70.

3. *Amarillo Daily News*, February 20, 1921.

4. See the fuller account in Ferenc Morton Szasz, *The Divided Mind of Protestant America, 1880–1930* (University: University of Alabama Press, 1982); the best book on the subject is George Marsden, *Fundamentalism and American Culture* (New York: Oxford University Press, 1980).

5. *Albuquerque Journal*, July 26, 1925.

6. R. Halliburton, Jr., "The Nation's First Anti-Darwin Law: Passage and Repeal," *Southwestern Social Science Quarterly* (September 1960): 123–35.

7. George E. Webb, "Tucson's Evolution Debate, 1924–1927," *Journal of Arizona History* 24 (1983): 1–12; Webb, "The Evolution Controversy in Arizona and California: From the 1920s to the 1980s," *Journal of the Southwest* 33 (Summer 1991): 133–50.

8. Shuler, quoted in Jules Tygiel, *The Great Los Angeles Swindle: Oil, Stocks, and Scandal during the Roaring Twenties* (New York and Oxford: Oxford University Press, 1994), 277.

9. Kenneth T. Jackson, *The Ku Klux Klan in the City, 1915–1930* (New York: Oxford University Press, 1967), 187, 215–31. See also Shawn Lay, *War, Revolution and the Ku Klux Klan* (El Paso: Texas Western Press, 1985).

10. Supreme Council, Knights of Columbus, "Report of Commission on Religious Prejudice," Oklahoma Historical Society, 1–3.

11. Stanley V. Litizzette, *A Catholic History of North Carbon County, Utah* (Helper: Pecauh Printing Co., 1974), 6–8; "The Hellenic Orthodox Church: The Assumption, Price, Utah, Description of the Present and Original Physical Appearance," typescript, Public Library, Price, Utah.

12. Ed Gill, ed., *Through the Years: A History of the First Baptist Church, Muskogee, Oklahoma, 1890–1965* (Muskogee: Hoffman Printing Co., 1966).

13. Patricia Brandt, "Organized Free Thought in Oregon: The Oregon State Secular Union," *Oregon Historical Quarterly* 87 (Summer 1986): 167–205.

14. Carlos A. Schwantes, "Free Love and Free Speech on the Pacific Northwest Frontier," *Oregon Historical Quarterly* 82 (1981): 271–93.

15. Wilfred P. Schoenberg, *A History of the Catholic Church in the Pacific Northwest, 1743–1983* (Washington, D.C.: Pastoral Press, 1987), 520–30; Lloyd P. Jorgenson, "The Oregon School Law of 1922: Passage and Sequel," *Catholic Historical Review* 54 (October 1868): 455–66; Thomas J. Shelley, "The Oregon School Case and the National Catholic Welfare Conference," *Catholic Historical Review* 75 (July 1989): 204–5.

16. Martin E. Marty, *Modern American Religion,* vol. 2: *The Noise of Conflict, 1919–1941* (Chicago: University of Chicago Press, 1991), 253.

17. Jay P. Dolan, ed., *The American Catholic Parish: A History from 1850 to the Present,* vol. 2: *Pacific States/Intermountain West/Midwest* (New York: Paulist Press, 1987), 43; Marty, *The Noise of Conflict,* 254–55.

18. Max Vorspan and Lloyd P. Gartner, *History of the Jews of Los Angeles* (San Marino: Huntington Library, 1976), 195, 207. See also Leonard Dinnerstein, *Anti-Semitism in America* (New York: Oxford University Press, 1994).

19. Neal Gabler, *An Empire of Their Own: How the Jews Invented Hollywood* (New York: Crown Publishers, 1988), 266–310.

20. Steven M. Avella, "Transformation of Catholic Life in the Twentieth-Century West: The Case of the Diocese of Sacramento, 1929–1957," *California History* 72 (Summer 1993): 151–69; Schoenberg, *A History of the Catholic Church,* 556.

21. Jeffrey M. Burns, "Building the Best: A History of Catholic Parish Life in the Pacific States," in Dolan, ed., *The American Catholic Parish,* 83; Gilbert G. Gonzalez, *Labor and Community: Mexican Citrus Worker Villages in a Southern California County, 1900–1950* (Urbana and Chicago: University of Illinois Press, 1994), 88–89.

22. Moises Sandoval, ed., *Fronteras: A History of the Latin American Church in the U.S.A. since 1513* (San Antonio: Mexican American Cultural Center, 1983), 241–53; Kay Alexander, *California Catholicism* (Santa Barbara: Fithian Press, 1993), 58–78; Francis J. Weber, *Catholic Footprints in California* (Newhall, Calif.: Hogarth Press, 1970), 107–8. See also Francis J. Weber, "Catholicism in California," *American Ecumenical Review* 159 (October 1969): 245.

23. *The Diocese of Oklahoma* (c. 1936), pamphlet, Vertical Files, Oklahoma Historical Society.

24. Undated clipping, Churches Folder, Public Library, Lincoln, Nebr.

25. *Las Vegas Review-Journal,* October 26, 1964; Fred Wilson, "Historical Sketch: First Methodist Church of Las Vegas, 1905–1955," Installment 21, Las Vegas Historical Collections, Las Vegas.

26. *Carlsbad Argus,* June 8, 1980.

27. *A History of the First Methodist Church: 75 Years of Christian Service, 1890–1965* (1965), Vertical Files, Public Library, Carlsbad, N.M., 16–18.

28. *Salt Lake City Tribune,* October 11, 1980: 4; Ada Duhigg mss., A2328, Utah Historical Society, Salt Lake City; *Salt Lake City Tribune,* October 7, 1938.

29. Judith R. Johnson, "A History of Embudo Hospital," *Menaul Historical Review* 21 (Summer 1983): 2–4; *Albuquerque Journal,* May 20, 1959.

30. Keith C. Peterson, "Psychiana, Inc." *Columbia* (Fall 1996): 31–36. Thanks to Mark Trahant for this reference. See also Ferenc M. Szasz, "'New Thought' and the American West," in Ferenc M. Szasz, ed., *Religion in the West* (Manhattan, Kans.: Sunflower University Press, 1984), 83–90.

31. Russell R. Elliott, *History of Nevada* (Lincoln: University of Nebraska Press, 1973), 284–85, 34.

32. Meryl Deming, *First Congregational Church of Reno, 1871–1986,* pamphlet, Nevada Historical Society, Reno.

33. *History of First Methodist Church, Reno, Nevada, 1868–1968,* pamphlet, Nevada Historical Society, Reno.

34. Deming, *First Congregational Church of Reno.*

35. Editorial, *Oklahoma Journal of Religion* 2 (August 1944): 12.

36. For a good summary history, see Grant Wacker, "Pentecostalism," in *Encyclopedia of the American Religious Experience,* 3 vols. (New York: Charles Scribner's Sons, 1988), 2: 933–45; and John Thomas Nichol, *The Pentecostals* (Plainfield, N.J.: Logos International, 1966).

37. Stanley M. Burgess and Gary B. McGee, *Dictionary of Pentecostal and Charismatic Movements* (Grand Rapids, Mich.: Regency Reference Library, 1988), 11–36.

38. For a convenient list, see Edith L. Blumhofer, "For Pentecostals, a Move toward Racial Reconciliation," *Christian Century,* April 27, 1994: 445. See also Grant Wacker, "Playing for Keeps: The Primitivist Impulse in Early Pentecostalism," in *The American Quest for the Primitive Church,* ed. Richard Hughes (Urbana: University of Illinois Press, 1988), 197.

39. Wacker, "Playing for Keeps," 209.

40. James N. Gregory, *American Exodus: The Dust Bowl Migration and Okie Culture in California* (New York and Oxford: Oxford University Press, 1989), 203.

41. Bryan Wilson, *Religious Sects: A Sociological Study* (New York: McGraw-Hill, 1970), 90.

42. David Edwin Harrell, Jr., *Oral Roberts: An American Life* (Bloomington: Indiana University Press, 1985), 5.

43. *Daily Oklahoman,* April 27, 1978.

44. *Oklahoma Journal,* June 10, 1978.

45. George Harold Paul, "The Religious Frontier in Oklahoma: Dan T. Muse and the Pentecostal Holiness Church," Ph.d. dissertation, University of Oklahoma, 1965, 283.

46. From clippings in Oral Roberts Vertical File, Historic Biographies, box 11, Western Collection, University of Oklahoma Library, Norman.

47. Oral Roberts, *Expect a Miracle: My Life and Ministry* (Nashville: T. Nelson, 1995).

48. Harrell, *Oral Roberts;* see also David Edwin Harrell, Jr., *All Things Are Possible: The Healing and Charismatic Revivals in Modern America* (Bloomington: Indiana University Press, 1975), vii.

49. Dan Morgan, *Rising in the West: The True Story of an "Okie" Family in Search of an American Dream* (New York: Vintage, 1992).

50. Gregory, *American Exodus,* 218–20.

51. Demos Shakarian, *The Happiest People on Earth* (Waco, Tex.: Chosen Books, 1975).

52. See the overview in Harvey Cox, *Fire from Heaven: The Rise of Pentecostal Spirituality and the Reshaping of Religion in the Twenty-first Century* (Reading, Mass.: Addison-Wesley Publishing Co., 1995).

53. *Albuquerque Tribune,* February 29, 1990; Richard Rodriguez, "A Continental Shift," *Los Angeles Times,* August 13, 1989: pt. 5; *New York Times,* May 14, 1989: l.

54. *Albuquerque Tribune,* February 28, 1990; Rodriguez, "A Continental Shift."

55. D. W. Meining, "The Mormon Culture Region's Strategies and Patterns in the Geography of the American West, 1849–1964," *Annals of the Association of American Geographers* 55 (June 1961): 191–220.

56. Thomas Alexander, *Mormonism in Transition: A History of the Latter-day Saints, 1890–1930* (Urbana: University of Illinois Press, 1986).

57. Jan Shipps, "The Latter-day Saints," in *Encyclopedia of the American Religious Experience,* 663.

58. James B. Funsten, "The Making of an American on the West Side of the Rockies," *Outlook* 71 (June 1902): 452.

59. John Howard Melish, *Franklin Spencer Spalding: Man and Bishop* (New York: Macmillan, 1917), 166, 171–75.

60. *Deseret News and Telegram,* February 28, 1956.

61. Milford Randall Rathjen, "The Distribution of Major Non-Mormon Denominations in Utah," master's thesis, Department of Geography, University of Utah, 1960.

62. Theodore E. Martin and Marian E. Martin, comps., *Presbyterian Work in Utah, 1869–1969* (Salt Lake City: Wheelwright Lithographing Co., 1970), 68.

63. Arnold L. Mauss, *The Angel and the Beehive: The Mormon Struggle with Assimilation* (Urbana: University of Illinois Press, 1994).

64. R. Maud Ditmars, "A History of Baptist Missions in Utah, 1871–1931," master's thesis, University of Colorado, 1931, 59, 81–83.

65. Henry Martin Merkel, *History of Methodism in Utah* (Colorado Springs, 1938), 82, 97, 101, 120.

66. Kenneth H. Wynn, "The Mormon Region," in *Encyclopedia of American Social History*, 1: 1094, 1095.

67. *Salt Lake City Tribune,* October 7, 1938.

68. Garth L. Mangum, "Welfare Services," in *Encyclopedia of Mormonism*, 5 vols. (New York: Macmillan, 1992), 4: 1554–58.

69. Undated newspaper clipping, Utah Historical Society; *Deseret News,* December 31, 1947.

70. Frank J. Taylor, "The Saints Roll up Their Sleeves," *Saturday Evening Post,* October 11, 1957.

71. "Welfare," in *Encyclopedia of Mormonism.*

72. *Salt Lake City Tribune,* October 7, 1938.

73. *Logan Herald Journal,* May 30, 1977.

74. *Deseret News,* July 1, 1939.

75. *Logan Herald Journal,* May 30, 1979.

76. *Sunstone* 18 (December 1995): 90. Thanks to Mark Ashurst-Magee for alerting me to this citation.

77. Shipps, "Latter-day Saints."

Chapter 5. Western Religious Life of the 1940s and 1950s

1. Gerald D. Nash, *The American West Transformed: The Impact of the Second World War* (Lincoln: University of Nebraska Press, 1990).

2. Reinhold Niebuhr, *The Nature and Destiny of Man* (New York: Scribner's, 1955) provides his strongest statement.

3. *Rocky Mountain News,* November 7, 1943.

4. *Salt Lake City Tribune,* June 13, 1943.

5. *Congregational District News* 8 (February 1944): 5, Western Collection, University of Oklahoma Library, Norman.

6. *Salt Lake City Tribune,* June 17, 1946.

7. *Oklahoma Messenger* 3 (April 1941).

8. *Oklahoma Episcopal Messenger* 7 (June 1945).

9. Newsletter, National Conference of Christians and Jews (1944), Oklahoma Historical Society.

10. Henry A. Wallace, "The Church and the General Welfare," *Congregational District News* 8 (March 1944): 20, Oklahoma Historical Society.

11. *Littleton [Colorado] Independent,* July 15, 1960.

12. *75th Anniversary of the First Baptist Church, Carlsbad, New Mexico, 1890–1965,* 23, Vertical Files, Public Library, Carlsbad, N.M.

13. Franklin Ng, "America's 'Concentration Camps,'" *Books and Culture* (November–December 1996): 30–32, 39.

14. *Grand Junction Daily Sentinel,* August 30, 1942; Peter W. Williams, *Houses of God: Region, Religion and Architecture in the United States* (Urbana and Chicago: University of Illinois Press, 1997), 1–3.

15. See Dorothy Day, *By Little and by Little: The Selected Writings of Dorothy Day,* ed. Robert Ellsberg (New York: Knopf, 1993); and Paul Boyer, *By the Bomb's Early Light: American Thought and Culture at the Dawn of the Atomic Age* (New York: Pantheon, 1985).

16. Langdon Gilkey, *Society and the Sacred: Toward a Theology of Culture in Decline* (New York: Crossroads, 1981), vi ff.

17. Wilbur Zelinsky, "An Approach to the Religious Geography of the United States: Patterns of Church Membership in 1952," *Annals of the American Association of American Geographers* 51 (June 1961): 139–43.

18. Edwin Scott Gaustad, *Historical Atlas of Religion in America,* rev. ed. (New York: Harper and Row, 1976).

19. Zelinsky, "An Approach," 150, 152, 161, 164, 166.

20. William G. Loy et al., eds., *Atlas of Oregon* (Eugene: University of Oregon, 1976), 32.

21. Zelinsky, "An Approach," 164, 166.

22. Leonard Dinnerstein, "Anti-Semitism Exposed and Attacked, 1945–1950," *American Jewish History* 71 (1981): 136.

23. Quoted in Neal Gabler, *An Empire of Their Own: How the Jews Invented Hollywood* (New York: Crown Publishers, 1988), 276.

24. Elinor Tong Dehey, *Religious Orders of Women in the United States* (Ammand, Ind.: W. B. Corley, 1930). See also Susan Carol Peterson and Courtney Ann Vaughan-Roberson, *Women with Vision: The Presentation Sisters of South Dakota, 1885–1985* (Urbana: University of Illinois Press, 1988); and Anne M. Butler, "Mission in the Mountains: The Daughters of Charity in Virginia City," in *Comstock Women: The Making of a Mining Community,* ed. Ronald M. James and C. Elizabeth Raymond (Reno and Las Vegas: University of Nevada Press, 1998), 142–64.

25. Sister M. Lilliaka Owens, "Colorado's Pioneer Graduate," *Colorado Magazine* 14 (September 1937): 173; see also Thomas J. Noel, *Colorado Catholicism and the Archdiocese of Denver, 1857–1989* (Niwot: University Press of Colorado, 1989).

26. Steven M. Avella, "The Transformation of Catholic Life in the Twentieth-Century West: The Case of the Diocese of Sacramento, 1929–1957," *California History* 72 (Summer 1993): 151–69.

27. *Denver Post,* April 9, 1952.

28. *History of First Christian Church,* dedicatory folder, Oklahoma Historical Society.

29. *Denver Post,* November 3, 1957.

30. Ibid., January 16, 1960.

31. "Religions of Salt Lake City," typescript, Utah Historical Society, 45.

32. *Las Vegas Review Journal,* May 17, 1963: 28.

33. *Denver Post,* June 10, 1961.

34. *Lincoln Sunday Journal and Star,* January 14, 1968.

35. *Current Biography Yearbook, 1968* (New York: H. W. Wilson, 1969), 245.

36. *Rocky Mountain News,* August 4, 1948.

37. *Denver Post,* July 13, 1973.

38. *Rocky Mountain News,* December 7, 1952.

39. "The Churches of Denver," undated clipping, c. 1955, Vertical Files, Western Room, Public Library, Denver, Colo.

40. *Rocky Mountain News,* April 21, 1952, March 23, 1953; Central Presbyterian pamphlet, Vertical Files, Public Library, Denver, Colo.

41. "Amarillo Church History," typescript, Mary E. Bivins Memorial Library, Amarillo, Tex.

42. Juti A. Winchester, "A Sign of the Times: A Shrine of the Ages at Grand Canyon," paper delivered at the Phi Alpha Theta Southwest Regional Conference, March 22–23, 1996, New Mexico Highlands University.

43. John C. Scott, *This Place Called Saint Martin's, 1895–1995: A Centennial History of Saint Martin's College and Abbey, Lacey, Washington* (Virginia Beach: Downing Co., 1996).

44. *In Observance of the Bicentennial of the Dominguez and Escalante Expedition* (Salt Lake City, 1976), n.p.

45. Jay P. Dolan, *The American Catholic Experience: A History from Colonial Times to the Present* (Garden City: Image Books, 1985), 350–51.

46. John Bernard McColain, "Survey: California Catholicism's Neglected Gold Mine: A Report on Research and Writing, 1850–1960," *Church History* 29 (1960): 344–50.

47. Philip Gleason, "In Search of Unity: American Catholic Thought, 1920–1960," *Catholic Historical Review* 65 (April 1979): 189.

48. *Rocky Mountain News,* August 31, 1946, September 6, 1947, October 14, 1990; *Deseret News,* October 29, 1972.

49. *Deseret News,* September 26, 1945.

50. *California Intermountain News,* March 16, 1972.

51. *Salt Lake City Tribune,* April 8, 1956.

52. *LDS Church News,* week ending September 27, 1980.

53. Jan Shipps, "Mormon Metamorphosis: The Neglected Story," *Christian Century,* August 14–21, 1996: 784–87; Armand L. Mauss, *The Angel and the Beehive: The Mormon Struggle with Assimilation* (Urbana and Chicago: University of Illinois Press, 1994); *Albuquerque Journal,* October 4, 1997.

54. *Annual of the Baptist Convention of Oklahoma* (1951), 96–98.

55. Bill Hunke to Peggy Carnett, August 7, 1996, provided by Dan Carnett.

56. *Dallas News,* September 6, 1952, September 4, 1952.

57. Cited in Eldon G. Ernst, "Baptists in the Pacific Northwest: An Historiographical Frontier," *Foundations* (October–December 1969): 321.

58. *Denver Post,* April 20, 1973, June 23, 1978.

59. *Rocky Mountain News,* December 7, 1952.

60. There is no biography of Byrne. On McIntyre, see Francis J. Weber, *His Eminence of Los Angeles: James Francis Cardinal McIntyre,* 2 vols. (Mission Hills, Calif.: St. Francis Historical Society, 1996).

Chapter 6. Western Religious Personalities

1. William Miller, review of Epstein, *Sister Aimee: The Life of Aimee Semple McPherson, New York Times,* March 14, 1993: 11.

2. David W. Ryder, "Aimee Semple McPherson," *Nation,* June 28, 1926: 82; Nathan O. Hatch, "Foreword," in Edith L. Blumhofer, *Aimee Semple McPherson: Everybody's Sister* (Grand Rapids, Mich.: William B. Eerdmans, 1993), ix.

3. Morrow Mayo, *New Republic,* December 25, 1929.

4. Lately Thomas, *Storming Heaven: The Lives and Turmoils of Minnie Kennedy and Aimee Semple McPherson* (New York: William Morrow and Co., 1970), 96.

5. Jules Tygiel, *The Great Los Angeles Swindle: Oil, Stocks, and Scandal during the Roaring Twenties* (New York: Oxford University Press, 1994).

6. Schindler in *The Truth about Aimee Semple McPherson: A Symposium* (Girard, Kans.: Haldeman-Julius Co., c. 1920), 2.

7. *New York Times,* September 28, 1944, as cited in Earl Pomeroy, *The Pacific Slope: A History of California, Oregon, Washington, Idaho, Utah, and Nevada* (New York: Knopf, 1965), 229.

8. Richard Dyer, review of Epstein, *Sister Aimee: The Life of Aimee Semple McPherson, Boston Globe,* April 6, 1993.

9. Robert Bahr, *Least of All Saints: The Story of Aimee Semple McPherson* (Englewood Cliffs, N.J.: Prentice Hall, 1979), 239.

10. Louis Adamic in *The Truth about Aimee Semple McPherson,* 61.

11. Quoted in ibid., 57.

12. Blumhofer, *Aimee Semple McPherson: Everybody's Sister,* 384.

13. David L. Clark, "Miracles for a Dime," *California History* 47 (Winter 1978–79): 363.

14. McWilliams, *Southern California,* 262.

15. Hatch, "Foreword," x.

16. Daniel Mark Epstein, *Sister Aimee: The Life of Aimee Semple McPherson* (San Diego: Harcourt Brace and Co., 1993).

17. Quoted in Blumhofer, *Aimee Semple McPherson,* 344.

18. Steven M. Avella, "Transformation of Catholic Life in the Twentieth-Century West: The Case of the Diocese of Sacramento, 1929–1957," *California History* 72 (Summer 1993): 168.

19. Ralph Looney, "Brother Mathias," *Witness,* January 7, 1961: 3 (pt. 1) and January 14, 1961: 5 (pt. 2).

20. Carol N. Lovato, *Brother Mathias: Founder of the Little Brothers of the Good Shepherd* (Huntington, Ind.: Our Sunday Visitor Publishing Division, 1987), 68.

21. *New Mexico Register,* July 8, 1966; *Albuquerque Journal,* March 19, 1961.

22. *Albuquerque Journal,* March 18, 1961.

23. *Albuquerque Tribune,* July 16, 1968.

24. Lovato, *Brother Mathias,* 11–13.

25. *New Mexico Register,* July 8, 1966.

26. *Albuquerque Tribune,* March 18, 1967.

27. Pamphlet (c. 1944) by the National Conference of Christians and Jews, box 7, Oklahoma Historical Society, Oklahoma City.

28. Interview with Harry Rosenberg, spring 1989.

29. Frommer and Frommer, eds., *Growing up Jewish,* 58.

30. *Oklahoma Journal of Religion* 1 (January 1955): 13. A solid biography is Robert C. Cottrell, *The Social Gospel of E. Nicholas Comfort* (Norman: University of Oklahoma Press, 1997).

31. *Oklahoma Journal of Religion* 1 (August 1946): 9.

32. *Lime* 25 (June 1996): 1–6; *Albuquerque Tribune,* October 20, 1998; *Albuquerque Journal,* October 20, 1998.

33. William J. Parish, "The German Jew and the Commercial Revolution in Territorial New Mexico, 1850–1900," *New Mexico Historical Review* 35 (January 1960): 1–23 (pt. 1) and (April 1960): 129–41 (pt. 2); Henry J. Tobias, *The Jews of New Mexico* (Albuquerque: University of New Mexico Press, 1990). Quotation from *Albuquerque Journal,* April 22, 1990.

34. William Toll argues that the figures of intermarriage are much lower than previously thought ("Intermarriage and the Urban West: A Religious Context for Cultural Change," in Rischin and Livingston, eds., *Jews of the American West,* 164–89).

35. Weinstein interview.

36. Stanley M. Hordes, "The Sephardic Legacy in the Southwest: The Crypto-Jews of New Mexico," *Jewish Folklore and Ethnology Review* 15 (1992): 180; Hordes, "The Sephardic Legacy in New Mexico: A History of the Crypto-Jews," *Journal of the West* 35 (October 1996): 82–90.

37. Judith S. Neulander, "Crypto-Jews of the Southwest: An Imagined Community," *Jewish Folklore and Ethnology Review* 16 (1994): 164.

38. This is the opinion of Professor Frances Hernandez, *Albuquerque Tribune,* November 22, 1990.

39. Hordes, "Sephardic Legacy"; interviews with Stan Hordes.

40. *Albuquerque Journal,* March 31, 1991.

41. Examples may be seen in Hordes, "Sephardic Legacy."

42. Emma Moya, "Uncovering Jewish Roots," *La Herencia del Norte* 12 (Winter 1996): 1. The October 1996 issue of *Western States Jewish History* contains several articles on this theme.

43. Albert Rosenfeld, "In Santa Fe, the City Different," *Commentary* 23 (May 1954): 456–60; Morris Freedman, "The Jews of Albuquerque," *Commentary* 28 (July 1959): 55–62.

Chapter 7. Western Religion Confronts the Modern World

1. Robert S. Ellwood, *The Sixties Spiritual Awakening: American Religion Moving from Modern to Postmodern* (New Brunswick, N.J.: Rutgers University Press, 1994), 9.

2. Sydney E. Ahlstrom, "The Moral and Theological Revolution of the 1960s and Its Implications for American Religious History," in *The State of American History,* ed. Herbert J. Bass (Chicago: University of Chicago Press, 1970), 100.

3. Ronald B. Flowers, *Religion in Strange Times: The 1960s and 1970s* (Macon, Ga.: Mercer University Press, 1984); Ellwood, *The Sixties,* 10–13.

4. David G. Hacker, "Sociology of Religion and American Religious History: Retrospect and Prospect," *Journal for the Scientific Study of Religion* 7 (1988): 461–74.

5. Steve Bruce, *Religion in the Modern World: From Cathedrals to Cults* (New York: Oxford University Press, 1996).

6. Steve Bruce, ed., *Religion and Modernization: Sociologists and Historians Debate the Secularization Thesis* (Oxford: Clarendon Press, 1992).

7. Thomas Luckmann, "Shrinking Transcendence, Expanding Religion?" *Sociological Analysis* 50 (1990): 127–38.

8. Donald A. Luidens, "Fighting 'Decline': Mainline Churches and the Taxonomy of Aggregate Data," *Christian Century,* November 6, 1996: 1077.

9. Robert N. Bellah, Richard Madson, William Sullivan, Ann Swidler, and Steven M. Tipton, *Habits of the Heart: Individualism and Commitment in American Life* (New York: Harper and Row, 1985); *The Good Society* (New York: Vintage Books, 1991). A version of their new introduction to the ten-year anniversary edition was published in *Christian Century,* May 8, 1996: 510–15.

10. Dean M. Kelley, *Why Conservative Churches Are Growing: A Study in the Sociology of Religion* (New York: Harper and Row, 1972); Robert Wuthnow,

The Restructuring of American Religion: Society and Faith since World War II (Princeton, N.J.: Princeton University Press, 1988); James Davison Hunter, *Culture Wars: The Struggle to Define America* (New York: Basic Books, 1991).

11. Richard John Neuhaus, *The Naked Public Square: Religion and Democracy in America* (Grand Rapids, Mich.: William B. Eerdmans, 1984).

12. Robert Wuthnow, *The Struggle for America's Soul: Evangelicals, Liberals, and Secularism* (Grand Rapids, Mich.: William B. Eerdmans, 1989).

13. Daniel Bell, "The Cultural Wars: American Intellectual Life, 1965–1992," *Wilson Quarterly* (Summer 1992): 74–107.

14. Barry A. Kosmin and Seymour P. Lachman, *One Nation under God: Religion in Contemporary American Society* (New York: Harmony Books, 1993), 6.

15. Douglas T. Miller and Marion Novak, *The Fifties* (Garden City: Doubleday, 1977), 85.

16. George Gallup, Jr., and David Poling, *The Search for America's Faith* (Nashville: Abingdon, 1980), 80, 83.

17. *Albuquerque Tribune,* July 14, 1984.

18. Dennis A. Gilbert, *Compendium of American Public Opinion* (New York: Facts on File, 1988), 303.

19. *New York Times,* April 10, 1991.

20. *Los Angeles Times,* April 13, 1991.

21. Roger Doyle, *Atlas of Contemporary America: A Portrait of the Nation* (New York: Facts on File, 1994), 72–73.

22. Kosmin and Lachman, *One Nation under God,* 86.

23. *Albuquerque Tribune,* April 11, 1991.

24. Kosmin and Lachman, *One Nation under God,* 82.

25. *New York Times,* April 5, 1997.

26. Gustav Niebuhr, *New York Times* article in *Santa Fe New Mexican,* June 25, 1996.

27. *Salt Lake Tribune,* March 17, 1979; *Deseret News,* December 15, 1979.

28. *Pueblo Chieftain,* September 5, 1961, October 18, 1968.

29. *Las Vegas Review Journal,* October 9, 1965, October 10, 1967.

30. *Deseret News,* August 10, 1974.

31. Buddy Monahan, "Native American Urban Ministry," unpublished paper given at the University of Dubuque Theological Seminary.

32. Arnold Crompton, *Unitarianism on the Pacific Coast: The First Sixty Years* (Boston: Beacon Press, 1957); *Wall Street Journal,* March 4, 1999; conversations with Sidney E. Mead, 1980–82; David Robinson, *The Unitarians and the Universalists* (Westport, Conn.: Greenwood, 1985).

33. Interview with Al Lopez, 1995.

34. *Denver Post,* April 17, 1988, January 2, 1984, June 7, 1986; *Rocky Mountain News,* June 14, 1981.

35. *The Migrant Ministry,* pamphlet ms. 506, Idaho Historical Society, Boise.

36. "Hispanic Migrant Workers' Social and Educational Services in Idaho," Idaho Historical Society Reference Service no. 1092 (February 1965).

37. ICC Biennial Assembly (1962), 5, and Mrs. Eloise Ward, Evaluation Report, Caldwell Migrant Missionary (1965), mss. 100, both at Idaho Historical Society, Boise.

38. Max Vargas, "Report for Week Ending Dec. 30, 1965," mss. 100; Merle E. Wells, "Southern Idaho Migrant Ministry"; Wendell Peabody, "Report to the Board from the Executive Director, July 7, 1967," mss. 100, all at Idaho Historical Society, Boise.

39. See the excellent edited study by Gaustad, *A Documentary History of Religion in America since 1865* (Grand Rapids, Mich.: William B. Eerdmans, 1983, 1993).

40. Wade Clark Roof, *Community and Commitment: Religious Plausibility in a Liberal Protestant Church* (New York: Elsevier, 1978), 204.

41. Jaroslav Pelikan, *The Christian Tradition,* vol. 5: *Christian Doctrine and Modern Culture since 1700* (Chicago: University of Chicago Press, 1989), 1–10.

42. *Time,* August 7, 1995.

43. George M. Marsden, *Reforming Fundamentalism: Fuller Seminary and the New Evangelicalism* (Grand Rapids, Mich.: William B. Eerdmans, 1987), 2–5.

44. Ibid., 10, 263–65.

45. Wade Clark Roof, *A Generation of Seekers: The Spiritual Journeys of the Baby Boom Generation* (San Francisco: Harper San Francisco, 1993).

46. See Thomas C. Reeves, *The Empty Church: The Suicide of Liberal Christianity* (New York: Free Press, 1996); Christian Smith et al., *American Evangelicalism: Embattled and Thriving* (Chicago: University of Chicago Press, 1998); and Robert S. Michaelsen and Wade Clark Roof, eds., *Liberal Protestantism: Realities and Possibilities* (New York: Pilgrim Press, 1986).

47. Roger Finke and Rodney Stark, *The Churching of America, 1776–1990: Winners and Losers in Our Religious Economy* (New Brunswick, N.J.: Rutgers University Press, 1992), 237, passim.

48. *Christianity Today,* as reported in the *Rocky Mountain News,* December 19, 1994.

49. Pastor prefers to remain anonymous.

50. Dan Carnett, "New Mexico Baptists since World War II," ms.

51. *Rocky Mountain News,* December 19, 1994, December 21, 1994.

52. Mark A. Shibley, *Resurgent Evangelicalism in the United States: Mapping Cultural Change since 1970* (Columbia: University of South Carolina Press, 1996). See also Wade Clark Roof and William McKinney, *American Mainline*

Religion: Its Changing Shape and Future (New Brunswick, N.J.: Rutgers University Press, 1987).

53. *Albuquerque Journal,* June 5, 1993.

54. *Critical Issues* 1, no. 3: 1–8.

55. *Christian Century,* July 28–August 4, 1993: 723.

56. *Albuquerque Tribune,* February 20, 1995.

57. Ibid., June 5, 1993.

58. Ibid., February 19, 1993.

59. *Time,* February 12, 1990.

60. *Albuquerque Tribune,* November 1, 1990.

61. Virginia Culver, "Religious Groups Taking Sides," *Denver Post,* June 28, 1995.

62. *Lincoln Journal,* December 26, 1972.

63. Ibid., undated clipping in author's files.

64. Peter Berger, *The Sacred Canopy: Elements of a Sociological Theory of Religion* (Garden City: Doubleday, 1967).

65. Kathleen Norris, *Dakota: A Spiritual Biography* (New York: Ticknor and Fields, 1993), 94–101.

66. Kathleen Norris, *The Cloister Walk* (New York: Riverhead Books, 1996).

67. Norris, *Dakota,* 69–77.

68. Ibid., 78. See also Michael W. Spangler, "A Rhythm of Listening," *Christian Century,* October 9, 1996: 940–41.

69. Norris, *Dakota,* 23, 9, 121.

70. Norris, *Cloister Walk,* 212.

Chapter 8. Western Religion as Public Controversy

1. J. Gordon Melton, *Encylopedic Handbook of Cults in America* (New York and London: Garland Publishers, 1989), vii.

2. *Wall Street Journal,* March 2, 1971.

3. *Time,* January 24, 1972: 51–53.

4. *Rocky Mountain News,* July 12, 1972, July 26, 1972.

5. *Denver Post,* January 1, 1972.

6. *Denver Post Empire Magazine,* April 21, 1974.

7. David Snell, "Goom Rodgie's Razzle-Dazzle Soul Rush," *Saturday Review World,* February 9, 1974; *Denver Post Empire Magazine,* April 28, 1974.

8. *Denver Post Empire Magazine,* April 28, 1974.

9. Ibid., April 21, 1974.

10. *Denver Post,* April 21, 1974.

11. *Rocky Mountain News,* April 4, 1976; *Denver Post,* August 13, 1976.

12. David Chidester, *Salvation and Suicide: An Interpretation of Jim Jones,*

the People's Temple, and Jonestown (Bloomington and Indianapolis: Indiana University Press, 1986), ix.

13. Ibid., 1–11.

14. Herb Caen, "Epilogue: Why?" in Marshall Kilduff and Ron Javers, *The Suicide Cult: The Inside Story of the People's Temple Sect and the Massacre in Guyana* (New York: Bantam Books, 1975), 191–201.

15. Chidester, *Salvation and Suicide,* 10.

16. *Newsweek,* "The Cult of Death," December 4, 1978: 38–85; *Time,* December 4, 1978, December 11, 1978.

17. Caen, "Epilogue," 191, 201.

18. Chidester, *Salvation and Suicide,* 6.

19. James T. Richardson, "People's Temple and Jonestown: A Corrective Comparison and Critique," *Journal for the Scientific Study of Religion* 19 (1980): 239–55.

20. Doyle Paul Johnson, "Dilemmas of Charismatic Leadership: The Case of the People's Temple," *Sociological Analysis* 40 (Winter 1979): 239–55.

21. Lewis F. Carter, "Bhagwan Shree Rajneesh: Observations and Identification of Problems of Interpreting New Religious Movements," *Journal for the Scientific Study of Religion* 26 (1967): 148–72; John Updike, *S* (New York: Knopf, 1988); Hugh Milne, *Bhagwan: The God That Failed* (New York: St. Martin's Press, 1986); James S. Gordon, *The Golden Guru: The Strange Journey of Bhagwan Shree Rajneesh* (Lexington, Mass.: Stephen Greene Press, 1987); Kate Strelley with Robert D. San Souci, *The Ultimate Game: The Rise and Fall of Bhagwan Shree Rajneesh* (San Francisco: Harper and Row, 1987).

22. Frances FitzGerald, *Cities on a Hill: A Journey through Contemporary American Cultures* (New York: Simon and Schuster, 1986), 247–381.

23. Strelley and San Souci, *The Ultimate Game,* 358.

24. Carl Abbott, "Utopia and Bureaucracy: The Fall of Rajneeshpuram, Oregon," *Pacific Historical Review* (1990): 77–107, quotation on 90; FitzGerald, *Cities on the Hill,* 275.

25. FitzGerald, *Cities on a Hill,* 328.

26. *Scotsman,* July 29, 1994.

27. Abbott, "Utopia and Bureaucracy," 94–95.

28. Strelley and San Souci, *The Ultimate Game,* 377, 94–95.

29. "Future Is Uncertain for Commune after Rajneesh's Death," *Albuquerque Tribune,* January 20, 1990.

30. Strelley and San Souci, *The Ultimate Game,* 379.

31. *Albuquerque Journal,* August 16, 1998, December 1, 1998. Carmen Thompson tells of her "Memories of a Plural Wife" in *Good Housekeeping* 228 (March 1999): 118–20, 166.

32. Armand L. Mauss, *The Angel and the Beehive: The Mormon Struggle with Assimilation* (Urbana and Chicago: University of Illinois Press, 1994), 77.

33. Steven Naifeh and Gregory White Smith, *The Mormon Murders: A True Story of Greed, Forgery, Deceit, and Death* (New York: New American Library, 1985), 84.

34. Linda Sillitoe and Allen Roberts, *Salamander: The Story of the Mormon Forgery Murders* (Salt Lake City: Signature Books, 1988), 319–57.

35. Robert Lindsey, *A Gathering of Saints: A True Story of Money, Murder and Deceit* (New York: Simon and Schuster, 1988); Stillitoe and Roberts, *Salamander,* 487, 516.

36. Interview with Jan Shipps, fall 1991.

37. *New York Times,* January 24, 1987.

38. Naifeh and Smith, *The Mormon Murders,* 492–501.

39. Ronald L. Numbers, *The Creationists: The Evolution of Scientific Creationism* (New York: Alfred A. Knopf, 1992); George E. Webb, *The Evolution Controversy in America* (Lexington: University Press of Kentucky, 1994); Edward J. Larson, *Trial and Error: The American Controversy over Creation and Evolution* (New York: Oxford University Press, 1985).

40. Numbers, *The Creationists,* 238–39.

41. See the *Autobiography of Herbert W. Armstrong* (Pasadena: Worldwide Church of God, 1986), 2 vols.

42. "Geologist at Large," biographical notes prepared by Kirtley F. Mather (1977); "Evolution on Trial," radio talk by Mather, Station WNBC, December 11, 1925; statement by Mather, issued by Defense Counsel, *State of Tenn. v. John T. Scopes,* given to author by Mather's daughter, Florence Wengerd.

43. David B. Wilson, ed., *Did the Devil Make Darwin Do It? Modern Perspectives on the Creation-Evolution Controversy* (Ames: Iowa State, 1983).

44. Ronald L. Numbers, "Creationism in 20th-Century America," *Science,* November 5, 1982: 538; George M. Marsden, "Creation versus Evolution: No Middle Way," *Nature,* October 13, 1983: 572; John A. Moore, "Creationism in California," *Daedalus* 103 (Summer 1994): 175.

45. Calvin Trillin, "U.S. Journal: Sacramento, California," *New Yorker,* January 6, 1973: 56.

46. Francis J. Flaherty, "The Creationism Controversy: The Social Stakes," *Commonweal,* October 22, 1982: 555.

Chapter 9. Religious Personalities of the Modern West

1. William Stringfellow and Anthony Towne, *The Death and Life of Bishop Pike* (Garden City: Doubleday, 1926), vii. Pike's own writings include *The Other Side* (New York: Dell, 1968) and *If This Be Heresy* (New York: Harper and Row, 1967).

2. *Peace Pilgrim: Her Life and Work in Her Own Words* (Santa Fe: Ocean Tree, 1983).

3. *Albuquerque Journal,* December 6, 1992.

4. Mike Davis, *City of Quartz* (New York: Vintage Books, 1992); L. Ron Hubbard, *The Rediscovery of the Human Soul* (New York: L. Ron Hubbard Library, 1996), 14–15.

5. *Albuquerque Tribune,* August 17, 1990.

6. *Seattle Times/Seattle Post-Intelligencer,* February 12, 1987.

7. Irene S. Gonzales, "Indian Religious Liberty in the Late Twentieth Century," seminar paper, 1991.

8. Robert S. Michaelsen, "The Significance of the American Indian Religious Freedom Act of 1978," *Journal of the American Academy of Religion* 52 (March 1984): 93–96.

9. Ake Hultkrantz, *Native Religion of North America* (San Francisco: Harper San Francisco, 1987), 11.

10. Tim Giago, "Ancient Spirituality," *Albuquerque Journal,* March 20, 1993.

11. Peggy Pond Church, *The House at Otowi Bridge* (Albuquerque: University of New Mexico Press).

12. Barre Toelken, "Seeing with a Native Eye: How Many Sheep Will It Hold?" in W. H. Capps, ed., *Seeing with a Native Eye: Essays on Native American Religion* (New York: Harper and Row, 1976), 31–39.

13. *Albuquerque Journal,* May 7, 1991.

14. *Albuquerque Tribune,* September 21, 1992.

15. *Albuquerque Journal,* June 9, 1996.

16. Copy in author's possession.

17. AP story, *Albuquerque Journal,* August 12, 1993.

18. Francis J. Weber, *California Catholicity* (Los Angeles, 1979), 92.

19. See Raymond J. DeMallie, *The Sixth Grandfather: Black Elk's Teachings Given to John G. Neihardt* (Lincoln: University of Nebraska Press, 1984).

20. Name withheld. Information from *Gallup Independent,* September 1, 1995. James Treat, ed., *Native and Christian* (New York and London: Routledge, 1996) discusses an important aspect of the Native/Christian interaction.

21. W. E. B. Du Bois, "The Religion of the American Negro," *New World* 9 (December 1900): 616.

22. Woodson, as cited in Milton C. Sernett, ed., *Afro-American Religious History: A Documentary Witness* (Durham: Duke University Press, 1985), 1.

23. Quintard Taylor, *The Forging of a Black Community: Seattle's Central District from 1870 through the Civil Rights Era* (Seattle: University of Washington Press, 1994), quote on 36.

24. C. Eric Lincoln and Lawrence H. Mamiya, *The Black Church in the African-American Experience* (Durham: Duke University Press, 1990), 1–17.

25. Winthrop S. Hudson, "The American Context as an Area for Research in Black Church Studies," *Church History* 52 (June 1983): 160–68.

26. Garry Wills, *Under God: Religion and American Politics* (New York: Simon and Schuster, 1990), 193–269.

27. Wyatt Tee Walker, "Walk Together, Children, Dontcha' Get Weary," *Religion and Values in Public Life* 2 (Spring–Summer 1994): 1–3.

28. T. Oscar Chappelle, "The Negro Church," *Oklahoma Journal of Religion* (March 1944): 3–5, 12.

29. AP story by David Briggs, *Albuquerque Journal,* March 6, 1993.

30. Albert S. Broussard, *Black San Francisco: The Struggle for Racial Equality in the West, 1906–1954* (Lawrence: University Press of Kansas, 1993), 183–84.

31. Ibid., 188–89.

32 *Los Angeles Times,* March 11, 1990.

33. *Time,* November 19, 1990: 88.

34. *New York Times,* December 24, 1968; see also the biographical sketch in *Encyclopedia of African American Religions,* ed. Larry Murphy et al. (New York: Garland Publishing, 1993), 835–37.

35. *New York Times,* July 18, 1974.

36. Ibid., February 18, 22, 1974, April 16, 1974, May 16, 1975, May 17, 1975.

37. "Sunday Morning Improv," *Psychology Today* 28 (July–August 1995): 24–28.

38. Cecil Williams with Rebecca Laird, *No Hiding Place: Empowerment and Recovery for Our Troubled Communities* (San Francisco: Harper San Francisco, 1992), 22, quote on 1.

39. Herb Caen, "Epilogue Why?" in Marshall Kilduff and Ron Javors, *The Suicide Cult* (New York: Bantam, 1978), 193; Winfrey, quoted in Williams, *No Hiding Place,* 81.

40. Williams, *No Hiding Place,* 11.

41. Arthur Kempton, "How Far from Canaan," *New York Review,* April 21, 1994: 59.

42. *Las Vegas Review Journal,* December 26, 1996.

43. Harvey Cox, *Turning East: The Promise and Peril of the New Orientalism* (New York: Simon and Schuster, 1977).

44. Rick Fields, *How the Swans Came to the Lake: A Narrative History of Buddhism in America* (Boulder, Colo.: Shambhala, 1981), 73–75.

45. Thomas A. Tweed, *The American Encounter with Buddhism, 1844–1912: Victorian Culture and the Limits of Dissent* (Bloomington and Indianapolis: Indiana University Press, 1992).

46. Monica Furlong, *Zen Effects: The Life of Alan Watts* (Boston: Houghton Mifflin Co., 1980).

47. Charles S. Prebish, *American Buddhism* (North Scituate, Mass.: Duxbury

Press, 1979); Emma McCloy Layman, *Buddhism in America* (Chicago: Nelson Hall, 1976), 31.

48. Layman, *Buddhism in America,* 264.

49. See Brian C. Taylor, *Setting the Gospel Free: Experiential Faith and Contemplative Practice* (New York: Continuum, 1976).

50. Phyllis A. Tickle, *Re-Discovering the Sacred: Spirituality in America* (New York: Crossroads, 1995), 171.

51. *Albuquerque Journal,* June 23, 1996.

52. Paul Boyer, *By the Bomb's Early Light: American Thought and Culture at the Dawn of the Atomic Age* (New York: Pantheon, 1984).

53. L. Bruce van Voorst, "The Churches and Nuclear Deterrence," *Foreign Affairs* 61 (Spring 1983): quote on 828.

54. Bernardin, as quoted in Edwin S. Gaustad, ed., *A Documentary History of Religion in America since 1865* (Grand Rapids, Mich.: William B. Eerdmans, 1983, 1993), 598; Ronald G. Musto, *The Catholic Peace Tradition* (Maryknoll, N.Y.: Orbis Books, 1986), 244–64. For a more critical view, see Michael Novak, *Moral Clarity in the Nuclear Age* (Nashville: Thomas Nelson, 1983). The best overall study is Jim Castelli, *The Bishops and the Bomb* (Garden City: Doubleday and Co., 1983).

55. L. T. Mattheisen, "I Didn't Know the Gun Was Loaded," in Ronald J. Sider and Darrel J. Brubaker, eds., *Preaching on Peace* (Philadelphia: Fortress Press, 1982), 29–33, quote on 31–32.

56. *Amarillo Sunday News-Globe,* June 11, 1995.

57. Carroll Wilson, "Church and State," *Accent West* (November 1982): 47–49, 55.

58. *Seattle Post-Intelligencer,* August 1, 1981.

59. Raymond G. Hunthausen, "Faith and Disarmament," in Sider and Brubaker, eds., *Preaching on Peace,* 84.

60. Raymond G. Hunthausen, *Current Biography Yearbook* (New York: H. W. Wilson, 1988).

61. Wilfred P. Schoenberg, *A History of the Catholic Church in the Pacific Northwest, 1743–1983* (Washington, D.C.: Pastoral Press, 1987), 659–60, 730.

62. Matthew Glass, *Citizens against the MX: Public Language in the Nuclear Age* (Urbana and Chicago: University of Illinois Press, 1993).

63. Richard A. Schaeffer, *Legacy: Daring to Care* (Loma Linda, Calif.: Legacy Publishing Association, 1995) is the best history of the medical school. See also *From Vision to Reality, 1905–1980: Loma Linda University* (Loma Linda, 1980).

64. Rene Noorbergen, *Ellen G. White: Prophet of Destiny* (New Canaan, Conn.: Keats Publishing, 1974).

65. Ronald L. Numbers, *Prophetess of Health: A Study of Ellen G. White* (New York: Harper and Row Publishers, 1976), 198.

66. Ibid., 183–84.

67. "Loma Linda University," *Scope* (January–March 1991): 6–13.

68. Ibid., 12.

69. *Newsweek,* March 3, 1997; Peter Baker, "'Power Hour' Pastor Wins Big Convert," *Washington Post,* syndicated column in *Albuquerque Journal,* February 16, 1997.

70. Pamphlets obtained from 1993 visit to the Crystal Cathedral.

71. Dennis Voskuil, *Mountains into Goldmines: Robert Schuller and the Gospel of Success* (Grand Rapids, Mich.: William B. Eerdmans, 1983), 1–10; Arvella Schuller, *The Positive Family* (New York: Jove Book, 1982).

72. Robert H. Schuller, *Move Ahead with Possibility Thinking* (New York: Family Library, 1967), 20.

73. Voskuil, *Mountains into Goldmines,* 18; Sheila Schuller Coleman relates a slightly different origin story (*Robert Schuller, My Father and My Friend* [Milwaukee: Ideals, 1989], 41–45).

74. Robert H. Schuller, *Self-Esteem: The New Reformation* (Waco: Word Books, 1982), 12.

75. Ibid., 19.

76. Robert H. Schuller, *Believe in the God Who Believes in You* (New York: Bantam, 1991); Robert H. Schuller, *The Ten Commandments: A Divine Design for Dignity* (New York: Bantam, 1991), x–xxii, 16.

77. Robert H. Schuller, *The Peak to Peek Principle* (Garden City: Doubleday and Co., 1980), 107.

78. Robert H. Schuller, *It's Possible* (Old Tappan, N.J.: Spire Books, 1978), 10.

79. Schuller, *Believe in the God*; Robert H. Schuller, *Be Happy You Are Loved* (Nashville: Thomas Nelson, 1986), 82.

80. Robert H. Schuller, *Tough-Minded Faith for Tender-Hearted People* (New York: Bantam, 1983). Faith is

Trusting the unprovable
Dreaming God's dream
Assuming "it is possible"
Acquiring an appetite for beauty
Yielding yourself to God
Filling someone else's cup
Bowing out gracefully
Facing death unafraid.

81. Quoted in Voskuil, *Mountains into Goldmines,* 34.

82. T. D. Allman, "Jesus in Tomorrowland," *New Republic,* November 27, 1976: 7–9.

83. John M. Mulder, "The Possibility Preacher," *Theology Today* 31 (July 1974): 157–60.

84. Dennis E. Shoemaker, "Schuller Shooting," *Theology Today* 31 (January 1975): 355.

85. Marty, quoted in Schuller, *Self-Esteem,* 11–12.

86. "Hard Questions for Robert Schuller about Sin and Self-Esteem," *Christianity Today,* August 10, 1984: 14–20; "Schuller Clarifies His View of Sin," *Christianity Today,* August 10, 1984: 21–22.

87. Robert H. Schuller, *If It's Going to Be It's Up to Me* (San Francisco: Harper San Francisco, 1997), 240.

88. Wilfred Bockelman, "The Pros and Cons of Robert Schuller," *Christian Century,* August 20–27, 1975: 732–35.

89. Browne Barr, "Finding the Good at Garden Grove," *Christian Century,* May 4, 1977: 424–27; Bockelman, "The Pros and Cons," 732–35.

90. Quoted in Voskuil, *Mountains into Goldmines,* 62.

Epilogue

1. James B. Funsten, "The Making of an American on the West Side of the Rockies," *Outlook,* June 14, 1902: 452.

2. Newt Gingrich quoted in the *Guardian Weekly,* May 7, 1995.

3. Charles R. Morris, *American Catholics: The Saints and Sinners Who Built America's Powerful Church* (New York: Random House/Time Books, 1995).

4. *New York Times,* April 23, 1999: D3.

5. Michael Medved, *Hollywood vs. America: Popular Culture and the War on Traditional Values* (New York: Harper Collins/Anderson, 1992); Michael Medved, "Hollywood *vs.* Religion," *Imprimis* 18 (December 1989): 1–5; Cynthia Gronier, "Capturing the Culture," *Imprimis* 19 (January 1990), 51; Ferenc M. Szasz, "The Clergy and the Myth of the American West," *Church History* 59 (December 1990): 497–506.

6. *Albuquerque Journal,* October 25, 1998; *Toronto Globe and Mail,* April 23, 1999; *Seattle Times,* April 27, 1999; *Albuquerque Journal,* March 1, 1999.

7. Peter L. Berger, "American Religion: Conservative Upsurge, Liberal Prospects," in *Liberal Protestantism: Realities and Possibilities,* ed. Robert S. Michaelsen and Wade Clark Roof (New York: Pilgrim Press, 1986), 358, 359.

8. Arnold Mauss, *The Angel and the Beehive: The Mormon Struggle with Assimilation* (Urbana: University of Illinois Press, 1994); see also Jan Shipps, "Is Mormonism Christian? Reflections on a Complicated Question," *BYU Studies* 33 (1993): 438–65.

9. See J. Gordon Melton, "Another Look at New Religions," *Annals of the American Academy of Political and Social Science* 527 (May 1993): 97–112.

10. Peter W. Bakken et al., *Ecology, Justice, and Christian Faith: A Critical Guide to the Literature* (Westport, Conn.: Greenwood Press, 1995).

11. Donald E. Miller, *Reinventing American Protestantism: Christianity in the New Millennium* (Berkeley: University of California Press, 1997).

12. David Rieff, *Los Angeles: Capital of the Third World* (New York: Touchstone, 1991), 23.

13. Barbara A. Weightman, "Changing Religious Landscapes in Los Angeles," *Journal of Cultural Geography* 14 (Fall–Winter 1993): 1–15; Michael E. Engh, "'A Multiplicity and Diversity of Faiths': Religion's Impact on Los Angeles and the Urban West, 1890–1940," *Western Historical Quarterly* 27 (Winter 1997): 463.

14. Eldon G. Ernst, "Religion in California," *Pacific Theological Review* 19 (Winter 1986): 43–51.

15. Russell Chandler, "Californians: Spiritual but Not Conventional," *Progressions* 2 (January 1990): 8–10.

16. Gustav Niebuhr, "Land of Religious Freedom Has Universe of Spirituality," *New York Times,* March 30, 1997.

Selected Bibliography

Archives Consulted

Albuquerque Public Library
Amarillo Public Library
Arizona Historical Society
Boise Public Library
Carlsbad, New Mexico, Public Library
Colorado Historical Society
Fort Collins, Colorado, Public Library
Idaho Historical Society
Kansas Historical Society
Las Vegas, Nevada, Historical Library
Lincoln, Nebraska, Public Library
Menaul Historical Library, Albuquerque
Nebraska Historical Society
Nevada Historical Society, Reno
Panhandle-Plains Historical Museum, Canyon, Texas
Price, Utah, Public Library
Reno Public Library
Roswell, New Mexico, Public Library
Santa Fe Public Library
Sharlott Hall Museum, Prescott, Arizona
Western Room, Denver Public Library

Selected Secondary Works

Abbott, Carl. "Utopia and Bureaucracy: The Fall of Rajneeshpuram, Oregon." *Pacific Historical Review* 59 (1990): 77–107.

Ahlstrom, Sydney E. *A Religious History of the American People*. New Haven: Yale University Press, 1972.

Albanese, Catherine L. *Nature Religion in America: From the Algonkian Indians to the New Age*. Chicago: University of Chicago Press, 1990.

Alexander, Kay. *California Catholicism*. Santa Barbara: Fithian Press, 1993.

Alexander, Thomas. *Mormonism in Transition: A History of the Latter-day Saints, 1890–1930*. Urbana: University of Illinois Press, 1986.

Anderson, Douglas Firth. "Through Fire and Fair by the Golden Gate: Progressive Era Protestantism and Regional Culture." Ph.D. dissertation, Graduate Theological Union, 1988.

————. "'We Have Here a Different Civilization': Protestant Identity in the San Francisco Bay Area, 1906–1909." *Western Historical Quarterly* 23 (May 1992): 197–221.

Arrington, Leonard J., and Davis Bitton. *The Mormon Experience: A History of the Latter-day Saints*. New York: Alfred A. Knopf, 1979.

Atlas of the New West: Portrait of a Changing Region. New York: W. W. Norton and Co., 1997.

Avella, Steven M. "Transformation of Catholic Life in the Twentieth-Century West: The Case of the Diocese of Sacramento, 1929–1957." *California History* 72 (Summer 1993): 151–69.

Banker, Mark T. *Presbyterian Missions and Cultural Interaction in the Far Southwest, 1850–1950*. Urbana: University of Illinois Press, 1993.

Bellah, Robert, Richard Madson, William Sullivan, Ann Swidler, and Steven M. Tipton. *Habits of the Heart: Individualism and Commitment in American Life*. New York: Harper and Row, 1985.

Bennett, John W.. *Hutterian Brethren: The Agricultural Economy and Social Organization of a Communal People*. Stanford, Calif.: Stanford University Press, 1967.

Berger, Peter. *The Social Reality of Religion*. London: Faber and Faber, 1969.

Blumhofer, Edith L. *Aimee Semple McPherson: Everybody's Sister*. Grand Rapids, Mich.: William B. Eerdmans, 1993.

Bruce, Steve, ed. *Religion and Modernization: Sociologists and Historians Debate the Secularization Thesis*. Oxford: Clarendon Press, 1992.

Butler, Anne M. "Mother Katharine Drexel: Spiritual Visionary for the West." In *By Grit and Grace: Eleven Women Who Shaped the American West*. Ed. Glenda Riley and Richard W. Etulain. Golden, Colo.: Fulcrum Publishing, 1987, 198–220.

Carroll, H. K. *The Religious Forces of the United States*. Rev. ed. New York: Scribner's, 1912.

Castelli, Jim. *The Bishops and the Bomb*. Garden City: Doubleday and Co., 1983.

Chidester, David. *Salvation and Suicide: An Interpretation of Jim Jones, the People's Temple, and Jonestown*. Bloomington and Indianapolis: Indiana University Press, 1986.

Conkin, Paul K. *American Originals: Homemade Varieties of Christianity*. Chapel Hill: University of North Carolina Press, 1997.

Cottrell, Robert C. *The Social Gospel of E. Nicholas Comfort, Founder of the Oklahoma School of Religion.* Norman: University of Oklahoma Press, 1997.

Cox, Harvey. *Fire from Heaven: The Rise of Pentecostal Spirituality and the Reshaping of Religion in the Twenty-first Century.* Reading, Mass.: Addison-Wesley Publishing Co., 1995.

Dinnerstein, Leonard. *Anti-Semitism in America.* New York: Oxford University Press, 1994.

Dolan, Jay P. *The American Catholic Experience: A History from Colonial Times to the Present.* Garden City: Image Books, 1985.

————, ed. *The American Catholic Parish: A History from 1850 to the Present.* Vol. 2: *Pacific States/Intermountain West/Midwest.* New York: Paulist Press, 1987.

Ellwood, Robert S. *The Fifties Spiritual Marketplace: American Religion in a Decade of Conflict.* New Brunswick, N.J.: Rutgers University Press, 1997.

————. *The Sixties Spiritual Awakening: American Religion Moving from Modern to Postmodern.* New Brunswick, N.J.: Rutgers University Press, 1994.

Engh, Michael. *Frontier Faiths: Church, Temple, and Synagogue in Los Angeles, 1846–1888.* Albuquerque: University of New Mexico Press, 1992.

————. "'A Multiplicity and Diversity of Faiths': Religion's Impact on Los Angeles and the Urban West, 1890–1940." *Western Historical Quarterly* 27 (Winter 1997): 463–92.

Epstein, Daniel Mark. *Sister Aimee: The Life of Aimee Semple McPherson.* San Diego: Harcourt Brace and Co., 1993.

Ernst, Eldon G. "American Religious History from a Pacific Coast Perspective." In Carl Guarneri and David Alvarez, eds., *Religion and Society in the American West: Historical Essays.* Lanham, Md.: University Press of America, 1987, 3–39.

————. "Religion in California." *Pacific Theological Review* 19 (Winter 1986): 43–51.

Ernst, Eldon G., and Douglas Firth Anderson. *Pilgrim Progression: The Protestant Experience in California.* Santa Barbara: Fithian Press, 1992.

Etulain, Richard W., ed. *The American West in the Twentieth Century: A Bibliography.* Norman: University of Oklahoma Press, 1994.

————. *Religion in the Twentieth-Century American West: A Bibliography.* Albuquerque: Center for the American West, 1991.

————, comp. "Regionalizing Religion: Evangelicals in the American West, 1940–1990." In Raymond M. Cooke and Richard W. Etulain, eds., *Religion and Culture: Historical Essays in Honor of Robert C. Woodward.* Albuquerque: Far West Books, 1991.

Fields, Rick. *How the Swans Came to the Lake: A Narrative History of Buddhism in America.* Boulder, Colo.: Shambhala, 1981.

Finke, Roger, and Rodney Stark. *The Churching of America, 1776–1990: Win-

ners and Losers in Our Religious Economy. New Brunswick, N.J.: Rutgers University Press, 1992.

FitzGerald, Frances. *Cities on a Hill: A Journey through Contemporary American Cultures.* New York: Simon and Schuster, 1986.

Frankiel, Sandra Sizer. *California's Spiritual Frontiers: Religious Alternatives in Anglo-Protestantism, 1850–1910.* Berkeley: University of California Press, 1989.

Frommer, Myrna Katz, and Harvey Frommer, eds. *Growing up Jewish in America: An Oral History.* New York: Harcourt Brace and Co., 1995.

Gabler, Neal. *An Empire of Their Own: How the Jews Invented Hollywood.* New York: Crown Publishers, 1988.

Gaustad, Edwin S., ed. *A Documentary History of Religion in America since 1865.* Grand Rapids, Mich.: William B. Eerdmans, 1983; reprinted in 1993.

Gleason, Philip. "A Browser's Guide to American Catholicism, 1950–1980." *Theology Today* 38 (1982): 323–89.

Gonzalez, Gilbert G. *Labor and Community: Mexican Citrus Worker Villages in a Southern California County, 1900–1950.* Urbana and Chicago: University of Illinois Press, 1994.

Griffin, John J. "Yours in His Service: H. Orton Wiley, an Evangelical Theologian and Educator." Ph.D. dissertation, University of New Mexico, 1998.

Griffith, James S. *Beliefs and Holy Places: A Spiritual Geography of the Primeria Alta.* Tucson: University of Arizona Press, 1992.

Guarneri, Carl, and David Alvarez, eds. *Religion and Society in the American West: Historical Essays.* Lanham, Md.: University Press of America, 1987.

Hordes, Stanley. "The Sephardic Legacy in New Mexico: A History of the Crypto-Jews." *Journal of the West* 35 (October 1966): 82–90.

Hunter, James Davison. *Culture Wars: The Struggle to Define America.* New York: Basic Books, 1991.

Jorstad, Erling. *Holding Fast/Pressing On: Religion in America in the 1980s.* New York: Praeger, 1990.

Kelley, Klara Bonsack, and Harris Francis. *Navajo Sacred Places.* Bloomington: Indiana University Press, 1994.

Kosmin, Barry A., and Seymour P. Lachman. *One Nation under God: Religion in Contemporary American Society.* New York: Harmony Books, 1993.

Layman, Emma McCloy. *Buddhism in America.* Chicago: Nelson Hall, 1976.

Libo, Kenneth, and Irving Howe. *We Lived There Too.* New York: St. Martin's/Marek, 1984.

Lindsey, Robert. *A Gathering of Saints: A True Story of Money, Murder and Deceit.* New York: Simon and Schuster, 1988.

Loftin, John D. *Religion and Hopi Life in the Twentieth Century.* Bloomington: Indiana University Press, 1991.

Lovato, Carol N. *Brother Mathias: Founder of the Little Brothers of the Good Shepherd*. Huntington, Ind.: Our Sunday Visitor Publishing Division, 1987.

Luebke, Frederick, ed. *European Immigrants in the American West: Community Histories*. Albuquerque: University of New Mexico Press, 1998.

Maffly-Kipp, Laurie F. "Eastward Ho!" In *Retelling U.S. Religious History*, ed. Thomas A. Tweed. Berkeley: University of California Press, 1997, 127–48.

Marsden, George. *Fundamentalism and American Culture*. New York: Oxford University Press, 1980.

———. *The Soul of the American University: From Protestant Establishment to Established Nonbelief*. New York and Oxford: Oxford University Press, 1994.

Marty, Martin E. *Modern American Religion*. Vol. 1: *The Irony of It All, 1893–1919;* Vol. 2: *The Noise of Conflict, 1919–1941;* Vol. 3: *Under God, Indivisible, 1941–1960*. Chicago: University of Chicago Press, 1986, 1991, 1996.

Mauss, Armand L. *The Angel and the Beehive: The Mormon Struggle with Assimilation*. Urbana: University of Illinois Press, 1994.

May, Henry F. *Protestant Churches and Industrial America*. New York: Harper and Row, 1949; reprinted in 1967.

Melton, J. Gordon. *Encyclopedic Handbook of Cults in America*. New York and London: Garland Publishers, 1989.

Miller, Donald E. *Reinventing American Protestantism: Christianity in the New Millennium*. Berkeley: University of California Press, 1997.

Milne, Hugh. *Bhagwan: The God That Failed*. New York: St. Martin's Press, 1986.

Moore, R. Laurence. *Religious Outsiders and the Making of Americans*. New York: Oxford University Press, 1986.

Morgan, Dan. *Rising in the West: The True Story of an "Okie" Family in Search of an American Dream*. New York: Vintage, 1992.

Morris, Charles R. *American Catholics: The Saints and Sinners Who Built America's Most Powerful Church*. New York: Random House/Times Books, 1995.

Nash, Gerald D. *The American West in the Twentieth Century: A Short History of an Urban Oasis*. Albuquerque: University of New Mexico Press, 1977.

———. *The American West Transformed: The Impact of the Second World War*. Lincoln: University of Nebraska Press, 1990.

Noel, Thomas J. *Colorado Catholicism and the Archdiocese of Denver, 1857–1989*. Niwot: University Press of Colorado, 1989.

Norris, Kathleen. *The Cloister Walk*. New York: Riverhead Books, 1996.

———. *Dakota: A Spiritual Biography*. New York: Ticknor and Fields, 1993.

Numbers, Ronald L. *The Creationists: The Evolution of Scientific Creationism*. New York: Alfred A. Knopf, 1992.

————. *Prophetess of Health: A Study of Ellen G. White*. New York: Harper and Row, 1976.

Pascoe, Peggy. *Relations of Rescue: The Search for Female Moral Authority in the American West, 1874–1939*. New York: Oxford University Press, 1990.

Peter, Karl A. *The Dynamics of Hutterite Society: An Analytical Approach*. Edmonton: University of Alberta Press, 1987.

Quinn, D. Michael. "Religion in the American West." In *Under an Open Sky: Rethinking America's Western Past,* ed. William Cronon et al. New York: Norton, 1992, 145–66.

Rawls, James J. "The California Mission as Symbol and Myth." *California History* 74 (1992): 343–60.

Rischin, Moses. *The Jews of the West: The Metropolitan Years*. Waltham, Mass.: American Jewish Historical Society, 1979.

Rischin, Moses, and John Livingston, eds. *Jews of the American West*. Detroit: Wayne State University Press, 1991.

Rochlin, Harriet, and Fred Rochlin. *Pioneer Jews: A New Life in the Far West*. Boston: Houghton Mifflin, 1959.

Roof, Wade Clark. *A Generation of Seekers: The Spiritual Journeys of the Baby Boom Generation*. San Francisco: Harper San Francisco, 1993.

Rosenbaum, Fred. *Free to Choose: The Making of a Jewish Community in the American West: The Jews of Oakland, California, from the Gold Rush to the Present Day*. Berkeley: University of California Press, 1976.

Sandoval, Moises, ed. *Frontiers: A History of the Latin American Church in the U.S.A. since 1513*. San Antonio: Mexican American Cultural Center, 1983.

Schoenberg, Wilfred P. *A History of the Catholic Church in the Pacific Northwest, 1743–1983*. Washington, D.C.: Pastoral Press, 1987.

Scott, John C. *This Place Called Saint Martin's, 1895–1995: A Centennial History of Saint Martin's College and Abbey, Lacey, Washington*. Virginia Beach: Downing Co., 1996.

Shibley, Mark A. *Resurgent Evangelicalism in the United States: Mapping Cultural Change since 1970*. Columbia: University of South Carolina Press, 1996.

Small, Lawrence F., ed. *Religion in Montana: Pathways to the Present*. Helena: Falcon Press, 1992.

Sorin, Gerald. *Tradition Transformed: The Jewish Experience in America*. Baltimore: Johns Hopkins University Press, 1997.

Starr, Kevin. *Americans and the California Dream, 1850–1915*. New York: Oxford University Press, 1973.

————. *Inventing the Dream: California through the Progressive Era*. New York: Oxford University Press, 1985.

———. *Material Dreams: Southern California through the 1920s.* New York: Oxford University Press, 1990.

Szasz, Ferenc Morton. *The Divided Mind of Protestant America, 1880–1930.* University: University of Alabama Press, 1982.

———. *The Protestant Clergy in the Great Plains and Mountain West, 1865–1915.* Albuquerque: University of New Mexico Press, 1988.

———, ed. *Religion in the West.* Manhattan, Kans.: Sunflower University Press, 1984.

Szasz, Ferenc Morton, and Richard W. Etulain, eds. *Religion in Modern New Mexico.* Albuquerque: University of New Mexico Press, 1997.

Szasz, Ferenc Morton, with Margaret Connell Szasz. "Religion and Spirituality." In *The Oxford History of the American West,* ed. Clyde A. Milner II, Carol A. O'Connor, and Martha A. Sandweiss. New York: Oxford University Press, 1994, 359–91.

Taylor, Quintard. *The Forging of a Black Community: Seattle's Central District from 1870 through the Civil Rights Era.* Seattle: University of Washington Press, 1994.

———. *In Search of the Racial Frontier: African Americans in the American West, 1528–1900.* New York: W. W. Norton and Co., 1998.

Thomas, Lately. *Storming Heaven: The Lives and Turmoils of Minnie Kennedy and Aimee Semple McPherson.* New York: William Morrow and Co., 1970.

Tobias, Henry J. *The Jews of New Mexico.* Albuquerque: University of New Mexico Press, 1990.

Toll, William. *The Making of an Ethnic Middle Class: Portland Jewry over Four Generations.* Albany: State University of New York Press, 1982.

Vecsey, Christopher, ed. *Religion in Native North America.* Moscow: University of Idaho Press, 1990.

Vorspan, Max, and Lloyd P. Gartner. *History of the Jews of Los Angeles.* San Marino: Huntington Library, 1976.

Walker, Randi Jones. *Protestantism in the Sangre de Cristos, 1850–1920.* Albuquerque: University of New Mexico Press, 1991.

Weber, Francis J. *California Catholicity.* Los Angeles: N.p., 1979.

———. "Catholicity in California." *American Ecclesiastical Review* 159 (October 1963): 233–51.

———. *His Eminence of Los Angeles: James Francis Cardinal McIntyre.* Mission Hills, Calif.: St. Francis Historical Society, 1996. 2 vols.

Williams, Peter W. *Houses of God: Region, Religion, and Architecture in the United States.* Urbana and Chicago: University of Illinois Press, 1997.

Wuthnow, Robert. *Christianity in the Twenty-first Century: Reflections on the Challenges Ahead.* New York: Oxford University Press, 1993.

———. *The Restructuring of American Religion: Society and Faith since World War II.* Princeton, N.J.: Princeton University Press, 1988.

Illustration Credits

German Reformed Church, Dempster, South Dakota. Photo courtesy of South Dakota State Historical Society—State Archives.

Saint Mary's Catholic Cathedral and pastor's residence, Cheyenne, Wyoming. Courtesy Wyoming Division of Cultural Resources, Meyers Collection B-916; photo no. 15731.

Holy Family Roman Catholic Cathedral, rectory, and school, Tulsa, Oklahoma. Courtesy Tulsa Historical Society.

Temple Square, Salt Lake City, Utah. Used by permission, Utah State Historical Society, all rights reserved; photo no. 6387.

The Boston Avenue United Methodist Church, Tulsa, Oklahoma. Courtesy Tulsa Historical Society.

Temple Mt. Sinai, El Paso, Texas. Courtesy Southwest Collection, El Paso Public Library.

Rabbi William S. Friedman of Denver. Courtesy Denver Public Library, Western History Collection.

Rev. Oral Roberts, c. 1965. Courtesy Oral Roberts University, Tulsa, Oklahoma.

All Souls Unitarian Church, Tulsa, Oklahoma. Courtesy All Souls Unitarian Church.

An architectural model of the Mormon Temple in Los Angeles. Used by permission, Utah State Historical Society, all rights reserved; photo no. 8068

Aimee Semple McPherson playing with her son, Rolf. Courtesy Seaver Center for Western History Research, Los Angeles County Museum of Natural History; image 4891.

An early-twentieth-century tombstone. © 1994 Cary Herz Photography.

A dance at Santa Clara Pueblo, New Mexico, c. 1930. Courtesy Center for Southwest Research, General Library, University of New Mexico; neg. no. 994-045-0043.

Dr. Robert H. Schuller. Courtesy Crystal Cathedral.

The Crystal Cathedral, Garden Grove, California. Courtesy Crystal Cathedral.

The Buddhist temple Higashi Honganji. Courtesy Security Pacific Collection, Los Angeles Public Library.

A classroom in an Islamic school. Courtesy Shades of L.A. Archives, Los Angeles Public Library.

Index

About the Author

Ferenc Morton Szasz has taught history at the University of New Mexico in Albuquerque for over three decades. Currently professor of history, he has written or edited over eighty articles and seven books on a variety of subjects. The scientific, cultural, and religious history of the American West is his chief area of interest.